# BATTALION COMMAND

## Dare to Lead

(REVISED EDITION)

## READERS' REVIEWS

A book of immense professional value by the man who has always practised what he preaches. General Sengar, through absorbing real-life examples, has admirably compiled what it needs to command a battalion with pride, passion and purpose. This book is a readymade recipe for all aspiring commanding officers to chew, digest and practice. A must-read for officers of all ranks and positions.

**—Lt General SK Patyal, SM**
**Former DA to Pakistan and Corps Commander,**

* * *

I do admit at the very outset that both the books (*Battalion Command-Dare to Lead* and *Leadership Foundation and Self-development for Junior Leaders in Uniformed Services*) deserve serious reading as they are a 'Gold Mine'. The initial perusal has drawn my attention to the centrality of 'fearlessness' and 'selflessness' as the 'raison d'etre' of any command. The *Leadership Foundation and Self-development for junior Leaders in Uniformed Services* is, without any doubt, an excellent guide for junior leaders who aspire to lead with passion and commitment.

**—Maj General Sudhakar Jee (Retd), Deputy Commandant,**
**Army War College, Jun 2019**

* * *

The book has been written from the heart of a soldier who has shared his experiences as a Commander. As per the author, Battalion Commander is a 'Tiger' who has to take care of his (Battalion including the families) therefore he has to behave like a Tiger, Fearless and Ruthless, depending upon the situations. Had I read this book before the command of my regiment, I am certain to have commanded it better. General Sengar knows the way, he has taken the way and through his book, he is showing the way. A must-read book for every officer of India.

**—Brig Tarun Ohri, Armoured Corps**

* * *

"Written by the author of the popular book, *Militarily Crazy...*, this book reveals the professional side of General Sengar. Important aspects and nuances of command have been elaborated in this book based on his experiences and his command philosophy. True incidents of war and peace in the Indian context lend credence to the theme. Written with the conviction of a man who 'Walks the Talk', it is a must-read for all commanding officers, sub-unit commanders and leaders at the executive level in all walks of life."

**—Colonel KK Arun, SM (Veteran)**

* * *

This is not a book. It is an EMOTION. It is a holy text which will inspire military leaders. It is a workbook for military officers who aspire to lead with passion and commitment. Personal examples given in the book make it a reader's delight. Absolutely unputdownable story of leadership.

**—Col Shashi Upadhyaya, Regimental Commander, Army Air Defence**

* * *

The author presents practical and value-based leadership skills expected out of a combat leader. Battalion Command is a book that enables a Military Commander to take effective decisions in challenging situations during operations and peacetime. The book is the first of its kind written by any Indian Military General, who has illustrated each aspect of leadership with numerous real-life examples, he experienced during his four-decade-long career. It served me as a mentor during my Battalion Command.

**—Col AP Singh, Battalion Commander- The GUARDS**

* * *

I am witness to the Author's inspirational command of 5 GUARDS and 22 Infantry Division. What he has preached is what he practised fearlessly. His six books are my constant companion and I have read them, chewed them and digested them many times over. **I say this with full responsibility that they have changed my life**. This book *Battalion Command, Dare to Lead* is my BIBLE on unit command. If you ever find yourself at a crossroads in command, go to this book, it will navigate you safely home on a pitch-dark night.

**—Lt Col Manoj Kharayat, Artillery**

* * *

# THE REVISED EDITION: WHAT IS NEW?

*Battalion Command: Dare to Lead* was first published in 2016. Since then a lot of water and blood has flown down the Galwan river. I have written four books since then, which include, *Leadership Foundation and Self Development for Junior Leaders* and *The BE-KNOW-DO of Generalship*. There are important issues that I covered in detail in those books, while they were dealt with briefly in the *Battalion Command: Dare to Lead.*

Since May 2020, the Indian Army has lost three commanding officers, killed in action. One, in the Kashmir Valley during a counter-terrorist operation, one in the face-off against the Chinese in Galwan, Eastern Ladakh and one in an ambush in Manipur. Tragically, in the last incident, the wife and child of the battalion commander also lost their lives. No commanding officer was killed in the high-intensity Kargil War 1999. It is time to critically draw lessons from both.

The Galwan incident created a new paradigm for battalions on the borders and exposed the vulnerability of the commanding officer in a seemingly no conflict situation. These incidents have thrown up lessons for commanders at all levels that need to be deliberated, which have been included here as relevant to a battalion commander.

The US withdrawal from Afghanistan, the Yemen civil war and the ongoing Russia-Ukraine war have serious lessons for every level of command. The last few years have seen parroting of the line 'changing character of warfare'. What does it mean for the units? What do they need to do to be future-ready?

Other important aspects such as the Directive Style of Command, the importance of Emotional Intelligence etc. have been included in greater details as relevant to the commanding officers, which makes this book a comprehensive treatise on Battalion Command.

*Orders Appoint you to Command*
*No Orders Can Appoint you a Leader*
*Command does not sow the seeds of*
*Loyalty and Commitment,*
*Leadership does.*
(Reconstructed from different sources)

# BATTALION COMMAND

## DARE TO LEAD

(REVISED EDITION)

Major General Anil Sengar

PENTAGON PRESS

**BATTALION COMMAND: Dare to Lead**
*Major General Anil Sengar, YSM, VSM*

ISBN 978-93-90095-67-4

First Published: 2016
Revised Edition: 2022



**Disclaimer:** The views and opinions expressed in the book are the individual assertion of the Author. The Publisher does not take any responsibility for the same in any manner whatsoever. The same shall solely be the responsibility of the Author.

*Published by*
PENTAGON PRESS
206, Peacock Lane, Shahpur Jat,
New Delhi-110049
Phones: 011-64706243, 26491568
Telefax: 011-26490600
email: rajan@pentagonpress.in
website: www.pentagonpress.in

Printed at Aegean Offset Printers, Greater Noida, U.P.

*The book is dedicated to the magnificent young officers of the Indian Military, on whose broad shoulders rides the security of India*

*and*

*To my parents*

I could have been

A civil servant – But I valued people 's trust

A diplomat – But I hated the laissez faire

A politician – But I valued morals and ethics

A policeman – But I wouldn't be one

I wanted to be a God But I couldn't be one

So

I chose to be the next best thing.

# I BECAME A SOLDIER

# CONTENTS

# ACKNOWLEDGEMENTS

I wish to thank the readers of my books. Their feedback through calls and messages have been gratifying. My first book, *Militarily Crazy: The Lighter Side of Life in the Indian Army* helped many to deal with tragic times, because of the effortless reading that brought smiles on their faces. One lady from the USA sent me a mail to say that she felt like jumping on the sofa as she read this book with pride on the Indian Army. So many responded to convey how they startled their wives with their midnight laughter from this book.

The response to this book on *Battalion Command* has been most satisfying as it is helping the next generation to develop into better and more conscientious leaders. A fading soldier cannot ask for more.

This book is essentially a product of my practice of leadership from platoon to division command over almost four decades. My interactive nature helped me resonate well with men that gave me an insight into the lives and minds of soldiers.

My obsession with military values occasionally brought me into conflict with my superiors in command assignments that have been used to draw lessons for battalion command.

I would like to express my thanks to Col KK Arun, an exceptionally dedicated Rajput officer, for his diligent efforts in helping me with this book. I also convey my gratitude to General Vinod Vashist, another outstanding officer and a gentleman, who shared with me his advisories as a divisional commander.

I wish to thank General (Dr) VK Singh, PVSM, AVSM, YSM (Retd), former Chief of the Indian Army and Minister of State for Foreign Affairs for Overseas Indian Affairs and Statistics and Programme Implementation (Independent Charge), who readily consented to write the foreword of the book when first released.

I need to acknowledge the pivotal role my battalion 5 GUARDS has played in making my military career a delightful journey. Those wonderful men helped me grow as a professional soldier and a grounded human being. They were my silent gurus and this book is primarily based on the experiences of what happened there and with them for over two decades. The relationship built with my men in all command assignments has been the greatest takeaway from my career.

Finally, I acknowledge with deep gratitude the role of my parents for their love, sacrifice and the good values they gave us. My mother prayed for the well-being of all other children first and then for her own children.

These values were the foundation of the path I chose in my life and career. They enabled me to serve with pride and purpose and leave a legacy that I am proud of.

जनरल (डा.) विजय कुमार सिंह
पी वी एस एम, ए वी एस एम, वाई एस एम (से.नि.)
**General (Dr.) Vijay Kumar Singh**
**PVSM, AVSM, YSM (Retd.)**

सांख्यिकी एवं कार्यक्रम
कार्यान्वयन राज्य मंत्री (स्वतंत्र प्रभार),
विदेश राज्य मंत्री एवं प्रवासी भारतीय कार्य राज्य मंत्री
भारत सरकार, नई दिल्ली
**Minister of State for Statistics and Programme Implementation (Independent Charge), Minister of State for External Affairs & Minister of State for Overseas Indian Affairs Government of India, New Delhi**

# FOREWORD

I read this book by Major General Anil Sengar on battalion command with great interest. Very aptly, it has been titled *Battalion Command: Dare to Lead*. Battalion Command has been considered the golden hour in the career of an officer. As the author says, battalion command is less about command and more about leading. The commanding officer has the greatest responsibility of all in that on him depends the effectiveness of the army. Good commanding officers make good battalions while bad commanding officers make bad battalions. Seven hundred men look up to him, and for them, their world ends with him. Notwithstanding his young age, he is known as the proverbial 'Old Man,' because he is expected to have the wisdom and maturity to command a battalion. That also sums up the expectations from him and the challenges he faces.

The socioeconomic changes are bound to have an impact on the military as the men come from the same society with ever increasing awareness and aspirations for their families. The men today face far greater domestic challenges than before. The changing environment demands that the Army transacts its business with more transparency, fairness and empathy.

The author has very lucidly emphasized on the centrality of character, integrity and courage as the core traits that define leadership and the importance of military values as sine qua non for success of the army. The future battlefield contours will make military command more challenging. The biggest impact will be felt at the unit level – the cutting edge and they will need to adapt the leadership style in accordance with the rapid changes.

The book reflects the author's experiences and the path he chose in his career. His passion towards soldiering and military values is reflected in this book. The author, a man of courage and conviction himself, believes that the battalion commander, known as the Tiger in the army, must be fearless and act like one. I couldn't agree more. There can be no other way.

I compliment General Sengar for an impressive work on a topic of great significance to any army. I found it an absorbing read and believe it is an appropriate guide for a passionate commanding officer to command his battalion fearlessly with pride and passion, and leave behind his legacy.

**General VK Singh (Retd)**

# PREFACE

The Military remains the most challenging profession because it demands the highest standards of moral and professional conduct and subconsciously drives a moral burden on the soldier to answer the nation's call with supreme sacrifice without a word. It places upon the soldiery the greatest of responsibilities; the security and honour of your country . In no other profession is it understood that your buddy will give his life to save yours and he trusts you to do the same. Nowhere else does the family of a man undergo deprivations and hardships the way a soldier's does. And above all, a soldier is expected to sacrifice his all for nothing more than just duty as he understands it.

This profession deals with the direct leadership of men in the face of extremely challenging circumstances, which may lead to certain death, or worse, the possibility of their being maimed and disabled for life. Men will execute such tasks willingly and give their all, only when you lead them into the cauldron of melting lead – not if you order them into it.

Amongst all the command and leadership assignments during service, the command of a unit remains the finest and most challenging as also the most exhilarating experience for an officer. The proverbial finest hour in the life of an officer. The term 'battalion' used in the book refers to units of all arms and services known by different names. It is a life time engagement and you will be remembered as long as the battalion exists. A great grandson can walk into the battalion where he will be offered a drink and told more about his great grandfather than he knows himself.

The commanding officer is charged with the most onerous responsibility of nurturing the unit to be prepared to face death without a blink, on his orders. Attaining the stage when the men trust your character, competence and judgment, and are prepared to follow you willingly is the acme of command. The commanding officer leads eight hundred men from varied backgrounds, who hail from an ever increasing materialistic society with growing aspirations. Values which are the foundation of the army do not make much sense outside. So how does a commander motivate and lead his men in such an environmental paradox.

Leadership in this environment is a challenging assignment. Different levels of leadership demand different kinds of traits. The lower the level of command, the more direct is the contact with men, the greater the need for exemplary personal qualities, the lesser the margin for errors in personal conduct, the greater the exposure to personal dangers in combat and, thus, the greater the need for leadership by personal example.

The battalion commander is the most important pillar of any army. In combat arms, the challenge is far greater because threat to life is a constant companion in battle arm chair leadership will not work. It is here that an officer has to display far greater professional competence, physical and moral courage, and leadership and motivational skills.

He carries on his shoulders the sacred responsibility of ensuring that his unit is operationally fit for war in all respects. A failure of command at this level will mean a national embarrassment in war and many lives lost. A quick job card analysis of the commanding officer highlights the magnitude of his responsibilities:

- Ensuring operational preparedness of his command. Broadly, it relates to high state of training of the men, developing future ready junior leadership and equipment serviceability.
- Ensuring a high 'Human Quotient.'
- Meeting the aspirations of his command in professional and personal development.
- Managing the environment.

Each of this aspect is a subject of study by itself and implementation on ground; a monumental task requiring dedication , commitment and, above all, passion.

What makes me qualified to write a book on this subject? I chose to write this book because, while a lot has been written on military leadership, not much has been written with special focus on unit command. I am comfortable writing this because, as the commanding officer and later in higher command assignments, I practiced every word that I have preached in the book.

I had the opportunity to experience the dynamics of command and leadership in varied challenging environments. The leadership style that I adopted as a company, battalion, brigade and the divisional commander extracted the best from my command – voluntarily, making every challenge feel like fun.

One particular incident motivated me to write this book. I was non-empanelled in the promotion board to Brigadier. A commanding officer whom I had hardly known walked into my office. He expressed his disappointment on the result of the promotion board and said, "Sir, I have not known you personally. It is only here that I met you, but I have heard so much about your style of battalion command that we are trying to emulate what you did as a battalion commander." This was not the first time I was given this compliment. When I reflected as to what was so special about my command of my battalion, 5 GUARDS, I remembered a few caveats I had laid for myself on assuming command and these were:

- Battalion command is a payback time; an opportunity to give and not to take.
- As a Commanding Officer, I would be scared of nobody not even God.
- I would command my battalion from the head, but lead straight from my heart. I will place the interests of my battalion, officers and men above everything else. I, as the Commanding Officer, will come last, always and every time.

- My battalion would be the best battalion in the formation. On every count I must leave the unit better than what I inherited.
- This is my last rank; I aspire no more.

This book is based not only on my experiences but also of many others who commanded their units with similar zeal and passion. The characters of each episode are referred as Captain Passion or General Passion as applicable.

My command assignments, starting from my platoon to 22 Infantry Division were passionate love affairs. How I wished they would never end.

Battalion command can be fun, if you see it as a milestone and not a mill stone, or a stepping stone. It will be fun when you see it as a calling and have a purpose in command that goes beyond you.

I was standing at the Amar Jawan Jyoti, India Gate, in uniform with a few officers and men. Large number of tourists got themselves photographed with us. A young mother also walked up with her infant son for a photograph. Handing him over to me, she said, "Can you hold him sir; he will be blessed, and God willing, he will be an army officer one day."

We were no celebrities. They wanted to be photographed with officers of the Indian Army. That is a reason enough to be proud and we can never let them down. The country trusts the military and has expectations, and the military always delivers. The entity that has made this possible is a battalion. Good commanding officers good battalions, poor commanding officers poor battalions. Good battalions good army, poor battalions poor army.

I am a soldier of the old school. I strongly believe that no matter how the world and society may change, the fundamentals of command, leadership and soldiering cannot change. They were no different a millennium ago and they will be no different a millennium into the future. This is my humble effort to share some ground level experiences for the benefit of those who seek to leave their legacy through an honest commitment and devotion to their units.

The government has the responsibility to ensure that the army is well catered for on all counts so that the soldier can dedicate himself to the security of the country without worrying for his kith and kin. Unfortunately, that is not the case. The despicable manner of handling of the one rank, one pension issue (OROP) despite decades of tall promises by all kinds of government, and repeated slighting of the military in pay commissions is there for everyone to see. *The government must remember that how well the present generation of soldiers responds to the nation's call will depend upon how it treats its veterans.* And the government must do so, without their asking for it.

Compare this with the spirit of the British reflected in this article by Lt Gen Baljit Singh (Retd), published in The Tribune, 18 December 2015.

The occasion: 50th Anniversary of the end of WW II, 1995, London, UK.

Six Victoria Cross winners attended the celebrations from India. As Subedar Major (Honorary Captain) Umrao Singh standing over six feet tall and of ramrod stance, flat bellied and broad chest, walked up to Queen Elizabeth in the Audience Hall of Buckingham Palace, any drill sergeant of the Cold Stream Guards Brigade would have been envious. Breaking the precedence of ceremonial etiquette, the gathering burst into spontaneous applause!

The following day, Prime Minister John Major was driving past some invitees and from the corner of his eyes caught the sun glinting on their VC medals. The Prime Minister had his car halted. Walking up to the veterans, he saluted and greeted each one of them with a warm handshake. In the UK if a veteran with a VC or a MC pinned on his chest were to walk out, chances are that nine out of ten passers-by would halt midstride, smile and nod in salutation. In India, not one in a thousand would know what a PVC, MVC or a Vr C looks like, leave alone greet its bearer.

Dismissing his car, John Major escorted them to the venue of the function. Striking a conversation, he enquired if the veterans had any hardships that needed to be addressed. Umrao told him that even though the exchange rate now was Rs 50 to a pound, yet the paltry pension was handed out at the exchange rate of 1945. He asked would it not be fair to revise the pension which was last fixed in 1945 and bring it at par with their counterparts in the UK. John Major was visibly upset at the injustice and promised corrective action.

Six months later, Christopher Thomas, South Asia Correspondent of The Times (London), drove to Umrao Singh's home in Palra Village (Jhajjar District) and informed him that His Majesty's Government had enhanced their VC pension from 100 pounds per annum to 1300 pounds per annum, to be admitted at that day's prevailing exchange rate or subsequent rate, which ever was higher, but never lower.

Umrao Singh brought two glasses of rum and drank a toast with the messenger; "This is for John Major, Prime Minister of Britain."

Mr President, Supreme Commander of the Indian Armed Forces, are you listening?

People who are charged with the security of the nation should better read this:

*The great prime Prime Minister of Magadha, Chanakya, told Emperor Chandragupta Maurya :*

> *"Pataliputra rests each night in peaceful comfort, O King, secure in the belief that the distant borders of Magadha are inviolate and the interiors are safe and secure, thanks only to the Mauryan Army standing vigil with naked swords and eyes peeled for action, day and night, in weather fair and foul, all eight praharas [i.e., round the clock], quite unmindful of personal discomfort and hardship, all through the year, year after year. To this man, O Rajadhiraja, you owe a debt: please, therefore, see to it, suo moto, that the soldier continuously gets his dues in every form and respect, be they his needs or his wants, for he is not likely to ask for them himself.* ***The day the soldier has to demand his dues will be a sad day for Magadha; for then, on that day, you will have lost all moral sanction to be the King!"***

It is for the well-being of the country that someone else must think about the soldier.

How does the Indian government score on this?

# The Regimental Days: Marching with the Fifth

It has been ages since I joined my battalion, the 5 GUARDS, in 1979, and fairly long since I relinquished the command in 2002. I remember most of my stay very clearly, as if it was only yesterday. I stepped out of the train at Jalpaiguri to join my unit on a warm sultry day in July 1979. I was received by a well turned out senior subaltern, Lieutenant SJ Singh. I climbed up in the rear of the vehicle, called 1 Ton, the Second World War petrol guzzler, anxious, wondering what lay ahead. Guardsman Harka Bahadur, a solid muscular Gurkha driver, slammed the tail board. The vehicle rolled off because of the impact, as the hand brake, while pulled up tight was only ceremonial. Instantly, the thought crossed my mind, 'Wow, with such men, it has to be a solid battalion.' And it was. Harka Bahadur stopped the vehicle by brute force. The vintage 1 Ton refused to start as if protesting the punishment meted to its tail board by the driver. After the alternative starting mode of 'danda' start, a technology lost over the years, also failed, I was told to get down and push the vehicle. That was The Infantry, an arm driven on man and will power, thus never failing. That is how I push started my regimental life.

As we bumped along to the unit, an hour's drive away, I asked the jawan sitting with me in the vehicle, what he did. He said he was the 'danda man' of the vehicle. Not wanting to expose my ignorance, I sat quiet, wondering what the 'danda man' was all about and what his duties in the service of the nation were. For me, coming fresh from the academy, every single soldier at all times was in the service of the motherland.

5 GUARDS was a 'pahari' (highlanders) paltan, with men drawn from across the length and breadth of Himalayas. The more time I spent in the battalion, the more I fell in love with these men. They were superb soldiers.

The commanding officer visited my company in Sikkim. He entered one room and asked whose sahayak (buddy) stays here? I said, 'No sahayak sir, I stay here.'

'Why can't you stay in a bigger room?'

'The bigger room has been given to the men, we are short of accommodation.'

That was the way I began, and that was the way I lived. The men always came first.

In the larger part of my unit life, we were out in the field and/or operations. The Hurricane lantern was our companion for the most part when the sun parted company every day. Patromax, the luxury of the days was expensive at Rs 400. It would need a Harvard returned buddy, called batman those days, to have its mantle last more than a day. The pumping technique was complex and very few mastered the art. Net result, mantle not being available easily in those remote areas, and costly at one rupee a day, patromaxes were packed and forgotten, only to be taken out on a marriage anniversary. Generators were still non-existent in the battalions and inverters not heard of in the army. So, there was little to do in the high altitude once the sun went down.

The unit life was great and there was so much fun with those men. When on leave, we waited to get back to the unit; it was a home away from home.

These wonderful men bore everything with a smile despite the fact that we were repeatedly in tough assignments. The battalion fought every war since raising, from the liberation of Goa to the Kargil war with distinction.

In extreme conditions high in the mountains, they would give you the first hot cup of tea, brewed over a smoky fire of wet twigs. Served with smoke blackened hands and watering eyes, it carried the fragrance of their devotion and love that refused to wither with time.

We were on Siachen glacier in 1986. Those were early days. Our officers stayed in winters in the tattered snow tents and improvised shelters made from parachutes. The odd fibre glass huts that were there were given to the men. That was the culture of the unit. The commanding officer carried his own 'pithoo.'

The battalion also launched the unknown attack to capture a village in Poonch sector in 1991, in less than six hours after a stupid surprise order by the divisional commander, when deployed over 20 km in mountains.

After the attack, we held on to the defences dangerously dominated by the enemy from three sides. My buddy, Guardsman Noni Hazong, seeing that I was awake all night and sleeping with the men on the ground in flea infested gujjar hut, decided to make me comfortable. He fabricated a rough pillow. I slept on it for two months, not bothering to ask how he had managed one. When we were finally falling back, I saw my pillow was made of two sand bags full of 2 inch mortar shells, all of them without safety caps and most without even the safety pins. When I looked at him enquiringly, he burst out laughing, '*Saab, kuch toh karna tha, mera saab ke liye,*' (I had to do something to make my officer comfortable). I smiled then and we still laugh over it when we meet even today.

We address each other in the unit with respect as *aap*. If the commanding officer had to punish a soldier, which was rare, he would say, '*Aap ne galti kiya hai, iske lie mein aap ko quarter guard saza sunato hoon,*' There were no raising of voices and no cursing. It was a cheerful happy battalion. Officers and men greeted each other with smile with a resounding 'Ram Ram *saab*' from miles. The taste of *langar chai* and *dal* soup still lingers. The melodious sound of the pipe band and the lilting notes of the jazz band, practicing under a shady tree still ring in the ears. The noisy training area was a delight, with the mortar platoon being the noisiest. The battalion *bara khaana* was a cultural journey across the Himalayas, from J&K to the North East. A Kashmiri dancing the *Bihoo* and a Naga doing the Kumaoni dance was an utter delight. The officers and men mingled and it was an occasion for the men to let their hair down. They were wonderful simple soldiers bringing special skills and culture from all corners of Himalayas.

When we were in the valley combating insurgency, there were no bullet proof jackets for the first few years. In 1993 the first lot came and all battalions were issued thirty each for the officers. The officers declined to wear them because the men were right up with them. The men too declined to wear them for the same reason. Funny or stupid, no one wore them and they lay in the store till we had enough for both officers and men to wear. That was the wonderful spirit.

I had that wonderful buddy, Naik Mahesh. He would shield me bodily whenever we came under fire.

I said, 'You do that all the time, with no bulletproof jacket. You too have two little girls, like I have two little boys.' He said, 'I am your buddy. I am responsible for you. I will never be able to live in peace if something ever happens to you without the bullet going through me.' Not many are fortunate to have such top rate soldiers. Creditably, when the battalion was to move out from Sopore, the hottest insurgency spot in the valley, where it had been deployed for long, a delegation of locals appealed to the Governor of J&K that this 'chiddy fauz' (Garuda emblem) should remain there and we did.

Hav Rajinder Neog , an outstanding musician, suffered long from blood cancer when I was commanding. A little before he died, he said in English, 'Saab, 5 GUARDS is great.' That was the sense of ownership in all ranks. There was that simpleton and illiterate Subedar Major Dewan Singh who declined to proceed on leave on his daughter's death, because there were soldiers' cremation to be done in the unit the next day. Rising to this rank purely on loyalty, honesty and dedication, you could trust your last ten bucks on him. Who needs an educated man when you have such fine specimens as soldiers?

We converted to a mechanized battalion in 1994, after I had put in sixteen years of service as an infantryman. With that ended the adventurous infantry life.

These men applied their own logic at times and that made life fun. Guardsman Kapson Pao, from Nagaland, returned three days late from leave. When he reported to the company Junior Commissioned Officer (JCO), he was told that he would be punished for coming late. Kapson Pao could not be traced the next day as the company looked for him everywhere. Pao reappeared after thirty days. When marched up and asked where he had disappeared after reporting to the unit, he said, '*Saab, main toh ghar ka problem se thora late aya. Senior JCO bola teen din late ho ya tees din, saza barabar milega. Toh main socha agar saza barabar hee milega toh poora tees din late aatta hoon, aur wapas ghar chala gaya. Ab tees din ke baad theek report kiya saab. Aap jo saza dena hain, de do.*' (I was late by three days due to domestic problem. Senior JCO told me that late was late. The punishment was the same for late from leave, whether three days or thirty days. So I thought if the punishment was the same, I decided to come thirty days late and went back home. You can give me any punishment you want.)

Havaldar Ram Bahadur Nepali was an outstanding soldier. When his retired father, also from the paltan, wrote to the commanding officer that his son had not come on leave since long, plainly confessed that he had not gone home for nine months. When apprised that he had been on casual leave, said, fifteen days is too less to go to Nepal, since his village is two days' walk from the road head. So, he has married twice, one wife he keeps at Delhi for casual leave and one in Nepal for annual leave.

These men were a different breed. They were not perfect but they were simply as good as it can get. They were absolutely honest, truthful, loyal, hardworking and dependable. You were sure they will never let you down and they never ever complained of anything, and that made us more concerned for their well-being.

Out of twenty three years, I served about fifteen in the unit. There was no scope for a façade or double standards. We knew what the other was under the skin, and we were honest. We could recognize each other from the shadows and silhouette. The command of the battalion was absolute bliss. Young kids, who were toddlers when I joined the unit, were my young officers, with a large number of second generation men.

I commanded the battalion based on the caveats I had set for myself. My style occasionally brought me in conflict with higher commanders, but they respected me for my convictions. The command had its challenges, having commanded in Op Vijay, Op Rakshak and Op Parakram. Occasionally, the battalion got un-implementable orders, but they were dealt with appropriately. There was never 'yes' said when military wisdom said the reply should be 'no.'

Our men made the regimental experience an absolute pleasure. The universal ever smiling faces are etched in memory. I was most fortunate to have the finest team of officers and men that one can ask for. These *paharis* were just lovable troops and we were one big family. There was passion in everything we did. The battalion was all that mattered and it excelled on all counts.

During a holi celebration in the battalion, I had two drums filled with rum. I invited the men to a 'no holds barred drinking.' The Subedar Major cautioned me that these men will lose control and create trouble. I said, I know them well, they won't. Surprised at the incredible offer, they hesitated. As I filled my mug with rum and drank, the men filled theirs and drank to their fill amongst much fun and chatter. Drenched in and out, they went to the barracks and went to sleep. There was not one untoward incident.

The four legged Guardsman, Badshah Khan, a Great Dane mascot, became an integral part of the battalion and brought everyone lots of joy. He would run BPET, receive visitors with a hand shake, stand on hind legs and accompany the battalion battle cry with a synchronized bark. He was part of the battalion PT display team. Gradually he rose to the rank of a Naik, a rank bestowed on him in the unit *sainik sammelan*. Men often joked how Badshah was senior to them.

It was extremely sad to part ways from the band of brothers after twenty three years in the battalion. Every day in the battalion was great fun and each of these *paharis* was a gem.

*Oh God; why don't you turn the clock back in Time,*
*So I can be a battalion commander just one more Time.*

# FIELD MARSHAL KM CARIAPPA, OBE

(Excerpts from the first letter written by Field Marshal Cariappa, the first Commander-in-Chief of the Indian Army (1949 1953) to all officers. As relevant today, seven decades later.)

I send all officers of the Army the following message. I earnestly hope that every officer in the Army today will take all that follows in the spirit in which it is written, and live up to the requirements stated, hundred percent in the service of our country.

## Welfare of Troops

Our troops have always been magnificent in their sense of loyalty to the Army and the country. We can ensure that this satisfactory state of affairs continues if we keep our troops happy and contented in every way. This calls for personal attention of every officer, to the welfare of the men placed under his command. Their needs are simple. If the *jawan* feels that he has an officer who is professionally efficient, a gentleman and a person in whom he can place his confidence to safeguard his personal and domestic interests, we officers will have gone a very long way to ensure that man's loyalty to the Army and our government. As I have often said, our *jawans* are absolute gems. I would like you all to make everyone of them feel that they are proud to serve under you as a commander, whatever your command may be, however big or small it may be.

## Civilians

We must make them all feel that we, as officers, are always ready to associate ourselves with them as citizens of the land in our common efforts to serve our country, in our respective spheres of activities. Please make quite certain that you do NOT lay yourselves open to criticism by our people for lack of courtesy and good manners in your general conduct both in public and in private. Pay due respect to civilians senior to you and be as courteous as you possibly can, as an officer and a gentleman, to those above you, equal to you and below you in civil life, for courtesy and good manners do NOT cost you anything. Let us set an example to the rest of our country in regard to the value of these two essential things, i.e., courtesy and good manners.

## Politics

Please do not get mixed up with party politics. Officers and soldiers should not take an active part in political matters. You will appreciate that if we did so, we will not be serving the government of the day loyally. Remember we serve the people of the country and, therefore, the government of the day is that government which is put in power by the people. This, however, does NOT mean that we, as citizens of the country, should neglect our understanding of various political parties and their objectives. Now that we have a right to vote, it is imperative that all of us, officers and men, should be quite clear in our minds in regard to exercising our privilege of voting.

## Economy

Every one of us in the Army must do everything we can to save every pie we can, so as to ease the present financial burden on our government. Economy of transport, petrol, supplies, equipment, accommodation, personnel will all go to help solve this problem. See that not one of these is used more than is absolutely necessary and essential to ensure the efficiency of the Army. Remember, as I have often told you before, we are the custodians of the tax payer's property. Everything in the Army such as the service of the personnel, supplies, equipment, accommodation, vehicles, animals, etc., all belong to him. It is our sacred duty to see that we do not misuse any of these for our personal use in any way whatever. The proper care and storage and the efficient maintenance of all stores, weapons, equipment and vehicles is our personal responsibility.

## Public Funds

Every officer must make quite certain that Public and Regimental funds are not misappropriated or embezzled. I would ask you all who are placed in charge of public funds, including your Regimental Funds of all kinds, to be scrupulously honest in the handling of these funds. Do not be tempted to use these funds for private purposes.

## Ex-Servicemen

Firstly, please deal sympathetically with all cases of ex-servicemen which come to your knowledge. If an ex-serviceman comes to you with a request for help, do not send him away by saying, 'No, this is NOT my job.' Tell him, if it is not your job and you cannot help him, where he can go and whom he should see for help. Remember, these ex-servicemen have done their stuff for the country. It is because of their grand work in the past, coupled with our humble efforts since we have been free, that our army today enjoys the respect, the confidence and the affection of our people. We cannot neglect the interests and welfare of our ex-servicemen. Go out of your way whenever possible to help them if you can.

## Professional Study

Your profession today is a very complex matter. The advent of mechanization and scientific warfare has increased your responsibility in regard to your being prepared as an efficient soldier and officer in the service of your country. It must be your constant endeavour to see that you are up to date in military teachings in so far as they affect, initially your own arms of the service, secondly the Army and thirdly the three services, Army, Navy and Air Force as a whole. This calls for very extensive and continuous study. Do NOT waste your valuable time on useless pursuits. Plan your time in such a manner that you allot adequate portion of it for study without forgetting time for recreation and relaxation.

You must take part in the organized games, both individually and with your men. If we are to keep pace with modern developments, we must give the question of scientific research and operational research our very serious thought. You must concentrate on ensuring that the basic training of the men you command is thorough in every respect. Do NOT be slip-shod in this respect. This means your spending more time on study and training. Do NOT waste time on useless pursuits, for every second you so waste in peace, you will pay for in blood in times of war, for the lives of the men you command are in your hands and lives are too sacred to be so used. In your training, pay very great attention to minor tactics because if your training in minor tactics is really sound and thorough, your problems in action will be made so much easier.

## Officers' Private Life

I would like you also to make quite certain that you do not overdo your amusements. By this I mean, do not indulge too much in lavish entertainment, too much dancing and things like that. I am very sorry to see that the object of club life is not being properly understood by a number of officers in the Army today. Please do not be under the impression that Club Life is designed mainly for DRINKING and DANCING. It is not incumbent upon you to drink alcohol when you go to the club. Remember, alcohol is expensive these days. Think of your children's education or of putting by some money for a rainy day.

## Officers' Mess

I would like to see the Mess life kept up with all its dignity, propriety and correctness. Do not make your messes cheap by inviting all and sundry to your parties. I regard Messes as excellent training grounds for officers of all ranks from the point of view of maintaining discipline, comradeship, teamwork and building up one's character. Make quite certain the Mess is treated as a home for the officers of the unit. Officers must be dressed properly at all times. Please also ensure that not only your ante-rooms are kept neat and smart but your pantries, kitchens, and washing places are also kept equally smart and tidy. As regards food in the Mess, it must be simple but wholesome, well cooked and properly served. I do not think it is attractive to see the table covered with bottles of all kinds of sauces, sliced onions, chutneys and pickles dotted about. All these can be kept on a side table and brought up as and when required. I wish to see Messes used, as I have said above, as a home for officers. Whilst maintaining discipline and propriety in regard to paying respect to senior officers and visitors, I do not wish to see Messes as parade grounds where officers click their heels and stand to attention whenever they talk to a senior officer.

## Security

You have often heard the old saying, 'Careless talks cost lives.' Every one of us has a very sacred duty to the people of our country whose security we have pledged to guard. Please be hundred per cent security-minded at all times. Do NOT talk loosely in public or even in private to show off, 'I am in the know,' merely to gain cheap popularity. I have already put over to you all, through your Army Commander, the desirability of not consuming alcoholic drinks at public parties. You know the reason why. You see some of us can take drinks and some cannot. It is amazing how one's tongue gets loose after a glass or two of whisky or some such other strong drink. I have heard, much to my horror, some getting a bit too talkative on service matters at public parties after they have had a few drinks. Surely, we can do without these drinks at these public parties when refusing drinks is indeed in the interest of the security of our people. It is not a matter to be ashamed of to tell your hosts when you go to a public party that you do not wish to take any alcoholic drinks. On the other hand, if your hosts know of the noble idea behind your refusal to take a drink you will be held in a greater esteem by them.

## Commissioned Officers

We are all members of one and the same team where good comradeship, fellowship, loyalty to each other and cooperation between all ranks at all levels, are absolutely essential for the good of our Army. Please do not get into the despicable habit of becoming ranks conscious. Take what job is given to you. Do NOT ask for jobs. Give your best, your very best, at all times. We have all got to do this if we want to serve our Army and our country well. I will ask you all again, please, NOT to indulge in another despicable habit, which is criticizing senior officers and indeed criticizing junior officers also. If we all did our normal work conscientiously and completely, no one can have a single spare moment left to indulge in such talk about each other.

## Junior Commissioned Officers

I would like every officer to see that Junior Commissioned Officers, who are the backbone of our Army, do receive their proper recognition as such and are given every facility and guidance to carry out their job well. They must continue to receive from every officer the same degree of courtesy and regard and respect as they used to enjoy before the War. Some people seem to think because we are a fully nationalized Army, there is no place for JCOs in the Army. They argue that JCOs were a necessary link between the rank and file and the officers during the British regime and that such a link is not essential now as there are no more British officers in our Army. People, who talk thus, miss the most important aspect of this matter. The JCO has always been, and always will be primarily a commander of a sub-unit under the command of a commissioned officer. These appointments, i.e., commands of sub units have been held by our JCOs most efficiently throughout the history of our Army. They withstood the test of two of the biggest wars fought in the last 200 years. I would like every officer to regard these appointments in the manner I have stated and in no other way.

Such JCOs who are considered fit to be promoted commissioned officers, have been in the past and will in the future, be so promoted. They will be given every help to ensure that they enjoy their full privileges as commanders of sub-units as they did in the past. Every officer in the Army will see that the *izzat* of our JCOs is maintained at all times.

Finally, as long as you remain in the Army, whether you are a regular or temporary officer, please give your very best in the service of the country until the very last second you are in the Army, working as a loyal, well disciplined and honest member of this big team, our Army, as an Indian and with no anti communal feeling of any kind whatever. Please do not allow the virus of communalism to get into the Army. Communalism is a most destructive parasite which, if allowed to grow in the Army, will spell disaster for the country as a whole. We must maintain and enhance the good name we are fortunate enough to have today, which has been so liberally and generously expressed by our people as being a high factor which has helped and will help to provide the security and safety for our country. I feel absolutely certain, with not an iota of doubt in my mind, that all officers in my team, of which I have the proud privilege and the honour today of being the Captain, will help me in the matters I have stated above to see that we have a first class Army in all respects.

*Do nothing in private that you will be ashamed to admit in public.*

—Field Marshal KM Cariappa, OBE

# CHAPTER I

# MAKE YOUR COMMAND COUNT

## Battalion Command: The Ultimate Honour

No level below the commanding officer has independent authority. No level above him has the direct authority.

The starting point of an enjoyable command is the realization that the privilege of commanding a unit is the highest honour that an officer can ever get. It is the last direct command of troops. I like to describe it as the commanding officer's 'Sultanate' where his writ runs in totality. He has the opportunity to leave a legacy that could become a folk lore in the unit. He would be looked up to by all his men for everything and believe that he has the solution to all their problems. Despite the young age of commanding officers today, he is known as the '*Gaon Burha*' or the proverbial 'Old man.' He is like a parent to his men, 'Mai Baap.' What does a parent do for his children. He provides love, education, safety, happy environment and grooming so that they have a good and secure future. They try to live their dreams through their children. The commanding officer has to do that for his men. He has the opportunity to put his dreams into practice. He can do what he always felt a good commanding officer should do.

At the end of the day, an honest introspection will tell him what he has left behind, either way. While every battalion commander would feel that he has commanded well, there is this litmus test; the longer your legacy lasts, the more selfless you have been in command. The more selfless you have been in command, more the guarantee that you have had a good and enjoyable command.

## Get your Focus Right: Hit the Ground Running

Let me suggest that the potential commanding officers do the following before taking over command.

**Vision:** Write down your vision for your battalion. Why do you think the officers and men of your unit should buy your vision?

**Mission Statements:** Write your mission statement for your command.

- What are your roles as the commanding officer and how do you plan to achieve them?
- How different is this responsibility from the ones in the past in terms of knowledge, competence and a leader? Are you adequately equipped or need to work on it?
- Write down the three most important things you need to do to make your battalion operationally effective.
- What are the three most critical things your men would expect from you?

**Farewell Speech:** Write down your farewell speech. What you would like to be said about you, if it was given honestly, without the courtesy of being nice to the outgoing commanding officer on the following.

- Professionalism
- Character and Integrity
- Selflessness.
- Courage.
- Compassion.
- Growth and development of all ranks and families.

Notwithstanding the changing socioeconomic scene, Indian soldiers are an excellent lot. With more than three decades of service, most of it in challenging environment, I do not remember our men letting us down anywhere. We, therefore, need to be worthy of commanding such fine men.

'Tears welled up as they looked at him, and they appeared not as an army visiting its king but one attending a funeral. The grief was especially intense amongst those who were at his bed side. Alexander looked at them and said: "After my death, will you find a king who deserves such fine men?"' Curtius, of Alexander the Great's farewell to the Macedonians on his death bed, 323 BC. The History of Alexander, John Yardley, 1984.

An officer has to be worthy of commanding men who repose unquestioned trust and faith in their commanding officer. The men expect him to be all knowing; almost godlike.

So how and when does an officer begin to start preparing for command? In the Indian context of regimental system, officers spend their entire regimental service in one unit. From a young lieutenant, he goes on to command the same unit. He has to demonstrate consistency of high professional and personal standards. He could not be living by different standards all his life and then suddenly demand high standards simply because he is the commanding officer now. In the unit in which he serves for nearly two decades, he is totally naked, watched by seven hundred pairs of eyes. You cannot fool so many eyes for too long. Such a commanding officer will still be obeyed, but he will not command trust and respect of his command the mortar and cement of soldiering that binds the senior with his juniors. Every officer who is commissioned must aspire to command his battalion – and no more.

Why not, would be the prompt question of many? What is wrong with having an ambition to command a division for instance? May be, part of the answer to that question lies in this conversation.

The British army has been a professional and an effective army for centuries. The British Raj owed its success to its professional military which enabled it to become a nation on which the sun never set. Much after the Second World War, people felt that the British army was no more the same professional force that it had been for centuries. When a journalist asked a retired General why it was so, he replied, 'Because, in the olden days, an officer aspired to command his battalion. Today an officer aspires to become a General.' While ambition is necessary to drive a person, over ambition leads to sacrifice of military values. It is certain that in pursuit of that illusionary goal, he will miss the greater pleasure that the journey offers and so will those unfortunate to be associated with him. On the other hand if he aspires to be a good commanding officer, he will do the right things and in all probability become a General as well; and a good one at that.

I know one such case where the individual, while still a cadet in the training academy, apparently would claim that the lowest rank he would reach is one star Brigadier. His father at that time was a senior serving officer. Cutting the story short, the individual was decorated for 'apparent' gallantry in a metro city; but was found grossly wanting when his battalion was inducted to Siachen Glacier. Result, he was compelled to quit the army very early. While this may be one example, it highlights the point. On the contrary, if the same individual had nurtured the ambition of becoming a good commanding officer, he would be looking forward to proving his mettle in battle and would not have had the ignominy of having to quit in disgrace.

Ambition is the tonic that propels a man to achieve his goals. Commanding a battalion is a legitimate ambition that every officer who marches past the portals of the military academies must harbour. The preparation for a good command must start early as a young officer. The first thing in that long journey is to become a man of character and integrity.

An officer needs to evolve himself from early days for the simple reason that good soldiering must become a habit and that habit is best and most easily inculcated at this early stage of an officer's career. Should then a young officer be told that he must have the ambition to be a commanding officer one day? Most certainly yes, for a young lieutenant, the commanding officer is a demi-God and to aspire to occupy that exalted chair and lead a body of hundreds of men into battle will motivate him to be a good and professional regimental officer. It is a stage based learning process as one grows in service. He has to begin with being a good tank commander, platoon commander, battery commander and then a good commanding officer. There are few indispensable traits that are the hallmark of a good commander, whatever be the level; the 4CsE, i.e., character, competence, courage (moral and physical), concern for your men and personal example. It is my strong belief that a foundation based on 4CsE will ensure that the young lieutenant will make a good officer, never mind the rank that he attains. Imbibing these qualities means that he has the right foundation for a solid leadership career. Good soldiering is based on good character and good character is 'what a man is in the dark.' Every officer must remember that your reputation travels faster than you do.

Does this mean that every officer aspiring to be a good commanding officer needs to lead a monastic life? Certainly not. Everyone is entitled to his share of fun and must have it. 'One hundred percent work and one hundred percent fun' is the right mix; perfectly achievable and acceptable.

When it comes to monastic living, every commanding officer must set standards that he will never violate, whatever be the cost – integrity, honesty, selflessness and unit interest. A good officer wears his code of ethics on his sleeves. He declares his values loud and clear from the roof top and displays his convictions in public. An officer has to be honest beyond an iota of doubt. He has to be one and seen to be one. We waste too much energy in things too small and of any worthwhile consequence.

The Chetwode motto inscribed in the Indian Military Academy is the best guideline for an officer to follow. You do that and I promise that you will love soldiering.

> *"The Safety, Honour And Welfare Of Your Country Come First Always And Every Time.*
>
> *The Honour, Welfare And Comfort Of The Men You Command Come Next.*
>
> *Your Own Ease, Comfort And Safety Come Last Always And Every Time."*
>
> —Sir Philip Chetwode

I asked some officers as to what was their idea of a good commanding officer? Here is the summary of what they said:

- Accomplishes the mission against all odds.

- Is selfless and places organizational interests before his own.
- Uses his resources most economically in accomplishment of the mission.
- Allows full freedom to his officers to do the task.
- Looks after the welfare of his men and families.
- Some listed a vast number of good qualities.

A good commanding officer is a bundle of good qualities. If I were to construct a man using all the characteristics highlighted above, I would finish sculpting a near perfect leader. While perfect leaders will be far and few to find, can we train good leaders? To paraphrase William Somerset Maugham, 'There are three rules for creating good leaders. Unfortunately, no one knows what they are.'

He may have said that in some context at a different time in history. As far as the army is concerned, leadership is a choice to walk the talk. A choice to live by certain values and practice them in thought and action. While there are no set rules to make a good commanding officer, qualities of a good officer or a good commanding officer are easily identified as listed by officers above. Anyone who has the desire and the will to become a good officer can improve himself. Certain facets of personality that have a bearing on leadership are intrinsic and would need strong internal desire to change and change you can.

Analysis of the above perceptions highlight the following aspects of a good commanding officer:

- Trains his unit to near perfection.
- Professional competence to frame the right plans and accomplish the mission with maximum economy of effort.
- Invests in professional development of his command and gives freedom to his subordinates to function.
- Courage of conviction to stand up to his beliefs in the genuine interest of his battalion, but equally understands the larger perspective.
- Prepared to subordinate his interests for his unit's.
- Is genuinely concerned for the welfare and growth of his men.
- Loves his men as he does his children.

I would add one quality that in my scheme differentiates a great commanding officer from a good one. And this quality is the selfless **passion** for his battalion. For me, soldiering is a calling. Calling means, it is something that goes beyond you. It means utmost trust and faith. It means putting service before self. It means physical and mental deprivation. It means the ultimate honour to serve and if need be to die for your buddy and your battalion. It means a belief in the ethics and values of the army. The biggest manifestation of this calling is the regimental service. For it is here that maximum sacrifices are made. Thus, battalion command is a calling like none other. The whole concept goes beyond 'yourself.'

Men should have the confidence in an officer's ability and trust in his character to lead them in battle. While it is hard to be an excellent commanding officer, it is easy to avoid being a bad one. What are the worst faults a commanding officer can have? Conversely, the traits of a bad commanding officer are the following:

- Sees his battalion as a stepping stone for personal progression and looks for short term gains.
- Puts himself above his officers and men and sets different standards for himself than others.
- Neglects operational preparedness of his unit by accepting too many mundane assignments at the expense of training.
- Thinks that he is the wisest man in the unit and that there is nothing he can learn from others.
- Allows his wife to be overbearing in the unit.
- Seeks credit and passes the blame to others; thinks all good is because of him and all wrong is because of others.
- Avoids taking decisions.
- Thinks 'I' and forgets 'We'.
- Allows superior commanders to interfere with his command.
- Kisses up and kicks down.

Qualities that a commanding officer must develop are impeccable character, sincerity of action, clarity of thought and courage of conviction.

Lieutenant Colonel Cariappa (Later Brigadier), an outstanding officer, known in Guards fraternity for his morals and ethics, was commanding

4 GUARDS. He was out on short leave. An accident took place in the unit during his absence. On his return, the brigade commander mentioned the accident, saying he does not think high of his second-in-command, and now that annual confidential reports are due, he should take note of this. Colonel Kipper, as he was known, said that he has known his second-in-command for sixteen long years and knew him well. He will do justice to the officer, the commander had his own column in the confidential report and he can do what he felt appropriate.

General Himmeth, another outstanding officer was commanding 4 GUARDS. The divisional commander visited the battalion when he was on leave. He commented that the commanding officer is always on leave when he comes. When Colonel Himmeth returned, his second-in-command, amongst other things, mentioned what the divisional commander had said about him being on leave. Colonel Himmeth, promptly called up the divisional commander and told him that it was inappropriate of him to discuss the commanding officer with his officers.

**Time and Temper Management:** Time management is critical for a commanding officer. In operations, it will always be the case. He cannot do everything himself. Time management goes well beyond efficient use of time alone. It is a function of having correct priorities and focus. It is about not doing the unnecessary and not wasting your time on trifles that do not contribute to your objectives. It is about focusing on major issues and delegating the rest. It is a function of concurrence in working and decentralization. For this reason, it is important that staff officers are selected on merit, employing the best man for the job. A commanding officer must be the master of his time and dictate how he uses his time rather than time dictating how and what he does.

A simple time management philosophy stated by Steven Covey will be useful. This suggests slotting an activity into one of the following four categories.

| | Urgent | Non-Urgent |
|---|---|---|
| Important | | |
| Not Important | | |

The commanding officer must understand the difference between important and urgent. He should prioritize important issues and identify those that must be addressed by him personally, those that can be delegated but need to be monitored and those that need no monitoring. This will facilitate organizing work systematically without creating stress and over burdening himself. Directive style of command facilitates time management and decentralization is the key to a happy and effective command. A monthly and quarterly planner helps avoid surprises.

Time and troop effort is a precious resource. It is necessary that economy of time and human effort is exercised by commanding officers. It is unproductive for any commander to hold back others just because he is required to sit late in the office. He must remember that while the head of the organization can choose his pace, subordinate officers do not have that luxury and may be required to address other commitments later in the day. It is also of utmost importance that the commanding officer, or for that matter every officer is punctual at all times. The benefit goes beyond what meets the eye. It is an effective way to demonstrate value of time and discipline to your command, a training by itself.

Anger in simple terms is an individual's response to an unpleasant development, act, news or a behaviour as it affects an individual or his beliefs. It would seem trivial to talk of such a mundane issue. People in authority will often be confronted with situations that have the potential to piss them off. It is important that such people respond to such situations in a mature manner or else they will only be sorry for their response.

Anger is the worst enemy of one self. People in authority, particularly the commanding officers, who deal directly with men, have to be men of patience, who should be prepared to think before acting. Looking back at my career, whenever I have lost my cool, which has been rare, introspection left me in no doubt that my response was unwarranted, poor and often disproportionate. As a commanding officer, one will quite often be confronted with situations that send our tempers soaring. Sometime it will involve superiors, sometime peers and sometime the subordinates in the unit. This may happen for a thousand reasons which could vary from lack of preparation for an event, lackadaisical attitude of some juniors or simply non-implementation of orders in a manner he expects.

Each commanding officer must evolve his anger control mechanism. The best way is to train yourself to walk away from the scene without a word, delaying the response to a later time when the mental turbulence has calmed. Sometimes un-implementable directions and unjustified demands from higher headquarters can send the tempers soaring for some commanding officers. The best action is to sleep over it for a day or two, if the time permits. Quite often the development will correct itself. If it does not, you will be addressing it with a more rational mind.

Remember, when a bullock cart wades through a pond, it creates turbulence, muddying the water. Return after a while, the waters are calm and the muck is settled restoring clarity in water. Likewise is the state of mind. Give yourself time, and the mind will settle down to rational thinking.

I was commanding my division. One spirited young officer, outraged by his soldier's refusal to box in the ring severely manhandled him. This turned into a major incident of mass indiscipline by the men, reported and debated in the national media. This is what I mean, while command is an emotional concept, the heart must never override the mind.

It is important that a commander trains himself to control his moods and temper. Ensure you use not one word of profanity for that does your position and dignity great harm.

**Perfection or Excellence:** One self-inflicted injury that leads to avoidable peace of mind is to be a perfectionist or a bad loser. I have seen some take pride in saying so. In both cases, these self professed traits did the unit more harm than good. It is a good idea to believe in the concept of excellence rather than perfection for, while excellence can be quantified and felt, perfection will often be a mirage to a perfectionist. A perfectionist will rarely be satisfied. In the bargain, he is only likely to bring misery to himself and his unit, leading to even poorer performance. I have seen that happen. A unit will not win every competition, but it can excel in most. Thus, a commanding officer must articulate the definition of success. One definition is, 'A deep sense of satisfaction achieved, knowing your battalion made the best effort you are capable of – that you could have done no more.' What was lacking in skill is what must be worked upon and you will be a winner next time.

A commanding officer may be under various kinds of stress, in peace and war. He must develop a calm mind capable of rational thinking.

A battalion command is an emotional concept. Yet a battalion must be commanded from the mind through intellect and not from the heart alone. Intellect may go with the heart, but emotions should not dictate the decision as emotions have a weakening effect. While a commanding officer must feel intensely for his men, yet should not allow that to cloud his judgment. (Demystifying Leadership, Lt Gen KB Kala)

A commanding officer must practice spirituality and not so much religion. Spirituality encourages development and growth of the mind and the soul. It helps a leader to maintain calm and balance when under duress and adversity.

## Military Values Vs Religious Values

One commanding officer had made the weekly mandir parade a voluntary affair, much to the chagrin of the unit religious teacher. It was based on one belief that if a soldier was to live by the military values and all that this profession and the uniform stood for, there was no need for any religion for motivation. These values placed far more demanding 'non-parochial' codes of conduct on a soldier than any religion does.

Unfortunately, today, the virus of communalisation is being spread in our society by some vested interests. Some incidents that have occurred in the recent past do not go with military ethos. The military can ill-afford to have this, for it can seriously rupture our biggest strength-camaraderie and brotherhood cemented together by military values and unity of purpose that transcend caste, faith, community and religion. All our units have soldiers from different faiths, regions and castes. While, generally speaking, there is no conflict between the military and religious values, the narrative being propagated by some vested interests against symbols of the national identity demands that our motivation be based on military values and not on religion, for soldiering is our religion. We saw the result of religious misguidance in some units during 'Operation Blue Star.' Also, the incidents of collective acts of indiscipline are invariably witnessed in one class composition units, where religion, caste or regional identity becomes the medium of exploitation.

## Command must be Fun

> *If you have some wrinkles on your face at the end of your command, they must only indicate where your smiles have been.*
>
> —Anonymous

When I took over the command of my battalion, Brigadier Ajai Pahwa, an officer of the battalion, sent me a congratulatory letter. Among other things he wrote, 'Command of a battalion is a heady wine. Sip it slowly and you will enjoy it. Gulp it down and you will have a headache.' I will explain what I made out of that.

It is going to be a wonderful experience provided one steps up to that position with maturity and a sense of responsibility without too much excitement. Unit command must be seen as a milestone and not a stepping stone in one's career. On assuming command, there is a major change in status, perks and privileges. On the uniform, there is additional brass and addition of collar tabs or 'lip sticks' as they are known in the army. That sets you up in a different league. Everyone gives the commanding officer that extra respect not available to other colonels. Sign boards such as 'Flag Cars and CO's Vehicles Only' says it all. On the other side, the commanding officer has some perks such as dedicated military transport and extra help at home. He assumes the power to write the performance report of the officers that could give a man a false sense of power to control others' destiny. The lady suddenly finds herself more equal among equals and more wanted by the unit officers and ladies. I remember reading a report that said; of all the problems that took place in the units, more than eighty percent had something to do with ladies. That says it all. My advice to the ladies therefore is – handle the trappings of power with maturity. You will be out of the exalted position before you realize.

There is no supervision over a commanding officer except his own conscience. The new found status has the potential to cause embarrassment if not handled with maturity. A person with weak integrity can easily slip into temptations.

Further, there may be few self serving officers who will be happy to lead you up the wrong path if you show even a hint of moral weakness. A commanding officer will do well to remember that he has no lien over any part of unit property or asset, and he will only be happy if he follows this advice. Remember the old saying, If the king plucks an apple, the public will take away even the roots.

So, a budding commanding officer and his lady wife must take a deep breath and tell themselves that he is just another officer in the long list of commanding officers before him. That it is a temporary phase and sooner than he realizes, he will be done with it and gone, and someone else will step into his shoes. So, he will be better off telling himself to sip the heady wine-slowly.

On the other hand, he has to be excited about the fulfilment of his dream to command his battalion. He has to be excited about leaving his legacy behind. He has to be passionate about making his battalion the best battalion in the formation. He has to be excited about paying back what his battalion has given him and, above all, he has to be concerned about leaving the battalion with the satisfaction that he gave it his all selflessly.

For the commanding officer, the whole battalion is his office. He will do well to spend most of his time outside the four walls of his (these days) plush office. Remember, all important unit activities happen out in the open and little inside the four walls of the commanding officer's office. The best feedback comes when one sees things for oneself and that will not happen sitting inside the office. The troops will be happy to see him and he will be able to impact his command through his personality, personal observations and timely mid course correction. The battalion commander must be thoroughly aware of what his companies are doing to be certain that his company commanders are singing from the same song sheet, composed by him.

The battalion commander needs to have fun and let his command have fun too. With the frequency at which our commanders change, out of the commanding officers, brigade commanders and the divisional commanders, there is one new man every four to six months. Each of these commanders has got a short command period in which to make his mark. Imagine the plight of the battalion, having to move at breakneck speed all the time. The commanding officer has to smartly do the balancing trick. I remember my battalion was posted in an active counter insurgency area. The battalion was doing well but the commander would allow us no respite; not a single day's break in the week for rest and refit. At that rate the battalion would have certainly lost enthusiasm and zeal, leading to complacency. The commanding officer would give us a break every week through innovative ways without disobeying orders. Likewise, every soldier must get one day off in a week to do what he wishes to and spend time with his family. He will deliver more the next week.

In the old days, it was common for the officers to eat out in some *dhaba* carrying their liquor and having fun. Calling on unit officers at the most odd hours of night was good fun and built camaraderie amongst officers. Young officers hunted in packs zooming off on their noisy bikes for fun.

Occasionally, the commanding officer's wife would cook something for the bachelors and send it to the mess. The commanding officer would land up in the mess for an occasional dinner that would last late. These activities made regimental life fun and built a happy team. Unfortunately, such team building activities have disappeared. Twenty hour TV and internet are the major culprits. Where has all the fun gone?

The commanding officer has to realize that his mood makes the difference between a good day and a bad day in the battalion. He must accept that things will go wrong. He does not have to get pissed off on everything. So make sure to start the day with a good mood, every single day. The commanding officer's wife has an important role to play in it.

A commanding officer must appreciate the power of smile. It is magical. Smile must be part of his wardrobe. He must develop one, if he is not blessed with one. He must drive into the battalion and return every salute with a cheerful smile and an enthusiastic *Kaisa hai Ram Bahadur?* (How are you today, soldier?)

I have seen commanding officers, do what you may, find something to get pissed off about. They do their cause no good. Commanding officers must divide his day into time to work and time to have fun. The office formality must be left there as he steps out of it.

## Command is All About Passion

Command will be great when the purpose is beyond you. When you understand that command is not about control, it is about empowerment of your subordinates, you sow the seeds of a great command...

> *During the Second World War, Colonel Darby was offered the command of a regiment with an increase of one grade in rank, but he refused to take it because he wished to stay with the men he had trained. On the same day, General Wedemeyer requested to be reduced to a Colonel so that he could take command of a regiment. I consider these two acts outstanding.*
>
> —General George Patton, Jr., *Patton on Leadership*

I too consider that brilliant leadership. Clearly, such ethos were the reasons for the astounding success of the Americans. German Army had similar ethos that ensured that they maintained cohesion till the last days.

The oxford dictionary describes passion as an intense desire for something. Passion is born out of dedication to a purpose that goes beyond you. In the context of the battalion commander, the purpose is the professional and social well-being of the battalion. Like the baby in the womb of a pregnant mother, it continues to grow till others can't help seeing it too. He will do things not for reaping personal benefits during his command, but for the long-term good of his unit, for one simple reason that it gives him intense satisfaction and pleasure. A true passion is an emotional bond with the purpose straight from the bottom of the heart. Can you develop passion in others? While it certainly will be everlasting if it is born from within, I do think that this can be cultivated in your subordinates. The honest passion of a leader, whose purpose is beyond himself, will be felt by his command and soon he will have collaborators who will spread his passion as if it was theirs. It is contagious and it will pervade the environment and subordinates. Nelson Mandela wanted to be a lawyer and practice law. He then identified a purpose beyond himself, which was to prevent the oppression of native people in his country. He never tried to raise an army of followers, he pursued the purpose with great passion and the people followed him because it was their cause.

Passion is the fire in the belly for a belief which generates unlimited energy, stamina and commitment and derives great personal pleasure and satisfaction. Nothing great in this world is achieved without passion, sometime bordering on the insane.

There is one story that in my mind best epitomizes passion. A wild life photographer had this ambition of capturing the maiden flight of a chick as it grew in a nest in some desolate forest. The mother would feed the chicks in that high nest. They would slowly grow and in time the chicks would be strong enough to take their maiden flight. That was the one precise moment that was never captured on video. An opportunity missed meant that he would have to wait for another year as that bird bred only once a year. This man would make a platform high up on a tree at a suitable vantage point. Stocked with provisions, he would spend weeks on that platform with his video camera trained to catch that maiden flight. It is quite incredible that he failed for thirteen long years to catch that magic moment. He eventually succeeded in his fourteenth year. Most would have given up. It is this kind of honest passion of the battalion commander for his battalion that I am referring to. And it is this kind of passion for uniform that I have always talked of inculcating in young officers. If you can do this, you would most certainly make passionate commanding officers.

Captain Passion was the young Adjutant of his battalion. He made sure the battalion put its best foot forward everywhere. He went to extreme extents. Even if a young officer was visiting his battalion, he made sure that the smartest soldier was placed on duty at the main gate. His passion for his battalion propelled him and it was soon that the battalion earned the compliment from the brigade commander that he had not seen a smarter regimental police section ever. That is the spirit of passion. A commanding officer does not have to be an extraordinary person, he simply has to have extra ordinary motivation and passion for his unit.

The compelling vision of a commanding officer is what his unit should be. He needs to first feel the heat inside him before he is able to inspire others to feel it. The vision must be aligned in keeping with the interests of the battalion that includes aspirations of its officers and men. A vision that only serves the future of the commanding officer will have no appeal for the rest.

The commanding officer must pick up the best to hold important appointments in the unit and empower them to do their best work. He should provide a working environment in which the junior leaders are able to reach their full potential and provide opportunities for work that builds confidence and raises self esteem of all individuals. The unrealized dividend of this is that it relieves the battalion commander to focus on what he should and serves the long-term interests of the unit.

The commanding officer must identify and nurture the potential in his subordinates. The real measure of a commanding officer is how much he is able to empower others to realize their own leadership potential. A unit will only achieve exceptional results when the majority surpasses their own potential. Maximizing JCOs potential is the key to nurturing an effective command.

Commanding officers can secure the loyalty of their subordinates by making an investment in their development, empowering them and helping them to become more effective in their professional and personal lives. Men entrusted with responsibility must be equipped with right tools. The authority to execute your orders, liberty to do it his own way and, above all, training them to handle their responsibilities. The position and authority of the JCOs and NCOs must always be upheld to ensure their effectiveness as junior leaders.

## Manpower Audit

The commanding officer must ensure that every asset of the unit is optimally utilized. Manpower is your greatest asset. You are for them. They are not for you. Every man must be utilized with purpose. During the course of my service I have seen units being criminally large hearted in frittering away their men for all kinds of jobs. Let us see this example as a case in point.

One unit had eighty five men on temporary duties. The unit had moved to the Eastern Command about a year ago, still had men attached in institutions in their previous command and some attached even outside their previous command. There were four men sent to Delhi for four trivial tasks which could be easily done by one. There are many economical and smarter ways of doing things such as the courier service, civil and military mail dispatch service, etc. An unpardonable waste that directly affects their training. Of the total strength of over eight hundred men in this unit, less than two hundred had been sent for pre induction training before deployment in anti-terrorist operations. No higher commander will ever decline his demand for his men to be made available for training. The unit had more than one hundred men on administrative duties in the rear with formation headquarters.

No self respecting commanding officer can allow his battalion to be treated as event managers. This large heartedness in pleasing everyone is disloyalty to your command and I have no doubt that it is done for self serving gains.

The sad part is that such incompetence gets rewarded. Deployed on the LAC in Arunachal Pradesh, this unit on its own had done nothing operational because none of the higher commanders demanded anything. Later, the brigade was orbatted under our division, where I was the Deputy GOC on raising. The brigade was put through the 'Op Alert' practice, an unpleasant surprise. They had never done one here. The companies of the unit could not reach their defended localities which were visible from the officers' mess lawn, for they had never gone there. They could not cross the nala less than half a kilometre from the mess, let alone prepare the defences. Everyone in the command chain got rewarded either by nomination to career courses or promotion. Lucky, they left before getting a report from us. Sad commentary.

When I questioned the commanding officer, his reply was as stupid as it can be, " It was nobody's KRA." So, as the commanding officer on the LAC facing the aggressive Chinese, he had no KRA because no one told him to have one. He was happy looking after the administration of higher headquarters and preparing his men to be slaughtered in the event of a war and bring national shame - 1962 in the making. It is a professional integrity issue. There is another lesson that such officers can become commanding officers in our system and then be nominated for Higher Command. What legacy will such commanding officers leave and what crop will they nurture?

Personally for me, the most obnoxious sight is a soldier taking officers' dogs for a crap with a mobile on the ear and sometimes struggling to control three dogs pulling in different directions.

With respect to one battalion, a brigade commander remarked in presence of others, 'It's a pleasure to see the men of this battalion. I am yet to see one obese or poorly turned out soldier from this battalion.' Would this just have happened by itself? Certainly not. The commanding officer of this battalion would impress upon the men that they belonged to the finest regiment and in that finest regiment they belonged to the best battalion, and they were the best soldiers who ever wore the hobnailed boots. The men believed him and took that extra care that the battalion voluntarily put its best foot forward at every level, every single time. The sentry post would have a set of brass polish kits. Each vehicle leaving the unit would carry a similar kit, and every soldier who was out of the unit for more than six hours would polish his buttons if he was close to a brass polish kit. A smart uniform instils self confidence and pride. A smart soldier with a good soldierly bearing and conduct on the street is a good ambassador of the army; a poor one neutralizes efforts of ten good ones.

Command is not a popularity contest. This does not mean that the commanding officer has to be a bully. A good commanding officer is a good leader. A good leader does not force change; he leads the change, often unnoticed. The commanding officer must set exacting standards in training and discipline. One should never accept compromise where compromise is unacceptable. It is important that the battalion is groomed with an aggressive 'never say die spirit' and a winning habit. It starts with the body language and demeanour of the commanding officer. While one should accept defeat with grace, the defeat must hurt the unit's pride and propel them to do better next time through fair means. It is this attitude that will become a winning habit and cultivate the perseverance required in battle when the situation looks hopeless. A battalion must always display a professional military outlook and a professional military environment must be maintained. Small activities done with military pride, precision and custom help to maintain that sharp military culture. I have visited units who either borrow buglers from others or mount ceremonial quarter guard without a bugler. Bugle calls signify warrior ethos and military traditions. It is a form of communication and a constant reminder to the men that they are a special breed and much is expected of them. It instils pride and discipline. Compare a retreat and lowering of the flag in the unit quarter guard with and without buglers. Most important, that is the most visible part of military funeral, the honour that is given to a martyred soldier. As a commanding officer of a combat unit, I would be damned if I were to borrow a bugler for a military funeral of my soldier.

Great things are done, when one loves what he is doing. Battalion command must be a passionate love affair...

## Junior Leadership Must Deliver

There's nothing worse in the army than a leader who cannot perform effectively in combat.

The JCOs and NCOs have an extremely important role to play. They are the backbone of the unit. They carry a huge amount of experience with them. They have the responsibility of training and administering their detachments and sub units. In war, they carry immense responsibility as they will command sub units that will dictate the outcome of the mission. In war, good JCOs and NCOs must guide young officers and soldiers who join the unit in battle. I have seen many young officers get in the harm's way for want of correct guidance in operations. While the JCOs are seen to be less than effective, they are here to stay. They must be given their due respect they have earned through years of service. In the present day, when the commanding officer himself is young, and the rest very junior, it is desirable that admonition of JCOs be done only by the commanding officer. It will avoid undesirable situations.

To be effective they need to be empowered through training and qualification, raising their self esteem and confidence. Thereafter, they must be given responsibility, held accountable and made to earn their pay.

As a sector and divisional commander I ensured that the JCOs earned their bread. I did that by ensuring that my visits to the units were focused on JCOs and the officiating allowance as company commander did not come for free. It had to be earned.

Visiting one of my units, I ticked off an overweight JCO. He replied that age was catching up and was about to retire. He was forty five years old and still three years from retirement. Do not allow them to get into the holiday mode so early. The commanding officer must ensure the JCOs deliver through empowerment and accountability.

> *'Don't tell people how to do things, tell them what to do and let them surprise you with their ingenuity.'*
>
> —George S Patton

One often hears that our army has become a 'zero error' army. This statement has been made to me by many officers. In the extremely competitive environment, it is easy to be left out on the wayside if there is a blot on one's record of service. Gen VK Singh, former Army Chief, as a corps commander put it in perspective, 'If that was true, none of the Generals would be where they are.' We all have made all kinds of blunders during the course of service, in peace and in counter insurgency operations, but have not been prosecuted where the intention was right and things went wrong because of error of judgment or faulty execution. Where the intention itself is wrong, the individual deserves no sympathy.

Incidents of the type of Colonel Ketchup or Booze General, molestation of women and fake killings are obnoxious and fall in this category.

Very often one hears that the JCOs are below par and cannot be trusted for any important job. When I hear this, I remind them that all of them are heads of the family. They have raised their families, put their children through education and a vast majority have done extremely well for their children. A fair percentage of officers in the army are the wards of JCOs and NCOs and doing very well. These are the people who purchase land and build houses in towns, all complex assignments. Where are we going wrong that the JCOs today are not delivering as expected?

If it is the issue of right selection, then it is none but us to blame. A NCO becomes a JCO after almost twenty years of service. That is a long time to assess his true worth. If he was a deserving NCO, why does he become an underperforming JCO. Selection in promotion is the key and everyone must be compelled to earn his pay. An undeserving NCO, if promoted, will be your headache for the next decade and deprive others of promotion.

I recollect an incident during my battalion command that triggered a major policy decision. My battalion was tasked for reception of senior officers at the airport including providing a cup of tea. Against instructions, I directed that JCOs will be made responsible for this unproductive duty. Strangely, JCOs found that a difficult job. In one case, a JCO asked my second-in-command as to which officer is going to be with him for this task, i.e., receiving one senior officer at the airport. If a JCO could not conduct the reception of one officer after briefing, it was time for them to get better. Deviating from the unit practice of selecting ten JCOs from fifteen attending the cadre, I cast the net wider and extended the JCO promotion cadre to fifty eligible NCOs. Of these, we selected only the required number purely on merit. There was some resentment in the battalion but it sent the message loud and clear that you could get faster promotion if you deserved. The deadwood opted out realizing that they did not measure up to the requirement. Men worked harder to get better. It changed the age profile and quality of JCOs with exponential gains. They shouldered much greater responsibilities and produced results without looking over their shoulders for directions. That made life simpler for the officers and enabled the directive style of command; junior leaders who understood their commander's mind and applied theirs to accomplish the commander's mission.

So, right selection is the first key. Empowering them through training and self esteem is the second and giving them responsibility, authority and holding them accountable is the third. Wherever there are free lunches and a guaranteed salary, there will be inefficiency. The army is planning to increase the number of JCOs in units as part of cadre review. I am not too sure that is a good idea.

The sub unit commanders must be made responsible to train their sub units with a clear end state defined. The objectives to be achieved must be spelt out through the SAT based training. Operational audit guidelines and job description cards as discussed later in the book will facilitate this. Appropriate monitoring by the training team will provide the necessary guidance and mid-course corrections. If he understands that there are no free lunches, he will deliver.

## Unit Tarteeb – Sticking to Basics

Unit tarteeb has become the buzz word today in our army for the right reasons. Broken into two words, it means unit, i.e., the battalion and *tarteeb* meaning procedure. Thus, unit tarteeb means following unit procedures. The first thing that starts the unit tarteeb is the morning PT parade. If that is the first thing done smartly in the morning, you are bound to have good day. You may realize that your lousiest day could be a Sunday, because you get up rather late and your bed keeps lying unkempt till late morning. Surprisingly, do up your bed and have a wash and you raise your spirits and mood instantly.

A number of activities fill up the day in the unit and they must be done religiously. This means that unit command channel must remain effective. Regimental activities such as regular interviews of men moving in and out of the unit, *sainik sammelans*, roll calls, periodic inspections and visits to stores and lines, cook houses, intercompany competitions, document checks, etc., keep the unit in good shape. It is extremely important that a unit has good operating procedures that help the men to organize their affairs better. A soldier must be warned a year in advance about his posting and where. Leave plans and course detailments, etc., must provide adequate time for him to plan and organize his personal affairs such as disposal of his family, schooling of his children, his move plans and reservation, etc.

One neighbouring unit lost five pistols. The enquiry could not establish whether the weapons were lost a day before or six months back, yet all *kote* documents were in order. Clearly commanders at all levels were playing the fool. No one checked the weapons physically for months, simply signed the *kote* register, and the officers signed the registers sitting in their offices. This is why it is necessary that unit *tarteeb* must be followed strictly. It will keep the unit sharp and avoid embarrassment.

While we talk of trust in the army, blind trust without verification can cause trouble. Trust those who have earned that trust over time.

Units must evolve good drills. When a unit moved from the field to a peace station, it would conduct reorientation drills for all unit activities such as quarter guard mounting, stand to procedures, firefighting drills, *kote* procedures, central roll calls, etc. This ensured that correct drills were instituted and unit reorientation to the changed environment achieved in quick time. This was also a quick learning process for the young officers and soldiers.

With changing times, the concept of *bara khana* in the unit has changed. Unlike the olden days, units outsource entertainment and other arrangements. While the justification of keeping the men out of arrangements is sound academically, *bara khanas* were meant to re-energize regimentation and have fun. Veterans were invited, old regimental stories were relived; some leg pulling of officers and JCOs, troops' culture were show cased and officers and men let their hair down with a peg of rum. Today, item dancers, not too civil, entertain the men in presence of unit families. Beer and whisky has replaced rum, and the purpose of *bara khanas* seemed to have been high jacked. It is important to reset the right focus.

# CHAPTER II

# COMMAND: LEADERSHIP AND MANAGEMENT

## Command: The Leadership and Management Equation

Command is the legal authority exercised by the commander over his troops to accomplish his mission. It carries with it the responsibility for planning, organizing, training, directing, coordinating and controlling military forces to accomplish, implied or inherent missions together with administrative responsibility for supply, health, welfare, morale, discipline, assignment and relief of personnel. (Indian Army Doctrine 2004) Military leadership is the process of influencing others to accomplish the mission by formulating achievable plans, providing purpose, direction, and motivation.

Management is related to running or controlling an organization. It is the skill to deal with people and situations. The term manage normally refers to accomplishing something despite odds. Leaders and managers have been described in different ways. In the corporate world a manager sees the bottom line, a leader sees the horizon. A manager sees the present, a leader sees the future. A manager does things right, a leader does the right things. A manager sees short term, a leader sees the big picture. A manager is about seeking power, a leader is about empowering others. A manager is about manipulation. A leader is about inspiration.

Management deals with planning and employment of resources towards accomplishment of the goals of the organization. It is a term which is understood to include a vast spectrum of activities. Leadership is about pursuing a purpose beyond yourself, it is about leading men, it is about creating trust, it is about aligning organizational vision with the aspirations of the men, it is about accepting responsibility, it is about the future. In the military, mission accomplishment is a complementary function of command, management and leadership. In this equation leadership plays the most important part; command and management by themselves cannot assure success.

> *'Leadership is an art that makes possible what the science of management says is not.'*
>
> —General Colin Powell

The most important equation between the soldiers and their commander is trust. Command cannot create trust. Trust is created by good leadership, i.e., accepting responsibility for your actions and orders, empowering subordinates, sharing the same hardships, sacrificing your interest for your men and leading by personal example. A US marine unit was caught in a firefight in Afghanistan. Some marines put their life in extreme danger to rescue others, getting grievously injured in the process. One marine rescued an injured marine from under fire, kissed him on the forehead and rushed to rescue the rest. The incident was recorded through the helmet mounted camera. When asked, why they risked their lives, they all said the same thing, 'In their place they would have done the same.' It is all about trust.

Indian Army is the same. I have seen many officers and men in my unit extricate soldiers putting their own life in extreme danger. There are innumerable examples of such kind. All men in the unit trust their comrades to do the same.

In a battalion, or for that matter in any military command at any level, command will do what the commanders want them to do, if he can make them believe what he believes. And convinces them why he believes what he believes.

The military environment is characterized by all kinds of restrictions and vulnerabilities. In this environment, the men must feel safe and this sense of safety will bring to the fore the most vital element trust, between the men and the command. And when there is trust, the men will give their sweat, blood and life. A commanding officer must not be feared by men of his own command, rather he should be feared by the enemy. He must be predictable to his command, so that there is no anxiety and stress. This will help the junior echelons to do their duties more effectively and in a happier frame of mind.

Battle represents the severest test of a commander's mastery of leadership. It is here that the leadership role overrides the command role. Command vests the leader with authority to lay down the mission and order its accomplishment. Accomplishing the mission in this high risk environment requires the additional influence of leadership which provides voluntary collaboration of subordinates.

Ideally, the leader must set the standards for command through personal example, by sharing the same hardships, risks and sacrifice. He must, therefore, demonstrate trust and confidence in his subordinate leaders and men. If he has created trust amongst his command in his competence, judgment and his concern for their safety above his personal interests, his authority and decisions will never be questioned.

Military leadership is a continuous process and its application and cultivation starts from the time a soldier or an officer joins the unit as a new rookie. One suddenly cannot become a good leader when appointed as the commanding officer. Leadership defies precise definition, but what it involves and demands is easy to comprehend. Good leadership is built on – character, competence, courage, experience, discipline and personal example among a dozen other virtues. Application and practice of these traits completes the concept of leadership.

## Leading by Personal Example

I will not send troops to dangers which I will not myself encounter.

The Duke of Marlborough (1650-1722), quoted in Sir Winston Churchill, Marlborough, 1933.

One officer slated to take over the command of the battalion asked me, what is the best way to command a battalion? My answer, 'At the unit level you do not command, you lead and lead by personal example. And when you do that, command-plus happens.'

I wish to quote a few incidents that demonstrate what leadership by personal example means and clearly tells us what good leaders should do:

> "*I hated it in the rear. It was a cesspool... You saw the worst there. The commander was living in luxury. They were in the middle of the war, but his superiors had an army of servants, ate with silverware at tables covered with white cloth and had tea parties and dances with Red Cross girls...certainly not the right example to set for American and Vietnamese soldiers while Vietnam was being blown apart.*"
>
> —General Schwarzkopf, quoted in 'In the Eye of the Storm'

An inspiring story of Alexander the great will drive the point I am making. Marching across a scorching hot desert, his men were falling from dehydration. Alexander was no better. When the marching column halted, a soldier rode off and managed half a helmet of water from somewhere and offered it to Alexander. Knowing the state of his troops due to lack of water, he took the helmet, and in full view of his troops, emptied it on the scorching sand. That small gesture to share their hardships was like a drink to his army and all they needed to bear the unbearable thirst in the scorching desert.

Why is it that many officers find battalion command a burden, a necessary evil that needs to be gone through and move on, earliest possible. Clearly such officers are not enjoying the command and seeing the battalion as a stepping stone in their career. I have no doubts these officers lack true passion for the battalion, and would have done little for the long term good of their units.

Why should officers be running away from what I described as the ultimate honour. Some reasons that may make the command an unpleasant experience are professional incompetence that makes him perpetually uncomfortable, difficult superior commander, shortage of officers that may be putting additional burden on him, poor unit environment amongst officers and ladies, an awkward subordinate and a self-serving commanding officer leading to problems. Let us examine these aspects.

**Incompetent commanding officer:** Normally by the time an officer reaches this rank, he has put in adequate service and if he has kept his wits about him, he should have acquired enough knowledge to get by, except if he has to lead the battalion in combat. This situation is the worst of all which has no real remedy and has to pay for his incompetence. Nevertheless, there is hope if he acknowledges his shortcomings, at least to himself and exploits the competence of officers and JCOs under his command. As for the battle, he can partly compensate by display of physical courage which, in certain situations, could be the spark to get the difficult job done. There is little doubt that the battalion will pay for his incompetence. If his predecessors have done their job of training the battalion well, it will manage one weak commanding officer with good officers and JCOs.

Colonel Chauhan was commanding 5 GUARDS in the Kashmir valley in an intense counter insurgency area. He was a hard task master demanding the last ounce from his command. He would be out in the freezing cold with the battalion the whole night. There was no question of him seeking the warmth of a house or fire. Whenever the battalion crossed a freezing stream or a river, he would be the first one to enter the water, stand in mid-stream till the last man crossed and join the tail. Compare this with a young company commander of a neighbouring battalion who would cross the stream piggy back on a soldier's back to avoid getting his boots wet. Nothing more needs to be said on this score. Incidentally, this officer was removed from command of a unit later. Unfortunately, the men of the unit suffered; a natural consequence of poor leadership. On the other hand, in 5 GUARDS, while everyone dreaded the commanding officer's strictness, he commanded absolute respect for his readiness to share the same hardships and more.

Nothing can be achieved without pain. Going back in history, there has been no great captain of war like Alexander the Great. An extract of a speech by Alexander as he faced the mutiny of the Macedonians at Ophis in Babylonia in 323 BC, quoted in Arrian, The Campaigns of Alexander, 7.10, c AD 150, tr. Aubrey de Selincourt, 1987.1

> *'Perhaps you will say, that in my position as your commander, I had none of the labours and distress which you had to endure to win for me what I have won. But does any man among you feel that he has suffered more for me than I have suffered for him? Come now if you are wounded, strip and show your wounds, and I will show mine. There is no part of my body but my back that has not a scar; not a weapon a man may grasp or fling the mark of which I do not carry upon me. I have sword-cuts from close fight, arrows have pierced me, missiles from catapults bruised my flesh. Again and again I have been struck by stones or clubs and all for your sake for your glory and your gain. Over every land or sea, across river, mountain and plain I led you to the world's end, a victorious army.*
>
> —Dictionary of Military Quotations by Peter G. Tsouras

Today there are no more battles of the kind Alexander fought, but the equation is no different. There is a commander and his command. Commander's mission is to train his command to fulfil its mission in battle. You may not be the fortunate one to lead your battalion in battle, but must approach your duties as if you will. In whatever we do, whether command in peace, field, counter insurgency or war – if you can stand in front of the battalion, look them square in the eyes and say that you have suffered the same hardships and risks and that you have subordinated your interests to theirs, your battalion will have faith in your command.

During a get together in the battalion, a soldier walked up to Colonel Passion and said, 'Saab, you need to simply signal, ninety nine percent of the battalion is ready to die on your one command.' Colonel Passion was disappointed that one percent were not. He saw it as a personal shortcoming as a leader. When he asked why not hundred percent, the soldier replied, a small number of such characters will always be there, whatever you may do.

What is it that this commanding officer did to build such kind of a following. This officer, I know, has always lived by the highest standards of military conduct, putting his men and command above himself, no matter the cost. Add to that sweating when his men sweated, shivered when his men did, never abandoning his men when they were exposed to danger or harsh weather, thus developing absolute mutual trust and confidence.

We have fine examples closer home. Brigadier Ashok Handoo, the famous Guards General, was commanding an infantry brigade during the Indo-Pak war in 1971. Brigadier Bisht, Gurkha Rifles, then a young Captain, was staff officer in the brigade headquarter with him. One evening the enemy started shelling his headquarters. This being the first incident of shelling, there was utter chaos as everyone ran helter skelter for cover. Brigadier Handoo stood on a bump as shells fell all around him. When he saw Captain Bisht taking cover under a military truck, he walked up to him, pulled him out and said, 'Stand here with me my son and be a man.' The story transformed his brigade into a fearless team. General Handoo, later an Army Commander was one of the most charismatic Indian Generals who left the Prime Minister's office because he was kept waiting after having been given an appointment.

The Kargil war is another brilliant example of leadership by personal example against terrible odds by our young officers. The country cannot thank them enough.

Small gestures relating to judicious use of perks and privileges, carrying your own rucksack, running BPET with men, putting a hand on the man's shoulders when you talk to one and projecting yourself as one among equals will send the right signal. In simple terms, the commanding officer may have some perks and privileges, but there are no different standards for him than what applies to others in his unit.

Your battalion will be what you want it to be, provided you do what you should be doing.

## Moral Courage: Stand up When you have a Cause

> *"The soldier must say "Yes" when he thinks "Yes," But when many say "Yes" and think "No", or when they feel forced to say "Yes" though they think "No", or when they say "Yes" for the sake of their career, their comfort or self-interest, while their conscience tells them "No", the point has been reached where true soldiering dies out altogether."*
>
> —Lt Karl Krafft (Officer Factory, Hans Helmut Kirst)

A commanding officer must not obey every order blindly. He must analyze the orders given. If they are un-implementable or going to put your men at avoidable risk in war and unjustifiable inconvenience in peace, have the courage to take them up with superior commander. He should be prepared to bend rules when necessary.

The commanding officer has to balance his obligation to the unit with his career interests. A good commanding officer will disregard his personal interest for the unit when necessary. He has to realize that eight hundred men expect him to have the courage to call a spade a spade, live by high moral and ethical standards, and protect the unit's interests. It is quite simple. If the commanding officer expects his men to risk their lives on his judgment and command, he bloody well risk his career for their well-being and the unit's interest. No moron needs to be educated which of the two is a bigger sacrifice.

A commanding officer's legacy will last, only when he correctly balances the unit's interest with his own, balance always tilting in favour of the unit. And if push comes to shove, sacrificing his personal interests altogether.

No commanding officer should permit his seniors to directly intervene in his command. While the unit is also the brigade commander's command, all instructions for employment of the unit resources must pass through the established chain of command. It is necessary to avoid confusion and maintain the sanctity of the command channel. There will be times when this will be necessary even at the cost of annoying superiors.

The commanding officer should have the courage to stand up against an unjust order. It may have its consequences, but that has to be accepted as command responsibility. That is why in the olden days the commanding officer was known as *Mai baap*; for the men, the world ends at the commanding officer.

Colonel Passion was commanding his battalion during Op Parakram, the deployment of the army on the Indo-Pak border after the terrorist attack on parliament. The issue facing the commanding officer was a serious one. The possibility of war at that stage was high with the units awaiting orders to be launched. The company commanders of this battalion, deployed in the forward zone, were ordered by the division commander for full time staff tasks in the brigade headquarters, without even reference to the commanding officer. The commanding officer and the second-in-command themselves were already employed on full time staff tasks in the divisional headquarter that kept them away from the unit for days.

The commanding officer, who was briefing the divisional commander every day, represented against these directions. He stated that given various factors, the company commanders will not be in a position to do justice to their tasks at this critical time if they were employed for staff jobs in the brigade headquarters. The General heard him and rejected the request directing that the company commanders will take over the responsibility at the brigade headquarters and find time to command their company as well.

Colonel Passion deliberated over the issue. He decided that we were talking war. He had a responsibility to the unit and to his men. The decision of the divisional commander was neither in the operational interest of the battalion, nor the division. The issue, he was convinced, needed to be represented in writing. Colonel Passion made a written representation to the divisional commander. The excerpts of the representation are reproduced below:

> 'The GOC's directions have devoid the unit of all its command elements; all command elements including the commanding officer having been pulled out for staff functions in the brigade and divisional

> headquarters. The unit has serious issues with serviceability of equipment and the serious nature of tasks of the unit. That the unit, deployed along the 130 km forward zone in platoon detachments will fire the first shots of the battle and take the first casualties of the looming war. The unit has been effectively reduced to a staff officer's battalion. In the absence of command elements, the companies have been left to inexperienced lieutenants and JCOs to fight the war under. The battalion's effectiveness directly impacts the success of the division in the impending war. In the absence of command elements, I regret my inability to accomplish the tasks given to me by the GOC. I owe it to my battalion, that in this warlike situation, I strongly request for re-consideration of GOC's directions and the order be rescinded. I and my company commanders be reverted to lead the unit in war. I will provide suitable officers to perform the tasks at the formation headquarters, as the GOC desires.'

The representation was handed over to the Colonel General Staff of the division, who was stunned by the tone and tenor of the letter. He saw this as suicidal, given the fact that the GOC had already overruled the request the same morning. He also mentioned that the commanding officer's confidential report was with the GOC. Col Passion replied that he would rather go home as a Colonel who had the courage to stand up to the unjust order, than be part of battalion history as the commanding officer who got his men killed in pursuit of the next rank. Victory in case of war, meaning unit's professional reputation was more important than anything else, not to mention the loss of men, which was bound to happen without the command elements.

Colonel Passion was summoned by the GOC.

Quote, 'I have gone through your letter. I am disappointed that despite giving directions on this issue earlier, you still represent in writing,' said the GOC.

'You are right sir, you gave the decision the other day. I felt that I did not have the opportunity to present my case properly and arguing there would have been wrong. The fact that I have decided to represent shows how adversely, I feel, the decision is going to impact my battalion's ability to accomplish the mission the GOC has given me. War is a real possibility as of now. I felt it was my moral duty to put forth my point clearly as it has serious consequences for my battalion, in case the conflict breaks out,' replied Colonel Passion.

'I have deliberated on your case. I have decided that you cannot be relieved from the task at the divisional headquarters, but your company commanders need not take over the tasks at the brigade headquarters,' said the GOC.

Col Passion thanked the GOC. He was happy that he had the courage to place the interest of the battalion and the division itself above his own, at a time when his annual confidential report was to be initiated. With his company commanders back with their companies, he was confident of dealing with the enemy. As for his annual report, it was of no consequence under the circumstances.

Did it impact the unit? Yes it did. Everyone's appraisal report was well below what they genuinely deserved. Does Colonel Passion regret his action? No, he felt bad for the few company commanders, who richly deserved to command the unit but never made it to colonel. At that stage, war with Pakistan looked imminent. If the war had broken out, this battalion would have suffered grievously in every way if he had not questioned the divisional commander's orders.

> '*Tell the King that after the battle my head is at his disposal, but in the meantime I hope he will permit me to exercise it in his service*!'

General FW Seydlitz, to Frederick the Great, quoted in Christopher Duffy, The Military Life of Frederick the Great, 1986.

The point is that if you have a case that you are convinced about, make your point with due military courtesy. Most senior commanders will see your point, if there is merit, unless egos come in the way. If they do not, accept the decision and implement it with full commitment. You would have done yourself justice and earned a reputation that will give you a reason to stand taller and look your men in the eye, forever. Better, you earn yourself a lasting peace of mind for having the courage to stand up in the interest of your men. There is no better feeling.

Atilla the Hun was a young king who achieved great military successes. His military chief, a middle aged hugely experienced man was rudely frank in his disagreements with his king. When Atilla pointed this out to his chief, he said, 'This way I serve you better, my king.'

That was a near war situation. Let us see a peacetime predicament of a commanding officer.

Located at Jammu, Colonel Passion was having a blissful sleep one night. Around midnight, the Colonel General Staff (Colonel GS) came on the line. He asked Passion to send one company to secure Vaishnomata shrine by seven in the morning, as a VIP was landing by helicopter the next day at eight.

'That cannot be done,' said Colonel Passion.

'Why not?' asked Colonel GS, taken aback.

'It is midnight. You have given me no early warning for this task. The time and space itself indicates that even if my company was to start right away, they will not be there before midday. My men are asleep, they need to be selected, organized, draw weapons and ammunition, for which the *kote* and magazine need to be opened in the middle of the night, and also top up vehicles with fuel. They will be out for two days in wilderness, need to be self-contained. All this needs time, particularly when you are giving me this task at mid night without any notice. This cannot be done by seven in the morning,' said Colonel Passion.

'Are you disobeying my orders?' asked Colonel GS.

'No I am not. I am telling you that your orders are unimplementable in the given timeframe. I will be committing a bigger sin by accepting the task and risking the life of the visiting VIP,' said Colonel Passion.

'I am sure you realize that when I pass orders, I do that on behalf of the divisional commander. Should I tell him what you are telling me?' retorted the Colonel GS.

'Most certainly, the issue does not change, never mind who ordered it,' I said.

He then asked the commanding officer to start preparing for the task, while he sought clarification. The commanding officer politely refused, stating that he saw no reason in waking up the battalion, when the task itself was unacceptable. He said he will wait for the call, only then will he take further action.

The Colonel GS, possibly realizing the futility of pushing Col Passion, said he will get back. Half an hour later, he was back on the line asking Col Passion to stand down.

The moral is, higher headquarters sometime cover up their follies by putting impossible timelines on the unit. The battalion commander must weigh the task and, if it is impractical, have the courage to stand up, rather than put his men to unwanted misery. I am told the VIP, in this case the corps commander, was informed of Colonel Passion's stand. The visit was cancelled. If the person who created the faux pas of failing to inform the battalion in time paid for it, Col Passion couldn't care a damn, but not put his men to misery for someone else's incompetence.

In March 2020, Captain Brett Crozier commander of USS Theodore Roosevelt was relieved of his command after warning superiors about the danger of COVID-19 spreading among his crew – a message that got leaked to the *San Francisco Chronicle.*

He wrote: "We are not at war. Sailors do not need to die. If we do not act now, we are failing to properly take care of our most trusted asset – our Sailors."

He added: "Decisive action is required. Removing the majority of personnel from a deployed US nuclear aircraft carrier and isolating them for two weeks may seem like an extraordinary measure.

This is a necessary risk. It will enable the carrier and air wing to get back underway as quickly as possible while ensuring the health and safety of our Sailors. Keeping over 4,000 young men and women on board the TR is an unnecessary risk and breaks faith with those Sailors entrusted to our care."

While this became a controversy, it is worth considering that this commander would not have taken this decision if it was not necessary. The last line reveals the essence of military leadership – '*faith with those sailors entrusted to our care.*'

This decision must not have been easy and he would have known the consequences. This is moral courage.

Such decisions will invariably bring you head-to-head with the authority, military or the government and as the commanding officer, you are the one most likely to take the hit. This is a price worth paying to build, retain or restore the trust of the men in their commanders.

Even when one man has the spine to do it, it strengthens the system as men develop hope and trust in the system. Yet, it can only be sustained when this 'strong spine behaviour' becomes a culture amongst the officers. And, it starts top down.

*As a battalion commander, your command will never be fun, nor will you be the 'proverbial tiger' if you are not prepared to put your life and career on the line for your men.*

## Decision Making: Why the Dilemma?

> Being in command means making tough decisions. Not being in command means being silent and doing what you are told...
>
> —Artenris Fowl
>
> (quoted in the Infantry Magazine Dec 2014)

The commanding officer is the last post in the unit. The buck stops here. Decision making is his prime responsibility. This can neither be outsourced, nor can it be kicked up to the higher headquarters. Decisiveness is the ability to take timely decision that clearly enunciates the course to be adopted in a given situation. Decisiveness does not mean taking immediate decision.

One officer went to the mess for breakfast. As he settled at the table, the waiter asked,

'What kind of egg will you like to have, saab?'

Clearly irritated, he retorted, 'What the hell! Asking for a decision early in the morning. In the office they keep pestering me, and here, you are asking which egg to eat,' and continued, 'Get anything you like.'

Well, the officer found it so difficult to decide the type of egg to eat. If he had to leave the inconsequential decision to the waiter, what prevented him from blurting out something?

What is the dilemma in decision making?

There are two aspects of poor decision making, procrastination and vacillation. I suppose, people find it difficult to take a decision when they are not confident of justifying their decision with a professional logic or, simply put, because of pure incompetence. This results because of the inability to comprehend the problem and analyze it in its correct perspective, or when they try to align their decision with the higher commander's thought process, or when they are worried about making mistakes. Indecisiveness also breeds out of being risk averse, or too cautious by nature, seek unnecessary inputs, leading to procrastination. In the process they tie themselves in knots leading to mental paralysis.

Why decision making is important is obvious. It is the starting point of every activity. When a decision is delayed, it reduces the time available to prepare for the task. It results in avoidable haste and keeps the men in a state of anxiety. In battle, it could spawn fear and rumour mongering, with undesirable results. Worse, in battle, delayed or poor decisions can result in failure, loss of lives, loss of personal and unit's honour. Therefore, while there may be times when the decision has to be pended, the command must be kept informed of the delay and the reason for it. It must be ensured that the command is never seen to be indecisive.

Decision making in peace and war are two different cups of tea. The decision making in war is a big challenge at all levels, because the stakes are very high and there is rarely a scope for mid-course correction. Yet, during the course of my long service, I have seen that decision making in peace itself is a challenge for many. There are two major ingredients for decision making and these are professional knowledge and competence. Even when these ingredients are there, it is the fear of things going wrong that makes decision making difficult for many. The other factors that play an important part are the commander's character and personality. Bolder the commander, more decisive he is likely to be. The risk taking ability of the commander plays a major part in his ability to make the decision. More cautious the man the more vacillating he is likely to be as a decision maker, looking for far too many inputs, quite often not relevant to decision making.

I was told of a formation commander under whom woollen socks were under trial in high altitude. The trial never reached conclusion because of unnecessary details that the unit was asked to go into, e.g., time taken to dry up under different ambient temperatures, effect on the socks when washed in water of varying temperatures, etc. The unit got fed up and waited for the formation commander to be posted out.

What makes decision making difficult is the fact that the more critical the decision, the more likely that the information is void and uncertain. Anything better is plain good luck. In combat situations this will always be the case, irrespective of the level. The fog of war and communication breakdowns will further compound the confusion. The increased battlefield transparency does not necessarily mean more clarity. It could mean information overload compounding the confusion of war. The biggest operation to kill Osama Bin Laden was launched, without a hundred percent certainty that he lived there, despite a decade of surveillance by the most powerful military in the world. The situation in future will be similar. The commanders at all levels need to develop the art of decision making and cultivate the propensity to take calculated risks, as did the USA for Osama. This requires developing the fine art of putting the finger on the centre of gravity of any issue and having the courage and character to make the decision.

Decision making becomes simple if the problem is approached systematically. What is the task? What does it involve to accomplish? What do I need to do to accomplish it? What resources do I have to do it? Do I need more resources than I have? How much time do I have? What are the terms of reference and what are my options? What information do I need to make the decision? What are the information voids and how do I get them. The systematic analysis clearly brings out the options. The command acumen lies in selecting the correct option to the best of your judgment at that point in time. The emphasis is at that point in time. After the event everyone is wiser, but that should not bother you, for the decision was taken in the given circumstances.

Every commander must look at decision making in the following manner. Routine decisions within your area of influence. Decisions, whose impact may not go beyond your area of influence, but have significant impact in the unit, such as those relating to promotions of individuals. Then there will be decisions which you may need to justify to your superiors.

Thus, apropos, I do not see any reason why should there be decision problems in the first case, i.e., routine decisions within your area of influence. Yet, I was told by a young officer that, as a food member, he did not have the freedom to decide desserts for dinner. Developing independent mind and decision making is part of training your command for combat. The mess secretary should better give the young officer broad guidelines and leave him alone. This will help him grow in confidence and enjoy doing his job. The heavens will not come down if the dessert was *rasogolla* instead of *rasmalai*.

The commanding officer, having deliberated on a decision within his area of influence with no major fall out, has no reason to procrastinate. When the decision has impact and accountability beyond his area of influence, he needs to develop the attitude that he has the justification for the decision taken at the given time. The superior commander may look at it differently for decision making is impacted by personalities and experience. Invariably, the higher commander will have more inputs than a subordinate commander and many more issues to factor in and, as such, his decision may be different.

**Decision making in battle:** Decision making in battle will never be easy, simply because of the stakes involved. There will invariably be lack of clarity in the situation. The battlefield transparency that we talk of will not be transparent enough. In future, there is a danger of higher commanders interfering with lower levels because of more information. There are two aspects of decision making in battle: the decision itself and the timing. There is a right time to make a decision. Finding the right time is the most difficult part. A decision taken too early or too late is a mistake. The biggest mistake is not to make a decision. Even a bad decision can carry the day given the dynamics of the battlefield.

A commanding officer must remember that the fog of war, uncertainty and anxiety applies equally to the enemy. The side that is bold and takes the initiative will have the last laugh. In both the Iraq wars, despite the fact that there was no enemy air force active, US jets shot their own helicopters or aircraft on more than one occasion. That also speaks of the fickleness of technology.

In peace, a commander must delegate as much as practically possible based on the ability of the subordinates. In war, decisions of consequence, wherever feasible, must be cleared by him, yet this must in no way inhibit the freedom of junior leaders to act on their own when they deem necessary. A superior commander must remember that if he has approved the decision or plan of the subordinate commander or delegated the authority to act, it becomes his plan and, therefore, the responsibility also becomes his.

My unit while serving in the valley faced a critical situation. Operating in a built up area, we lost an officer and three men to foreign terrorists in the space of half an hour, without eliminating even one terrorist. What does the commanding officer do in this situation? Operations in a built up area are always risky. Up against battle hardened Afghan terrorist was even more. Yet, how does a battalion explain four losses without accounting for even one terrorist. The commanding officer had to take a decision; take the risk of suffering more casualties in order to restore parity or bear the ignominy of a one sided contest with attendant impact on the morale of the soldiers that no self respecting battalion is comfortable with. We went for it, eliminating all six foreign terrorists in the built up area without any further loss. It worked; it quite easily could have backfired, for the dangers of built up area are known to all. Thus, calculated risk taking ability is not only an important part of decision making but of battalion command itself. There will always be more than one option, and you can never be sure that your chosen option will guarantee success. There will be some factors that will keep drawing you to the other option. The weight of responsibility is heavy. The decision must lay down clear directions leaving no scope for misinterpretations and confusion.

The basic consideration in planning and decision making in battle should be the fact that nothing may go according to plan the moment first round is fired. Therefore, the plan and the decision must have inherent flexibility and cater for responding to exigencies. It is important that all commanding officers develop creative and innovative qualities. A conformist approach will provide no surprises to the enemy and surprise is the most lethal weapon of war. Risk taking ability will enable commanders to seize fleeting opportunities.

**Importance of passing clear orders:** Passing of clear unambiguous instructions that leave no scope of misinterpretation and their understanding seems a trivial issue. Over the years, I am convinced this needs to be included as an important aspect of training at the unit level.

The story of Halley's comet truly brings out the theme of the point I am making. As the division commander, I often experienced that despite passing instructions in a comfortable office in an environment of free two way dialogue, instructions were quite often wrongly implemented. Over the years, I have experienced that there is a general failure to misunderstand oral orders. These misunderstanding are bound to have serious consequences in operations. Map board exercises and sand model discussions do not factor the infirmities of war; fatigue, anxiety, lack of sleep, hunger, poor communications, casualties and stress, etc. Add these and you have a perfect recipe for confusion. The contents suffer from misinterpretations as they are passed down the chain. Thus, it is important that commanding officers include this aspect amongst key result areas of training for junior leaders in the units. A simple guideline will help;

No important orders must be passed on the move or in haste by any commander in the unit. They must be passed standing and deliberately.

That gives the recipient an opportunity to note the details and seek clarifications. As a matter of drill, important aspects of the orders must be noted in a diary by the recipient and checked back by the commander passing orders. Memory is fickle and prone to confusion. Time spent in passing clear unambiguous orders, is time saved in effective execution.

The unit is the cutting edge of the sword. It is here where the blood and sweat mix and it is here that the cold steel of bayonets will meet the enemy's. Of all the places, it is here that the potential for misinterpretation of orders is the maximum, as they will be passed in an environment of confusion, uncertainty and often poor communications, when troops are under all kinds of stress.

Consequences of misinterpretation of orders can be disastrous as this incident below shows.

The army had that unforgettable experience during the Indo-Pak stand off during Operation Parakram in 2002. One strike formation was launched from the staging area based on the understanding of the orders from the higher headquarters. The situation was retrieved before the damage was done. An order which the Corps was sure was given by the Command Headquarters. An order which the Command Headquarters maintained was never given or meant. A misunderstanding, for whatever reason, could have resulted in a war between India and Pakistan. No better example that highlights the dangers of poor communications of orders.

Knowing when a risk is warranted is a hall mark of military wisdom. Young officers are prone to taking risks which must be tempered. In battle, there will be decisions that do not warrant taking undue risks, while there will be situations where calculated risks will need to be taken. In all such situations, decision will be difficult. A commander must remember that the enemy is as much in the dark as he is. In case of doubt be bold and choose the option that makes the enemy react and achieves maximum surprise. However, do not rush your unit into action without preparation, unless there is good reason to do so. In battle, things move slowly. The decision must be deliberate but the execution must be expeditious, yet not hasty.

Competence is the key to effective decision making. The commander will find himself caught in a clutter and maze of information. He must, with experience and training, learn to identify the centre of gravity of the given situation. He must have a clear mind and be above the clutter.

Rank like age, doesn't enable a person to always have all the answers. In the JCOs and senior NCOs, there is huge amount of experience which must be leveraged by commanding officers.

Indecision is a fatal flaw in a combat leader and it often causes needless loss of lives. Indecision leads to frustration in subordinates. When required to make a decision, make one and stick to it, right or wrong.

## Crisis Management

*Truth sets you free.*

—The Bible

Crisis is defined in the Oxford dictionary as 'a time of great danger, difficulty or confusion when problems must be solved or important decisions must be made. Some of the synonyms are catastrophe, calamity, cataclysm, disaster, etc. In the army's context, one could include untoward incidents that one finds difficult or embarrassing to report to the superiors.

Murphy's law is as true as truth itself. Things will go wrong at the most inappropriate moment. That is why it is said that when troubles come, they don't come in singles, they come in battalions. The crisis can be of varying magnitude. If the incident is manageable within your level without serious consequences, the crisis may not be severe. Sometimes, the development may carry the potential of blowing into a major crisis, but timely intervention at the middle or higher level can diffuse or control the situation. Sometimes, it may simply be beyond your control. The intrusive media can convert a manageable crisis into national news. At the unit level incidents can occur, while not being crisis in the literary sense, with severe overtones. They may or may not cause embarrassment. They may be related to accidents or loss of life due to omissions or commissions, related to group discipline or some other types. When that happens, the proverbial 'Regiment's *Izzat*' comes into play, leading the unit to cover up. And that will cause more harm for sure, in ways not understood by most. Any effort at cover up is only going to complicate matters and give you more sleepless nights. No officer aspiring to command a unit or a formation should believe that he can go through without a problem. Genuinely good and honest officers will occasionally be caught between upholding the military ethics and telling lies for the sake of the unit. Rationalization takes over and many would tell lies, genuinely believing that doing so for the unit is okay. Even when he wishes to be honest, he would find it difficult to be so, being the lone ranger. It is here that the commanding officer needs to play the part expected of him, to avoid creating this dilemma for his officers.

The Bible says, 'Truth sets you free.' My personal experiences convince me that this is the perfect principle for any commander to follow when things go wrong.

When stuck with a problem, consider these questions:

> In the problem, what is the main issue? Is it the cause or the symptom of a larger one? Are the dynamics limited to your area of influence or go beyond. Will you be expected to keep the higher headquarter informed or is it entirely your call? Can the solution be delegated or you need to be involved and at what stage?

The commanders at different levels will make different deductions from the analysis above. As a commanding officer, one has to intelligently analyze the situation and the environment. When you decide that the problem must be addressed, it is best to address it promptly. Serious problems do not go away and become complex with time. In the present day of social media and media intrusiveness, no serious issues, as have occurred in our army in the recent past can be kept under wraps.

You will often experience that most problems are simpler than they appear from distance. A commanding officer must have the feel of the pulse of the unit. Small ripples in the unit environment or behaviour of the men must be picked up by a perceptive commanding officer. He needs to have a feedback system that bring to his notice men's worries and concerns that may not come through formal feedback channel. Major problems do not explode suddenly. They gestate and fester over time and an awkward incident triggers the explosion. His feedback system must warn him of pending troubles. The unit appointments, junior commissioned officers and senior NCOs are in daily contact with men and must shoulder the responsibility of early detection and, when they fail, held accountable.

Crisis management starts with the right attitude of the commander and good preparation for the given task.

A young officer asked his commanding officer, 'Sir, you are one of the few commanding officers whom we see smiling all the time?'

The commanding officer replied, 'Going by the faux pas that I have committed in my service, I grant two major faux pas to every soldier in a year. With almost seven hundred bodies in the unit, I am prepared for fourteen hundred blunders a year in the unit. That makes it almost three and a half major blunders per day. You are not even committing three in a month. Can I ask for more?' He added, 'When given a task, there is time to meditate and plan, time to prepare and time to execute. When you have prepared well, there is no need to worry. In the worst case, if things go wrong, give no excuses, accept responsibility and accept the consequences. There is no use worrying to death as crisis in peace is unlikely to cause loss of lives and the rest does not matter much.'

To err is human. Those who work will commit mistakes and these must be accepted in the right spirit. Promoting zero error syndrome curbs initiative and that becomes a habit, making us too defensive and indecisive, looking for direction at every step. This will have a devastating effect in battle. The commanding officer cannot fight the battle himself. He can only do this through his officers, JCOs and NCOs. War being what it is, all leaders from section commanders onwards will need to take their own decisions. They will conduct themselves in battle as they have been trained in peace.

**Back to handling crisis situations:** As I said earlier, things will go wrong, try what you may. And they will go wrong when it hurts most, be it peace or war.

Your shortest route to salvation from trouble is to speak the truth, stand like a man and accept the consequences happily. When one speaks the truth, the ball automatically lands in the superior's court. It is then his problem to decide how to deal with it. If your intentions are right, you need fear no one.

During my command assignments as a sector commander in the valley and later as a divisional commander, I would often be reminded by officers of the 'zero error syndrome,' I would ask them, 'Please cite one case where an officer has been penalized for a mistake when his intentions were right. Not once could anyone quote me an incident. The zero error syndrome is rarely a function of the superior commander. It is more a self creation of a self seeking commander who wants to make a perfect impression on his superior. An officer lands up doing what a JCO should be doing and a JCO does what an NCO should be doing. In that process, he does incalculable harm to his organization by denying the opportunity to the appropriate level to perform and execute the job, which itself is on the job training for war. A senior officer will never penalize anyone if a junior officer or a JCO or an NCO commits an honest mistake. He will be given the allowance for his inexperience. In my units as sector and division commander, all training briefings were conducted by the JCOs and NCOs even to the army commanders. They were never perfect, but did my cause no harm at all. The dividends were exponential as it raised the self esteem and confidence of my junior leaders and their ability to contribute in battle.

One unit was conducting field firing at the ranges. The commanding officer was given a shocker early morning that a soldier had died, even before firing had started for the day. The previous evening, a violent sand storm had struck the range. At the same time one gun got jammed due to electrical fault. The firing was called off to manage the storm. A live round remained in the chamber which went unnoticed by the crew. Early next morning, one soldier entered the combat vehicle to fix the problem. A while later, another soldier climbed on top of the vehicle and started cleaning the barrel. Having fixed the problem, he pressed the trigger to check out the gun, unaware that a soldier was cleaning the barrel outside. A big bang and a soldier dead in a second, a round having pierced right through his chest from less than three feet. A proud battalion that it was, the officers felt it would show the battalion in poor light. So what was the suggestion? The commanding officer asked. We will spin a convincing story so that the battalion's professional reputation is not tarnished. All officers were convinced that this was the best course of action.

The commanding officer made the following points:

- You will be asking the men to tell lies. When you do that, you weaken yourself as a commander and lose the moral authority to command. You will forfeit all authority to look them in the eye and take action against anyone for any violations in future.

- To conceal one lie, you will be telling hundred lies and you cannot conceal hundred lies being told by twenty men. You would have given official sanction to lying in the battalion. A despicable trait of a soldier and a disastrous character of a unit.
- Overall, you will invite more shame on the unit than this incident has done.

And that will be worse than what has happened, for it weakens the fabric of the battalion. In short, you will cease to be Tigers and will spend the rest of your service with the shame of lacking the courage to stand up and tell the truth. With what face will you command these men and ask them to live a soldier's code?

The commanding officer rang up the divisional commander and reported as follows:

> 'I am sorry to report a tragic news. I lost a soldier today morning in a range accident because of mistakes on our part. I will fix what has gone wrong in the unit. As far as the General Officer was concerned, the entire responsibility for the incident rests with me.'

The divisional commander said that no one would feel the pain more than the commanding officer. He told him to ensure that the next of kin was not put to any inconvenience and all the dues were promptly given and that the mortal remains were handled appropriately.

The matter was over in no time. The commanding officer can never forgive himself for the sad loss of life in peace time and the terrible consequences for the family. But he did not have to lose a moment's sleep from the guilt of not having the moral courage to stand up and asking his men to tell lies. Such guilt can be very painful and long lasting to a conscientious officer. A court of inquest was ordered by the divisional headquarter. No one was tutored. Every man said what exactly had happened. The inquiry was over in one day. I think that commanding officer showed the moral courage to accept the consequences and did his officers a great service by preventing them from falling from the grace of his men and weakening the battalion.

Compare this with another incident. I was commanding a sector in a counter insurgency area in the valley. One morning, one of my commanding officers called up to say that one soldier has been seriously wounded during an encounter with terrorists. He gave me more details of the encounter. My staff officer told me that he did not believe that the report given by the unit is correct. I said, I will go by the commanding officer's word, for I expect my commanding officers to speak the truth. Later it was proved that my staff officer was right.

When I asked the commanding officer how serious was the soldier, he said the wound was serious but he would possibly make it. A helicopter was requisitioned for evacuation from the helipad at my sector headquarters. The casualty was accompanied by an officer and his buddy. The buddy holding an IV bag in his hand was trying to give him mouth to mouth resuscitation. Seeing no doctor or nursing assistant with him, I asked the officer why there was no medical staff with the casualty. He told me that the encounter was continuing and the commanding officer had held back the medical officer there, just in case they have more casualties.

The casualty was evacuated but succumbed to his injuries during the twenty minutes flight to the hospital at Srinagar.

In the business of combat, some soldiers will die, sometimes due to unavoidable reasons and sometime out of negligence. In this case, the soldier had not died in an encounter with the terrorists. That was a total lie told to me by the commanding officer. The soldier had died during training of search operations close to the company base. The young company commander simulated a terrorist by dressing up a Sikh soldier like one, trying to escape. He had not briefed the platoon that this will be happening. Though he had ordered the magazines to be removed from the weapon, the magazines were kept by the soldiers in their pouches. When the platoon was tactically searching the heavily wooded *nala*, the scouts spotted the movement of this simulated terrorist. The leading scout loaded his weapon and fired a single shot. Murphy's law went into motion. The single shot fired from an extremely awkward position on a moving target got him in the neck. Compare this with the number of rounds expended to neutralize one terrorist.

In principle, the young officer did everything right as I had directed them to train. Only, he had not briefed the men properly and that cost the life of a soldier.

The issue here is not related to the mistakes of the young officer. The issue is related to the commanding officer. He fully well knew how the casualty had taken place, and that in this instance there were no terrorists in the equation. The company was half an hour drive from the helipad at the sector headquarters. The flight to the nearest military hospital was another thirty minutes. In all, it would take the casualty about an hour to get to the military hospital. And in that critical state, every minute of expert medical aid meant the difference between life and death of that precious soldier. And to deny that man that aid to cover up their follies and trail of lies, when the medical staff in the battalion was doing nothing, was a despicable unprofessional act. In pursuit of his ambitions, the commanding officer had denied that soldier an opportunity to live.

That commanding officer called me up at night to see me personally. When he met me, he said that he had been telling me lies about the incident the whole day. I told him I knew it all along and by now everyone knows it too. I told him what I had to. The next day the corps commander was visiting my sector headquarters. The divisional commander flew in earlier. I told him what had happened and apologized for the wrong report. He said, he had given the same report up the chain and who would now inform the corps commander? I replied that this responsibility is squarely mine and I shall do it. I told the corps commander when he arrived and took the responsibility for the false reporting without deflecting the blame on the commanding officer. Personally, I found that very disappointing. In counter terrorist operations, things go wrong very often. The units hide many things, but acts such as these, leading to loss of a soldier just to cover your follies, in the hope of the next rank is downright obnoxious. In brief, that commanding officer's lack of moral courage cost that soldier his life and life time misery to his family. A commander of conscience should be perturbed all his life for such acts of moral cowardice.

As for me, it broke the bond of trust with that unit commander. I verified anything of significance when it came from that unit in future. Commanding officers should watch out for false sense of unit's image. I am sure, more than the unit's image, they try to protect their own careers on this pretext. Often, there will be a conflict of interest between following the path of truth and unit loyalty. Manipulation of truth, misrepresenting facts, falsifying achievements for the so called unit's reputation are ethically wrong and unpardonable. Where it leads to loss of any life, it is absolute sacrilege. Such actions do great harm to the reputation of the officer class amongst the troops. It grooms junior officers with wrong values. Such commanders can have no claim to loyalty of their subordinates.

In handling major crisis in counter insurgency areas, there is no graduated response. During an operation in the Kashmir valley, one soldier had fallen in a *nala* on a freezing winter morning. He picked up some papers lying around to light fire to dry himself. A passing villager saw the bits of burnt papers which happened to be Quran pages. All hell was let loose. The committee formed by the villagers filed a FIR and deposited the burnt remnants in the police station. The commanding officer was told to meet the village elders and the *maulvis* and resolve the issue. Rather than going himself, he sent his company commander who was a very junior officer. The crisis snowballed. The commanding officer then informed his commander. The commander arranged for the village *maulvi* and the police officer to visit the site and see for themselves. They were convinced that the soldier was not at fault. The commander drove straight into a crowd of couple of thousand agitating villagers against all advice. He addressed the rampaging crowd along with the *maulvi*.

The villagers demanded that the erring soldier be brought to the village and be punished. The commander made it clear to the crowd that the Army has a system to investigate and take action. Prima facie, the Quran papers used by the soldier to light fire were lying around on the road. They had no business to be there. The prerogative to deal with the man was the commander's and there was no question of the soldier being brought in front of the villagers. The village was told that the inquiry will be completed in two days and the decision taken by the army on the soldier will be announced from the village *masjid* by the *maulvi* in three days. That the army prides itself in upholding the respect of all religions. That in the protection group of the commander itself, there were men from all religions. The massive crisis, with great potential to flare up was diffused in quick time. The villagers broke off after the commander's talk. The soldier was acquitted and the decision communicated to the villagers as promised. The higher headquarters was worried that the incident should not be reported by the media. The commander realized, in the present day environment, with sizeable hostile population, there was no way to prevent it from appearing in the media. He called media personnel and apprised them of what had happened. The next day, the incident was reported by only one paper in an insignificant corner. Lesson; if you do not tell the media your story, they will print other's story.

Remember Truth needs no rehearsals. You will speak the same thing no matter how often you have to repeat it. And that means a peace of mind.

Whatever be the situation, there is always humour around. Funny undoable suggestions came from higher headquarters. The divisional commander was very worried how the burnt remnants, no more than a few thumb sized burnt pieces of Quran pages would be disposed. When he was told that they will be buried as per Muslim practice, he was concerned that the villagers might dig them out and reignite trouble. He was assured that no such thing would happen as the remnants would be buried within the company location. When he still remained concerned, he was told that water will be poured to ensure that nothing is left of them by the morning. Clearly worried, he said that's fine, but they must be watered every hour through the night. He was put at ease by saying it will be done.

One of the situations that the commanding officers may be confronted with is dealing with a difficult commander. A commander of character and good ethics will never pass an unjust or amoral order. If he is difficult for professional reasons, i.e., expecting high professional and moral standards while following them himself, is a situation with which a good honest commanding officer will have no quarrel with. The others will have to shape up or ship out. The difficulty is when you have a superior who places unprofessional and amoral demands. The commanding officer has to take a call. Choose to sing his tune and lose self esteem and standing amongst subordinates or establish a red line of conscience and ethics that he will not allow to be crossed, no matter the consequences. You will be better off this way than trying the delicate balance. There have been cases where senior commanders have placed amoral demands and the subordinate commanders have played along to protect their self interest. They deserve no sympathy for they simply lacked the moral courage to stand up and be counted; the basic trait of a good leader. There are some kinds of behaviour that must not be accepted from superiors and must be reported.

A unit will sometimes get awkward tasks with unjustifiable constraints. In the given set of circumstances, do the best you can. There is no reason to fret and fume over it.

A seminar was being conducted in Jammu University on Kashmir. Many military and civil VIPs were to deliver talks. That was a very sensitive time in Jammu when many terrorist incidents had taken place. Colonel Passion was made responsible for security with many constraints. In that university no student or cars were to be frisked. No internal roads of the university were to be closed. No restrictions on the movement of students were to be imposed. No soldier would carry a weapon and the like. It was a perfect recipe for disaster. Colonel Passion's representations were overruled. He then decided what was best under the circumstances, prepared well and executed it. He tucked his men in civvies with pistols in all important places. On the day of the seminar, he sat nonchalantly near the entrance reading a newspaper. The Brigadier in charge walked up to Colonel Passion and said that he cannot see any signs of security arrangements and seeing him sitting without a worry, made him very worried indeed. Colonel Passion told him that he was given a task to be executed with both hands tied behind the back. Over the last few days he has done what he thought should be done and his time to worry was over. If the terrorists are smarter than him today, it will be their day, and the army would be looking for a head to roll and that head was his own. No sweat; worry won't help. The Brigadier said he liked his attitude and left him alone – how much assured, only God would know. The point here is that for any important task, it is important to prepare well in time and execute it well. A hassled and worried commander infects his command with anxiety and uncertainty. He has to always look in control and that would be very contagious in his command as well.

In battle, things will go wrong for sure. The test of character of a commanding officer is to accept his mistakes and take corrective action with the advice of his superiors. This will ensure damage control without further embarrassment and loss of lives. During the Indo-Pak war of 1971, the battalion manning the defences at Fazilka was surprised by the enemy creating a serious situation. The commanders in chain lacked the moral courage to accept the mistake and attempted to restore the situation without a coordinated effort, resulting in the avoidable loss of hundreds of lives of soldiers.

## The SOCS Approach to Crisis Resolution

As a battalion commander, you will confront odd situations and crises pretty often. They should never be a cause to lose sleep. There is a crisis and it has to be handled. These guidelines help to address difficult situations.

It is called the SOCS Approach. SOCS stands for SITUATION - OPTIONS - CONSEQUENCES - SOLUTION.

**Situation** - Critically analyse the situation.

- What is the issue and why did that happen?
- What was your role in the development of the situation?
- What is the best outcome for you?

**Options** - Consider all the options you have to resolve the conflict or the situation.

**Consequences** - Consider the consequences of all the options.

**Solution** - Implement the option that has the best *long-term* consequences for you (your men and battalion).

– ***Emotional Intelligence***, Daniel Goleman

Combine this with the undermentioned that I have stated elsewhere in the book and you will never have to unduly worry.

- Use the power of 'pause' to bring your rational brain into play.
- That truth is the shortest way out of trouble.
- Create an environment where the bad news comes to you as easily as the good news.

Finally, be prepared to face the consequences peacefully. It won't bring the sky down on you. In the worst case, they will sack you, but they can't hang you.

## Perks and Privileges

We often hear talk of perks and privileges of the higher ranks in the army. If perks and privileges are the motivation for serving then that man is in the wrong profession.

Perks are defined in the Oxford dictionary as something that you get as part of the job, in addition to your salary. In the corporate world, it could be a car and a driver or a free insurance policy, etc. In the army, perks is something you have which you ought not to have, i.e., it is not officially authorized. Perks have a purpose, that is, to enable you to discharge your duties better by conserving your time and energies through some facilities provided. It is fine to have those perks that have come to be accepted as a reasonable practice that strictly help you to do your job better and help you devote more time and energy to your organization. They are not meant to make the commanding officer's wife comfortable because of her husband's position. It is to enable her to focus her efforts on the well-being of the battalion families, and not to take up a job, because there is someone to cook at home. Sending children to the school or for tuitions in a separate military vehicle or a long line of men at home is not perks. It is simply misuse of the position and resources by the officer in authority.

**The air conditioned culture:** These days, it is rare to see a commanding officer's office and vehicle without an air conditioner. You could argue, what's the big deal. It helps the commanding officer to do his job better in a hot country.

One battalion was stationed in a hot weather zone. The second-in-command suggested that the commanding officer put an AC in his office.

'Where is the AC?' asked the commanding officer.

'We will take it out of the workshop lorry, it is not required there,' replied the second-in-command.

'My friend, I am a commanding officer of a combat battalion. My men train in the blistering heat. They sleep under fans and only few of them have coolers in the lines. I do not use AC at home and I cannot be sitting pretty in an air conditioned office and expect my men to be out in the sun. My simple belief is that as a commanding officer of a combat unit, I must share the same hardships and there is simply no room for an AC in my office.'

'No, sir I did not mean that. The papers do not fly around with an AC as they do with a cooler in the room,' said the second-in-command.

'Fifteen commanding officers before me have commanded this fine battalion with distinction sitting at this MES steel table without ACs, setting high professional standards and bringing glory. The whole battalion is my office. I spend very little time in the day in this room. I am fine with a desert cooler, the comfort that I am providing to the men. I do not mind you putting it in your office if you cannot live without one,' Passion replied. The chapter was closed, AC was never mentioned again nor did the second-in-command put the AC in his office.

Today the battalions get a lot more funds that enable them to indulge in such luxuries. That does not justify the dilution of military basics. The readers can take their call on the issue.

This second-in-command was also not happy with the commanding officer's vehicle. The vehicle in question was a soft top light vehicle, the way it came from the manufacturer, with bare essentials. He recommended to do up the vehicle smartly with an AC and a good music system. His logic was that when the commanding officer of the battalion moves, the station should know who is moving. Colonel Passion told him that he would be happy if the station said that this commanding officer has the worst vehicle but the best battalion in town. So he stayed with his simple vehicle, the way it came from the factory. One day the vehicle met with an accident. All that this commanding officer did was to pick up the first vehicle in sight to replace his vehicle, for all the vehicles were just the same. Indeed, with this approach, all light vehicles were his reserves. More importantly, the formation headquarters never asked for his vehicle when they needed to pool good vehicles for some event.

Colonel Passion's conscience would not allow different standards for himself. As for the battalion, it was referred as the model battalion in the formation, notwithstanding that the commanding officer had the worst vehicle in town. In today's context, people will see it as a trivial issue because AC is common place. At the battalion level, it is through small gestures that you convey big messages and that won't be lost on your command.

This officer later commanded a formation in counter insurgency area in the Kashmir valley. He told me he did without an AC or a heater in his vehicle for the same reason that his men were out on operations in freezing cold. While no one would grudge him that comfort and neither was his superior commander watching him, he thought it was the right way to command. I remember Lt Gen Vinod Bhatia, a para trooper, who commanded a Corps in the eastern part of India, did not permit the approach road to his office to be repaired. He wanted that to remain a constant reminder that roads up in the forward areas needed to be fixed.

A colonel justified ACs in the commanding officer's offices and vehicles on global warming since I relinquished battalion command!

Good sense of humour to say the least. I had commanded my battalion less than a decade back. It is all a matter of attitude.

So, while there may be funds to buy an AC for the commanding officer, small gestures of sharing your men's discomfort would go a long way in commanding the confidence and trust of the men, so vital to command unquestioned obedience under fire.

As a divisional commander, I had stopped the use of military vehicles to convey officers' wives to schools where they worked. This caused considerable resentment, as if I had deprived them of their authorized entitlement. I was told in the same station the other formation commander did not do so. They understood my point when I explained to them that by doing so, they were unknowingly slipping into dishonest habits. Also, like the resentment on my directions, they were only placing their happiness and mental peace in other's hands. That they can walk taller, look anyone in the eye and serve with pride by simply living correctly and conducting themselves with dignity. All of us can well afford to live on our own means. It only required the right attitude. The men keenly observe everything that an officer does. Misuse of resources while ignoring the genuine requirements of the men causes considerable resentment. There have been unpleasant incidents, best avoided, involving military transport, soldiers and officers' wives. Slowly, this is taken as the done thing and people graduate to bigger misappropriation. Slowly, one reaches a stage where 'the king can do no wrong,' and when that happens, trouble cannot be far behind.

Many officers set their own standards of perks and privileges as it suits them, fully knowing that it is not in order. It is good to remember the principle what applies to Sepoy Bhoop Singh, equally applies to General Roop Singh.

These practices are a legacy of the colonial era. Of all the services, it is the army which is the biggest culprit where even the retired officers keep clinging to unauthorized perks till forced to relinquish. These must be set right ruthlessly.

While we keep milking the system based on the colonial legacy, the British themselves have set exacting standards of conduct for the military which should be the standards everywhere. There is no midway; there is only one way and that is the right way and your conscience is the only effective moral compass.

In 2019, Captain Nick Cooke-Priest was relieved from the command of the British aircraft carrier for using the official car on a weekend. He was found guilty of an error of judgment, even though he paid for the petrol when he used that car.

*Source:* https://www.telegraph.co.uk, 17 May 2019.

How many officers in positions of authority will pass this test of integrity?

# CHAPTER III

# HUMAN QUOTIENT: THE ULTIMATE FORCE MULTIPLIER

## Human Quotient

*Victory is assured by maintenance of human spirit rather than by maintenance of machines.*

—Anonymous

The revolution in military affairs has seen fighting wars change in an incredible way in the last half a century. The future warfare will be driven by technology, but in the end it is the human element that will continue to make the difference. No military victory is ever secured without boots on the ground. With all the technological and material advantage, the US and NATO experience in Iraq, Afghanistan and Syria amply demonstrated that warfare of the future is man-driven, everything else is in a support role. Here, in the Indian context in particular, countering the existential and future security threats is all about marshalling the human resource. It becomes a function of men, driven by competent leadership and supported by technology. The human factor has always been and always will in future, be the critical factor. Technology can complement but never substitute either leadership or the men.

The military way of life curbs personal freedom. It puts many statutory restrictions on the officers and men. The do's and don'ts curb initiative and creativity. Living like this becomes a habit where 'not thinking too can become a habit.' How does one lead men in battle with aggression and arrogance when he has been brought up on a tight leash. The commanding officer must mentor his command to break free from this military contradiction. They must be mentored for the battlefield of tomorrow and not peace time demands of today. Even tigers brought up in captivity take time to act like tigers when released in the wild. How can junior leaders raised as pussies in peacetime suddenly act like tigers in battle.

As a formation commander, I defined my efficiency equation as under:

$$\text{Operational preparedness} \times (\text{Human quotient})^{n} = (\text{Operational Effectiveness})^{nx}$$

Operational preparedness is a function of many factors. Operational effectiveness is an exponential function of human quotient. In a stressful battle environment, it is the human quotient that will make that crucial difference and tilt the balance. Battle of Saragarhi, Rezangla are a few amongst many examples of human quotient transforming a small force into a deadly one.

What is it that makes the religious extremists sacrifice their all cheerfully. It is his high human quotient, a result of his belief in his cause, ideology and his means, even if misplaced from others' perspective.

So, how do you define HQ? My definition is, 'It is the intensity of the desire to accomplish the mission as an individual and as a team; a function of many factors, mainly belief in the cause, your personal, professional and organizational pride, and inspiring leadership.'

How does one develop the human quotient. In a formation, there are units that clearly stand apart. One can sense the hunger for excellence, while there are others who are contented to go along. I also had the unpleasant experience of major indiscipline in one of my units of the division. Earlier, during a visit to that unit I had mentioned to the commander that this unit did not have the same spark as the other units in the brigade.

The difference between the two units was in the manner of involvement of the officers, enthusiasm of its troops and the standard of military activities. While one unit was heart and soul into excellence, the other was simply participating. Eventually, when the incident took place, it was clear that there was a complete disconnect between the officers and men. The commanding officer, outstanding on paper, had no feel of the pulse of the battalion. He did not understand the unit's state of mind and the growing discontentment. When I drove into the battalion which was in a state of disarray, all the officers including the commanding officer had abandoned command and left the unit. While a handful JCOs attempted to control the men, most were happy bystanders and some even fanned the fire. The unit violated the basic tenant of treating the men with dignity and integrating the officers with their command. The men unanimously rejected to have the commanding officer and the officers back, except one young officer. When I told the commanding officer this, he said, 'Sir, I am greatly surprised that they feel this way. I was born and brought up in the battalion.' Here lies the rub, the commanding officer was totally out of sync with ground realities in the unit.

For things to go wrong in the unit, two conditions need to be met. There is a poor inter-personal environment between the leaders and the led and a trigger. In this unit, the environment was ripe. The manhandling of a soldier by a young officer during a boxing match provided the trigger. In both cases, the commanding officer and the young officer felt they had a great equation with men and while both may have worked hard, they were grossly wrong in their assessment of their standing with the men.

Many officers suffer from the self inflated opinion of their standing in the unit. The fact that the commanding officer lacked the confidence of sticking and facing his men shows immensely poor human quotient. In such a state, not much could be expected from this unit. The same battalion was awarded unit citation in operations earlier and a year later was in tatters.

The tenets of building a good human quotient are straightforward. A commanding officer must understand the difference between command and leadership. Command gives him the authority to issue orders but it is the influence of leadership that develops the human quotient. The commander should have a vision that in his command officers and men sincerely share. An organizational and goal oriented leadership that is not guided by self serving ambitions. An interactive leadership that creates mutual trust and camaraderie between the officers and men. A happy environment where a smile is exchanged between officers and men when a soldier salutes. An environment where a soldier is comfortable walking up to his officer to discuss his problems. Empowering the command through innovative and progressive training to accomplish the tasks expected of him in peace and war. And, above all, meeting the aspirations and basic needs of the men so that they can concentrate on their professional responsibilities without having to worry about domestic issues. Good units have worked out simple procedures that enable their men lead an organized life rather than being on fire fighting mode all the time. Simple drills like timely planning of postings, courses and leave etc that allow the men to organize their family needs of accommodation, finance, children education, leave and move, are examples of good administration that helps in building a strong human quotient in the unit. Every man has self respect and his dignity must be honoured. In my unit, a *pahari paltan*, the manner of addressing men is '*aap*' and not '*tum*' or '*tu*'. If the commanding officer has to punish a soldier, he would say, '*Apne yeh galti kiya hai aur mein is ke liye ap ko 28 din shakt qaid ki saza deta hoon.*'

As a division, we had evolved simple yet effective ways to build the human quotient. Officers and men always stayed with affiliated units when on outstation duty. Competitions were organized based on brigade tactical grouping. The division officers could be drinking beer at eleven on a working day after an impromptu rugby match after a heavy down pour, and the GOC himself would be covered in muck and grime. The formation was one integrated and a cohesive fighting force and not a division of twenty five units.

In the end, the strength of the human quotient will be determined by the quality of leadership in the unit.

One special forces team suffered serious losses during the Kargil war. Eleven soldiers brought back their nine dead colleagues, lugging them for days over an extremely inhospitable high altitude terrain and weather, and through hostile territory. A fine example of great human quotient. In a unit of good human quotient, the mutual commitment of trust and faith will be stronger than their marriage vows. When a soldier is stuck in a life and death situation, he knows his buddies will come when he needs them, no matter what.

## Teamwork: Think 'We' – Think 'Team'

No military unit can succeed without teamwork. For the team to succeed, each member will have to give up some self interest for the good of the team. Teamwork divides the task and doubles the success. No individual wins or loses, it is the team that does.

A team is a group of people having some unifying relationship, coming together to collaborate to reach a common goal for which they are mutually responsible and truly believe that they have a stake in it.

In a battalion, this goal is accomplishment of operational mission under any circumstances. A group of people does not become a team unless there is a high degree of interdependence and camaraderie.

Building a happy cohesive team is the secret to making an effective battalion. Teamwork generates synergy where members complement each other and the whole is far greater than the sum of individuals. Doing so is winning half the battle. Team members are deeply committed to each other's personal growth and success. In a battalion, with a good officers team, the positive vibes fill the air where everyone helps the others to grow and enjoy others' success. A fresh air of cheerfulness and energy is clearly felt when one walks into such a unit. The happy team outperforms all reasonable expectations given to its individual members. That is, the team has a synergistic effect where one plus one does not make two, it makes eleven. In a good team, each member feeds on others, where weakness of one is covered by someone and, as a result, the team has no major weaknesses, only strengths.

The commanding officer's task is to provide the glue that will bind the members of the team into a cohesive unit where everyone shares and participates in the others' growth and success. Simple group activities where all the team members including the families and children are involved will go a long way in building a good team. Impartiality, fairness, a good working environment and personal example helps build a good team.

The secret is for all officers to understand that no one is perfect and they learn to accept each other's shortcomings and compensate them. The military values of loyalty, self-sacrifice, mutual respect, discipline and esprit de corps are facilitators of effective team work.

Colonel Passion held a simple confidential exercise in the battalion. He asked all officers to write three strengths and three shortcomings of all other officers without mentioning the name of the writer. Colonel Passion then summarized the qualities on separate paper for each officer and handed over to them. Interestingly, there was consistency in assessment of each other. The exercise was found useful by everyone except one. Those who had the maturity to see it as a sounding board saw it as true feedback, which they felt should have come much earlier. There was one who said it was a vindictive feed back with no truth in it. Incidentally, he was the one who was the least of a team man, even though professionally competent as an individual.

## Team: The Goose Sense

Have you ever noticed how the geese fly. They fly in 'V' formation. You would wonder why they fly that way.

As each bird flaps its wings, it creates uplift for the bird immediately following. By flying in 'V' formation, the whole flock adds up to 71 percent greater flying range than if each bird had flown alone.

When a goose falls out of the formation, it suddenly feels the drag and resistance of trying to go it alone, and quickly gets back into the formation to take advantage of the lifting power of the bird in front.

When the leading goose gets tired, it moves back in the flock and another goose flies point. Finally, and this is as interesting as it is important...when a goose gets sick or is wounded and falls out of formation, two other geese fall out with that goose and follow it down to lend help and protection. They stay with the fallen goose till it recovers and is able to fly or until it dies, and only then do they launch out on their own, or with another formation to catch up with their group.

Unknown author (*www.friedsocialworker.com/imagery/sense* of a goose.htm)

What else can be a better lesson for soldiers whose success and security depends on teamwork. The commanding officer should think out of the box ways to build team spirit and sub unit cohesion. Why should the PT fall in not be done any differently? Why should the quarter guard or any other guard not be a cohesive section rather than a mixed one? I have seen regiments with class based sub units. I always returned with the impression of a unit of three sub units rather than one unit, each squadron with its own battle cry.

In the military units we share a common direction and goal. We will get to our goal faster and more easily if we travel on the thrust of one another and that is team work. It is sensible to take turns doing the demanding job, whether with people or with geese. Truly, the word TEAM rightly stands for Together Everyone Achieves More.

I have seen many people quite the opposite. While they will be happy to travel on the thrust of others, they are not willing to reciprocate. A unit had an officer who was relieved for close to eight months for each of the last two chances to prepare for a promotion examination. Two days after the exam finished, his commanding officer asked him to deposit his reading material with the adjutant for the other officers. The officer promptly replied that he has burnt all his material.

Taken aback, the commanding officer asked him, 'Burnt, and why?'

'I did not owe anything to anyone, so I was not obliged to give anything to anyone.'

The commanding officer was aghast, not quite believing what he was hearing. The officer was called to the office and given a dressing down. He was told that if he was relieved for eight months for two successive years, he owed it to other officers who shouldered his work. Besides, a battalion is not about give and take, it is all about giving without even the thought of getting something in return.

This is the worst example of team work that I have come across. There is no place for such people in the army.

A unit consists of numerous squads and crews. Each of this entity is a team. Together squads make platoons and troops. The platoons and troops and make companies/squadrons and batteries, and they make units. For the group to grow as a team, they must:

- Be capable of admitting to mistakes, weaknesses and insufficient knowledge.
- Speak up openly when they disagree amongst themselves.
- Confront behavioural patterns directly.
- Put the success and interests of the team and organization over their own.

Patrick M. Lencioni: 'The Trouble with Teamwork' Leader to Leader. Be, Know, Good.

Col Dandridge M Malone, US army, sums up the relationship of individual training, team work and leadership in this equation:

The sum of the performance of individual soldiers X the ability of the soldiers to work together as a team X the ability of the leadership to get all those teams to work together as a unit = THE PERFORMANCE OF THE UNIT.

## Grooming of Officers and Young Soldiers

*'Give a young officer the gift of a good start; guaranteed you have a good officer for life.'*

In the old days, there was a good system of the senior subaltern being made responsible to groom a young officer in the unit. Regretfully, this all important aspect is being neglected today. Of all the functions of a commanding officer, grooming of an officer in my opinion is the most sacred simply because, as they say, a battalion is as good as the officers are. Spending time and effort on a young officer is an investment, the benefits of which will be reaped not by the battalion alone but by this nation.

The human resource is the greatest asset of any army. Of them all, it is the officers who are even more, for one simple reason that on their competence and ability rests the fate of the army.

*A good commanding officer will inspire his men to have confidence in their commanding officer. A great commanding officer will inspire his men to have confidence in themselves. The task of the battalion commander is not to train his command to be good followers, his job is to train them to be good leaders.*

Kargil wars can only be won when you groom young officers to be tigers and not pussies. Allow them to growl once in a while, even if they are growling at you.

The men are at the very core of the army. Their ability to deliver depends on how they are trained, motivated, organized, equipped and, most importantly, led. The orientation cadre of young soldiers in the unit is an important function that must aim at developing military traits and soldierly pride in him. It must identify his aptitude, strengths and shortcomings. His section and platoon commander must aim to build on his strengths and work on his shortcomings.

The truth is that today a vast majority of officers and all men join the army not for passion of soldiering per se, but for a job like any other. The pyramidal structure of the army leaves a large chunk of officers with no career progression beyond the rank of Lieutenant Colonel. Supersession in the army cannot be wished away. Vast majority get seriously affected by supersession. The solution lies in grooming a young officer in a manner that, notwithstanding supersession, his self pride and pride in his profession keeps him motivated till the end. The army simply cannot have passengers, for there is not a man authorized without a job in battle. War apart, in peace; every soldier is an ambassador of the army. He must always walk tall, dress up smartly and conduct himself in a manner befitting the army - an officer and a gentleman. Every poor act of omission and commission in public place harms the army's image.

The first task before the commanding officers is to motivate their officers and men to believe in the nobility and piety of their profession. Nobility, because of the responsibility the profession puts on their young shoulders like none other. Piety, because the country trusts the soldier to sacrifice his all in performance of his duty, a demand no other profession makes on its cadre. Because every man trusts his life with his mates, because men trust their lives on your competence and judgment, and because the country trusts your judgment to take life in defence of its people and the interest of the country. The military officer belongs to that distinguished class, which unlike others has no problem with the question 'What difference have you made to your country and its people?' In no other profession is an officer commissioned by the direct pleasure of the President of India, the Supreme Commander, who reposes utmost trust in his loyalty, sacrifice and courage to serve the country at the cost of his life. The country trusts him to live and die by the highest values of the code of conduct even though such values are conspicuous by their absence elsewhere.

The uniform gives us our countrymen's love, blind trust and faith. I have experienced this on many occasions. While posted in Meerut, I stepped out from a military vehicle, in civil dress, to draw money from the ATM. A lady handed me her ATM card to draw money for her, simply because of her trust in a military man. How can we ever break that trust?

Grooming of a young officer is the single most important function of a unit. The responsibility rests on every one, for everyone can teach him something about his field of work when he joins the unit. The ultimate responsibility rests on the commanding officer. Different units have different ways of grooming a young officer. Regretfully, this important aspect is being lost sight of in a large part of the army. I have personally seen a fine young officer being destroyed in a neighbouring battalion by the most un-officer like treatment. The net result was that in less than six months, this simple highlander became a rogue with a 'I care two hoodt' attitude and quit the army after his mandatory short service. The commanding officer of this unit was rarely in the unit, more interested in organizing mountaineering expeditions. On the other hand, average cadets have been turned into proud competent officers by good grooming.

What then is the ultimate objective of grooming a young officer? In plain and simple terms, it needs to be understood that: 'Teaching a young officer his skills to command a sub unit, while necessary, is not the prime objective of grooming. The prime objective of grooming is to make him an officer of good character and integrity.'

Acquiring particular skill sets is the easier part and can be done at any stage, but achieving the former is time bound. The earliest it is done, the easiest it is done. You don't do it in the first two years of service, it is likely that you have missed the bus. If that is achieved, the rest will follow. Units can devise simple but effective ways to develop good character qualities amongst new officers, who without exception are highly motivated. Every young officer is a bundle of energy with very high morals and values. He truly imbibes the spirit of the Chetwode motto and is prepared to lay down his life. He is a perfect raw material to be groomed into a dedicated and committed officer of the army the cutting edge of the sword.

A young officer will be watched critically by his men to see what he is made of. Most soldiers will give him the respect and trust that he has earned by becoming an officer while they judge his mettle. True respect and confidence is earned through actions and the men will be closely observing him in order to determine his worth as a leader. He will have to measure up to high standards of other officers before him. An officer should remain 'true' as troops are very perceptive and can quickly see through the facade. You cannot fool six hundred men for too long. New officers must constantly work to improve themselves and become better leaders. Always remember, as the leader you are in charge. There are wonderful examples of average and below average cadets developing into good leaders through good grooming and self improvement.

What does a young officer need to do? The first thing a young officer must do when he joins the army is to fight a battle, and that battle is for the hearts and minds of his men. If he wins that battle and subsequent similar ones, his men will follow him anywhere; if he loses it, he will never do any real good.

Field Marshal Viscount Montgomery in *The Memoirs of Field Marshal Montgomery*.

The battalion needs to help the young officer to win this battle. What all does this encompass? To understand this, we need to do a reverse appreciation. Let me draw a portrait of what I believe a young officer should be after one year of his service. In my opinion he should be a best mix of the following:

- A highly motivated young man who is proud of the profession he has joined with high ideals.
- Is proud of the battalion and his regiment, and considers no sacrifice too great for the honour and glory of his battalion.
- Has won the trust of his sub unit to lead them into battle through his competence, commitment and courage.
- Holds his personal pride as a soldier in such high esteem that he shall not allow his honesty and integrity to be breached by any magnitude of temptation or threat.
- Is a team man.
- And, above all, loves his men and cares for them.

Summarizing the above, a man of character and integrity who lives by the military code and ethics and leads by personal example in every way.

A young officer is a motivated soul. All that he needs is the right guidance under a professionally competent and a motivated officer. A young officer is greatly influenced by his first commanding officer. He invariably imbibes the same values and traits that he sees in his first commanding officer. It is a special relationship that he cherishes his entire career. The commanding officer, therefore, must be conscious of this fact and conduct himself accordingly.

The young officers now joining the army increasingly hail from humbler backgrounds, thus the societal gap between the officers and men has reduced. The challenge forced by this change needs to be recognized and addressed through focused grooming of young officers. The Indian soldier still gives unquestioned respect to the officer, but that can be sustained only through high standards of professionalism and leadership. The bottom line: The background is of no consequence if one sets high standards of personal conduct and leadership. Young officers must give respect due to JCOs, NCOs and the men that they have earned through their years of service.

Possibly, my expectations from a young officer would make him a near perfect soldier. Yes, I strongly believe that the aim of grooming a young officer should be to make him a near perfect officer imbibing above qualities. The units must work out ways that gradually transforms this fine raw material into a fine soldier. Easier said than done, how does one do it today when the units are short of officers and seem to be perpetually over employed.

The officer has to be groomed to be a thinking and creative leader. Since the purpose of grooming is to make him a leader of character and integrity, focus must be laid on building their character. While most officers are above board, there have been some unethical incidents such as 'ketchup colonel' in pursuit of awards. Such incidents, though exceptions should not happen at all in the army because of our high moral values. It is here that character building and education of morals and military ethics is necessary.

In every other service, an officer trainee is called a probationer. In the military, he is called a Gentleman Cadet. An officer is referred to as an 'Officer and a Gentleman.' A gentleman is described as a person who is well mannered, honourable and of good breeding. In the days of chivalry, knights and officers were noted as well for courtesy and gentle behaviour, as for death defying courage. From their acts of courtesy and benevolence was derived the word, now pronounced as 'Gentleman.'

He is called so because the only way to be an officer is to be a gentleman. To be a gentleman is to be a man of character. A man of character is a man of great virtues. He is an honest person, a person with a sense of duty and responsibility, is truthful, treats others with respect and dignity, is considerate to the weak, is a man of principles with courage to stand by his convictions, a person with a sense of balance to take the good and the bad with maturity, is loyal and can be trusted.

In our context, the Indian army is deployed and operates within own country and we are dealing with own countrymen. There is, therefore, more the reason that soldiers must be 'soldiers and gentleman.' One single factor that costs nothing but pays maximum dividends in building confidence amongst people and earning their respect is good troop behaviour.

The grooming of the officer should be the concern of every officer. The process of grooming a young officer must begin from the time he joins the academy. A highly motivated Gentleman Cadet getting commissioned is proud of the Regiment that he has not even seen. What better gesture than a man coming from the battalion with a set of accoutrements and a welcome letter from the commanding officer or the colonel of the regiment, with a packet of company *shakarpara* packed in regimental colours. Many battalions do that, and I am sure that is a great start as the cadets share this with others. This simple gesture sets him up perfectly for good dispensation to his unit.

In the unit, the best way is to place him under a good company commander, who himself epitomizes good character and integrity, is professionally competent and a selfless officer. Add to that a senior subaltern who should be selected for similar qualities. They will deliver the result effortlessly if they have that magic quality called passion for the uniform and the values it stands for. Followed as a practice, it becomes a habit in the battalion as everyone in his turn passes it down as a matter of paying back to the battalion. This also develops close brotherhood.

Mentoring by a good company commander ensures that the young officer imbibes the right values of a good professional officer. When he sees that his company commander does not retire till the men are settled, he will do the same, or sees his commanding officer carry his own rucksack and run battle endurance tests with the men, he will do the same and not consider it below his dignity to run with his men, as some do. On the other hand, bad examples could be emulated even faster.

Performance on courses is a quantifiable aspect that can give the young officers the desired confidence and raise their self esteem. The most important area in this aspect is preparing the officer well for the first course that he does. If he does well on the first course, he gets a reputation to protect and he works hard to do so.

A young officer has to be groomed to become a troops oriented officer. He must care for his men at all times and put himself last every time. He needs to believe that while Ambanis and Tatas can a wear a suit costing a fortune, they cannot wear a uniform costing a few hundred rupees. That is an honour that cannot be bought but has to be earned. The uniform gives him that exalted status which commands respect reserved only for a soldier, instils a sense of security in his countrymen by his presence and earns their complete trust and faith. The youngster must be brought up to believe that his uniform and his profession are more sacred than temples, gurudwaras and mosques.

A young officer must be brought up as a bold, fearless and creative officer with the spirit of a wild horse. Minor infringements that are not related to morals and ethics must be overlooked.

I wish to narrate this experience of a young officer:

'I was commissioned in 79 and joined my unit at Siliguri (West Bengal). Those were the days when there was no internet, no ATMs, no TVs and very few banks. The PNB, the mother of all banks where we all had our accounts was twenty kms away in Siliguri. Dulabari on the Nepal border was not too far, from where people including officers got imported goods, electronics being the craze those days. The consumer market those days in the country was basic to say the least and hence the craze for imported goods available across the border.

Seeing others, I too decided to buy a "music system" as it was called. Hardly a system, it was a basic transistor sized Sanyo single cassette player. Those days it was the only entertainment available to a young officer. It actually cost a fortune, a whopping 900 bucks when my basic salary was Rs 750.

Bank being too far, and since I owned no transport, getting to the bank was like going on a pilgrimage. I sent my buddy to borrow Rs 400 from the unit *baniya*. The buddy returned empty handed, saying the *baniya* has refused to give money unless I gave him a bank cheque first. The mess was four kms away and on a Sunday I needed the money urgently. That was the first time I was taking money from the unit *baniya*, which was a regular practice because of the distance to the bank. The officers would give him a cheque which the *baniya* would encash and square up.

That hurt my pride. I was not running away from the unit for 400 bucks. As the luck would have it, I was the duty officer. I ordered the weekly firing fighting practice in his *baniya* shop. All the *jalebis*, *burfis* and *samosas* were declared unfit for consumption and thrown out of the window. The fire fighting party was told that the shop is on fire. Two fire extinguishers were let loose across his shop in full glory, turning his shop into stalactite. The *baniya* in chief, unable to believe what was going on, kept protesting to no avail. He was declared a severe burn casualty and ordered to be evacuated to the MI Room. The men understood what was going on, loaded him on a stretcher and took him round the unit on the chants of '*Ram Naam Satya Hai*.'

I got the *baniya* back and told him that I would not run away with 400 bucks. Don't ever make this mistake again.

The next day I was summoned by the second-in-command, Major Tuffy Marwah, a hard task regimental officer.

'The *baniya* complained to me what you did to him and his shop yesterday. Is that true?' he asked.

'Yes sir,' I replied.

'Why did you do that?'

I told him the story, emphasizing that I would not run away with 400 bucks. That he lives off the battalion and he cannot insult an officer by refusing to loan 400 bucks for a day.

'Why didn't you tell me rather than take this drastic step. You think I would not have taken appropriate action?' he asked.

'It hurt my pride as an officer. I did what I thought must be done so he dare not insult another officer. It is not in my nature to go complaining, and sir, surely you would not have done what I did.' I replied.

Major Marwah smiled and asked the youngster to dismiss without a further word. He ensured that this young officer's boldness and killer instinct was not killed. The matter ended there and nothing was ever heard of it again. If the commanding officer ever learnt of it, he never let it be known to the young officer. On the other side, this unit thereafter had the most disciplined and responsive *baniya*, for the regimental folklore never die.

Personal example and austerity in living is all part of young officers grooming.

I notice with dismay, the '*bada sahib*' culture in the army, the ever increasing needs of officers and men. Even young officers are received in units and headquarters by soldiers to carry their brief cases thirty yards to the office, and they happily let them do it. At a time when a hurricane hit the east coast of USA, leaving the entire area flooded and destroyed, a US four-star General was shown by the CNN eating his MRE sitting on the road side parapet. Young officers were discussing why we could not have such down to earth Generals too. Event management seems to have overtaken professionalism. Inter battalion sports prize distribution in our army is a bigger event than the grand slam Tennis prize distribution.

One battalion was on the field firing range for field firing. When the commanding officer approached the unit location, he saw a huge tented camp. He was told that it was the officers living area. He was surprised to see that each officer's living had three tents. One for living, second the bathing room and the third, the toilet. That was the arrangement for the commanding officer as well. That in effect meant that a very junior subaltern had the same facility as did the commanding officer. An officer of the old mould, he asked the second-in-command to accompany him to the troops living area. He was surprised to see that hundreds of men were accommodated in the same number of tents as used by eleven officers in the searing heat. Colonel Passion passed instructions that he will live in one extendable tent and use one small tent with a dug out floor for bathing and toilet. The rest of the officers should accordingly work out for themselves. A point was driven home as the officers' colony shrunk to one third. Tents rendered surplus were sent for the men. One simple step taught a useful lesson to the officers. Ignoring this major, yet seemingly innocuous violation, would have done them great disservice. They would have grown up assuming that it was the right thing to do. If there is poverty it must be shared by the officers.

We served one tenure on the Siachen glacier in 1986. Those were the early days with limited resources. The battalion headquarter at Kumar had only two fibre glass huts. One was given to the men and the other was used as the MI Room. The officers stayed in make shift tents made from parachutes in the freezing cold for the entire duration of the tenure. The snow tents, also in short supply, were given to the men. These are all part of grooming young officers into down to earth professional soldiers.

In a military station, the corps commander organized an officers' seminar attended by over two hundred officers. Among other things, the corps used to run a kind of an orientation capsule for the young officers. The capsule included a variety of useful aspects. One aspect related to financial stability and an exposure to creating a second source of income. This capsule was part of officers' grooming. Fully knowing that the entire capsule was the brainchild of the corps commander, one Colonel Passion disagreed with one aspect of the orientation capsule and this was the issue of finances and share market so early in life.

He made this observation that the first three years of the young officer must be dedicated to learning the tenets of soldiering in its entirety, regimental history and traditions, knowing the men, learning military ethos and customs, mastering company weapons, learning section and platoon tactics, etc. At the end of three years, he must so establish himself that the men trust his competence and commitment to lead them effectively in battle. He did not go with the idea of focusing on finances at this early stage. It was more important for him to be a good platoon leader first, who commands faith and trust of his men to follow him in battle. In the long career spanning over three decades, it would do him no harm if he started looking at finances three years later. In his closing address the corps commander did not agree with Colonel Passion. He explained the need of good financial standing that helped the officer to focus on his profession, citing his own example that although close to retirement, he still did not own a house. This clearly is an undesirable state of affairs, which certainly is not a result of lack of formal education in finances. The importance of good financial standing cannot be argued against, but I strongly believe that the first three years of service have to be dedicated to laying the correct foundation of the profession. Finance and money have never been the prime motivating factors. If a young officer misses this crucial foundation building, he would have missed an important bus. You cannot start learning after five years what you should have learnt in first three.

It is the pride in being a soldier that will make him the officer he needs to be, a man who will do the right thing expected of him in pitch dark, i.e., even when he is not being watched. To highlight this aspect I must narrate an interesting episode:

One officer had driven down to Mhow and offered his brother his car for the staff college course at Wellington. A bachelor owning a small car, he had plans to drive along the coast spending a month on the way. Sitting in the college bar, Colonel Subramanian from 4 MADRAS, posted in Infantry School got chatting with him. He learnt that this officer was here to drive the car thousand miles to Wellington. Subramanian then made a strange request. He said that his father was sick and he needed to be at Bangalore at the earliest, and at this short notice, he was not getting a reservation anywhere.

'Can you give me a lift ?'asked Subramanian.

'To where ?'

'To Bangalore?' replied Subramanian.

'How many persons?'

'Four in the family,' replied Subramanian.

He drove this family straight to Bangalore, over a thousand miles, cancelling all his holiday plans. A man he had never met before and a man he would never meet again, he had nothing to take from Subramanian. How many people do you know who will do this for an unknown man, will you? Is the army lacking, where such qualities of character count for nothing in the promotion system?

So, good leadership is all about good character. How does one define character. Numerous definitions exist. Simply put 'What a man does in the dark is his character.'

> *'Ninety percent of leadership depends on character. The entire emphasis in the education system of any civilization that has reached golden age is on building character based on universal human values.'*
>
> —Lt Gen M L Chibber

The commanders at all levels must keep abreast with the changing times and aspirations and model their approach accordingly. However, some things in the army must not change. This incident brings out an important aspect of officer grooming.

Field Marshal KM Cariappa, the former Chief of the Indian Army, was invited to visit the CMP Centre at Bangalore, in the 1980s, decades after he had retired. Colonel RS Katoch, JAK RIF, a 1947 commissioned officer was detailed as his liaison officer because of his vintage. Colonel Katoch reached former Chief's residence ten minutes earlier to escort him for the evening engagement. Cariappa was waiting in the lounge, dressed impeccably in a suit. He shook hands with Col Katoch, offered him a drink and then asked his servant to get a pair of scissors. Col Katoch, taken aback, wondered as to why the Field Marshal was looking for a pair of scissors. He mustered the courage to ask him why he was looking for one and if he could help. The former Chief, looking at Katoch's blazer with a stern look said, 'I can see that you do not need the buttons on your blazer, so I must cut them off.' Col Katoch got the message and quickly buttoned up his blazer.

This was decades after he had retired. Why did he feel the necessity to do so, for what many would see today as a trivial issue. The message, as far as the officers are concerned, there is only one way to do things and that is the right way. Officers are expected to live by a certain code at all times, both while in service and as veterans, for once a soldier, always a soldier. The Field Marshal had his blazer buttoned up as he stepped up to meet Col Katoch.

## Professional Study

*Power (confidence) comes from competence,*
*Competence comes from knowledge and,*
*Knowledge comes from reading, observing and learning.*

Reading and writing habits have been major shortcomings amongst officers in general for far too long which must be corrected at the unit level. Performance in promotion examinations is a direct reflection of professional study habits. The twenty four hour television and internet are the biggest time stealers, even though both have great knowledge potential too, depending on what one chooses to do.

In an era where the gap between officers and other ranks is reducing on the material plane, it is only the knowledge that will separate them as leaders. The same goes for the JCOs. With better educated men around, their authority can only be stamped by their character and competence, a function of professional study.

Commanding officers must make special efforts to cultivate this habit in their officers and it will have to be imposed. Soon officers will realize the benefits of reading and start doing it voluntarily. Nothing can convey the benefits of reading better than this quote:

> *'Preparation for war is an expensive burdensome business, yet, there is one important part of it that costs little, study'*
>
> —Field Marshal Slim

All officers must be encouraged to inculcate interest in military history. No General can truly be a great Captain of war without a good insight of military history. Similarly, no officer can achieve his true 'intellectual potential' without the knowledge of history, because it enables him to grow professionally in quick time without having to reinvent the wheel.

General Nanavati, former army commander, while commanding his battalion 2/8 Gorkha Rifles was very particular about this. Book reviews and talks by young officers preceded dinner every night in the field mess. I am sure his officers benefitted immensely from his imposed regimen. Officers and men of this battalion were known for good performance on courses. 4 GUARDS followed a similar regimen. I remember, while doing the commando course, my buddy, Lieutenant Ranjit, 4 GUARDS, got a letter from his battalion second-in-command asking for the book review for the month. Ranjit could only curse; struggling to get through the commando course in one piece, a book review was the last thing on his mind. The point is, such practices need continued efforts to sustain and keep them going. The battalion had a practice of reimbursing the officer for the book if the book review was written with interest and diligence.

These days, one often hears this common excuse, there is simply no time, and we are too busy. I have never been able to agree with that point of view. Officers waste a lot of their time on time stealers such as TV, internet and social media tools. While life gets busy in patches, there is enough time that can be harvested here and there as one waits at the airport, in the train, or waiting for all kinds of events, etc.

The battlefield environment is already pregnant with technology. It will continue to develop at a great pace. At the tactical level, the junior leaders will need to be creative and innovative, adept at exploiting technology with wider intellectual horizons. Revolution in Military Affairs (RMA) is a continuous process. Professional study is the only route to enhance competence to keep pace with RMA.

In the higher military echelons, senior officers will need to be more conceptual and analytical without being too theoretical. They will deal with problems that are more abstract, complex and uncertain. Dealing competently with multiple components of the government needs an in-depth understanding of foreign policy, diplomacy, political, economic, informational and military elements of national power, as also governance, human rights and global affairs. They will require a thorough understanding of perspective of war as required for executing integrated tri-service operations. They will need to be adept at exploiting the technology as part of war fighting philosophy. The technology will compound the stress on the battlefield decision making and, thus, the need to be prepared to work through it. They will need to be able to appreciate what lies beyond the horizon and prepare for the future war and not the last war. (Scholar Warrior 2016 issue).

In my view, there can be lack of intellectual challenge in the army. It is possible for an officer to get by doing just the routine and get to higher ranks. How many officers do serious study, research and writing? How many officers think out of the box? How many senior officers can be seen as role models by the subordinates? Senior officers must encourage genuine disagreements, for disagreements are the engine of growth. If all company commanders say yes to the commanding officer, most of them are redundant.

Thus, the need for thinking and well read officers at all levels. Scholar warrior is not a cliché. Senior officers will need to intellectually challenge themselves to be taken seriously. Reading habit is the brick and mortar that will build the structure of intellectual growth. The military system does not adequately provide for higher education for all. This habit must be cultivated early in an officer's career and it will stay. Captain Liddell Hart was the Captain who taught the Generals. He was no genius, he spent monumental amount of time reading, observing, thinking, analyzing and writing. Winston Churchill credited his professional growth to five years of voracious reading early in his career.

If a person reads one book a month on a subject, in five years, he will be amongst the top five per cent experts in the world. Quite simple and not too difficult.

> *The heights reached by great men and kept, were not attained by sudden flight. But they, while their companions slept, were toiling upwards in the night.*
>
> —Anonymous

## Understanding Soldiers

> *'The soldier is a man; he expects to be treated as an adult, not a schoolboy. He has rights; they must be made known to him and thereafter respected. He has ambition; it must be stirred. He has a belief in fair play; it must be honoured. He has a need of comradeship; it must be supplied. He has imagination; it must be stimulated. He has a sense of personal dignity; it must be sustained. He has pride; it can be satisfied and made the bedrock of character once he has been assured that he is playing a useful and respected role. To give a man this, is the acme of inspired leadership. He has become loyal because loyalty was given to him."*
>
> —General George C. Marshall, US Army

Indian society, like all others has undergone a major transformation that has affected soldiers in a major way. A soldier of today is far different from yester years. He faces greater domestic challenges, greater responsibilities and has greater aspirations. The social media has raised his awareness levels much higher. Every incident of the army goes viral through social media. The ever increasing welfare oriented military has raised his expectations and he is demanding more of them as his right. He, therefore, looks at his leadership differently and expects a lot more in every way than did his predecessors a decade ago. A soldier of today does not care much about military ethics and values. Inner discipline is nowhere as strong as before. The number of incidents of mass insubordination over the last few years speak for themselves.

He knows the rules that interest him and interprets them to his convenience. I was the deputy GOC of a division under raising. We strictly followed the military way of life in all aspects. Use of mobiles was banned in the office complex. I saw one soldier using a mobile less than ten yards from my office. When I asked him whether he knew that use of mobiles were banned in the office area, he replied he is not inside the office, he is outside the office.

The battlefield is a dangerous place. The chaos provides enough opportunity for the sloppy men to have an excuse for not being where they should have been. It is for this reason the fear of the system must remain.

I fondly remember Subedar Major Dewan Singh of my battalion. It was in 1986 that we were deployed on Siachen glacier. As the Adjutant, I had to break the tragic news of the death of his daughter in his village in the Kumaon region. When told to proceed on leave earliest, he declined, stating, 'Whatever has happened at home has happened. I cannot see the face of my daughter anyway. As the Subedar Major of the unit, it is necessary that I am present in the unit for the cremation of three soldiers (who had died due to enemy shelling the same day).' Such sense of responsibility will be rarer in future.

A young officer must clearly understand what his men expect from him and what he can expect from them. A famous address to cadets being commissioned as officers in the US Army, by Sergeant Major John G Stepanek, echoes the sentiments of soldiers all over the world. A young officer will do well to grasp the essence of this speech and the path he must follow:

> "I feel a tinge of regret that I am not young enough to be sitting out there as one of you. You have so many years of challenge and adventure to look forward to. So many of these years are behind me.
>
> Soon you will meet your platoon sergeants, your first sergeant, your sergeants major, your other non-commissioned officers and your troops. What do we expect from you as officers, commanders, leaders?
>
> We expect of you, unassailable personal integrity and the highest of morals. We expect you to maintain the highest state of personal

appearance. We expect you to be fair, to be consistent, to have dignity, but not aloofness, to have compassion and understanding, to treat each soldier as an individual, with individual problems.

And we expect you to have courage – the courage of your convictions – the courage to stand up and be counted – to defend your men when they have followed your orders, even when your orders were in error – to assume the blame when you are wrong.

We expect you to stick out your chin and say, 'This man is worthy of promotion, and I want him promoted.' And we expect you to have even greater courage and say, 'This man is not qualified and he will be promoted over my dead body.' Gentlemen, I implore you. Do not promote a man because he has money problems, because he has a bar bill. If he is not capable of performing the duties of his grade, do not do him and us, the injustice of advancing him in grade. When he leaves you, or you leave him, he becomes someone else's problem.

Gentlemen, we expect you to have courage in the face of danger. Many of you will soon be in Vietnam where there are no safe rear echelons. During your tour, opportunity will arise for you to display personal courage and leadership. Opportunities could arise from which you may emerge as heroes. A hero is an individual who is faced with an undesirable situation and is able to nullify or negate it.

Do not display recklessness and expose yourself and your men to unnecessary risks that will reduce their normal chance of survival. This will only shake their confidence in your judgment.

Now gentlemen, you know what we expect from you. What can you expect from us?

From a few of us, you can expect antagonism, a 'Prove yourself' attitude.

From a few of us, who had the opportunity to be officers, and didn't have the guts and motivation to accept the challenge, you can expect resentment.

From a few of us old timers, you can expect tolerance.

But from most of us you can expect loyalty to our position, devotion to our cause, admiration for your honest effort – endurance to match your endurance – motivation to match your motivation – spirit to match your spirit – a desire for achievement to match your desire for achievement.

You can expect a love of God, a love of country, and a love of duty to match your love of God, your love of country and your love of duty.

We won't mind the heat if you sweat with us. We don't mind the cold if you shiver with us. And we don't mind quitting after your cigarettes are gone.

Gentlemen, you don't accept us, we were here first. We accept you, and when we do, you'll know. We don't beat drums, or carry you off the drill field on our shoulders. But, may be at a company party we'll raise a canteen cup of beer and say, 'Lieutenant, you're okay,' just like that.

Remember one thing. Very few non-commissioned officers were awarded stripes without showing somebody something, sometimes, somewhere. If your platoon sergeant is mediocre, if he is slow to assume responsibility, if he shies away from you, may be sometime not too long ago someone shot him down when he was right. Internal wounds heal slowly, internal scars fade more slowly.

Your orders appointing you as officers in the United States Army appointed you to command. No orders, no letters, no insignia of rank can appoint you as leaders. Leadership is an intangible thing, leaders are made, they are not born. Leadership is developed within yourselves.

You do not wear leadership on your sleeves, on your shoulders, on your caps or on your calling cards. Be you Lieutenants or Generals, we're the guys you've got to convince and we will meet you more than halfway.

You are leaders in an army in which we have served for so many years and you will help us defend the country we have loved for so many years.

I wish you happiness, luck and success in the existing and challenging years that lie ahead.

May God bless you all."

—Sergeant Major John G Stepanek, US Army.

## Soldier in the Present Environment

In any army, the unit is the basic building block. In our army it provides identity to the rank and file and motivates them to stake everything for the reputation of the unit. It is through his unit that a soldier learns to respect the three Ns of the army *Naam*, *Namak* and *Nishan*, i.e., the name, the salt or the livelihood that the unit provides and the flag. However, the syndrome, 'What is in it for me?' is more important for the modern soldier than those of the past generation.

Notwithstanding the changing environment, our soldier remains one of the finest in the world. It has been demonstrated time and again, and last being the Kargil war in 1999. However, some things have changed in the recent past. The soldier of today, whether from urban or rural background, is better educated and far more aware than the soldiers of the past. The environmental and societal changes have raised his aspirations for his family and better future for his children. The nuclear families have removed the family support system which has brought greater responsibilities and pressures on him.

A major change that has occurred is that the social and material gap between the officers and the men has narrowed. Unlike in the past, more and more officers are coming from lower and middle class background. There are soldiers, NCOs or JCOs, whose brothers, cousins or sons are commissioned officers. Better pay has improved their quality of life. Use of expensive motor cycles by men is common and use of cars not uncommon. Request for ACs in the men's family quarters are beginning to be made. The army will need to start providing for increased aspirations.

In this era of the narrowing gap between the leader and the led, our junior leaders in the units find themselves in a unique situation of leading men, who are academically more qualified and more questioning. While the men of today may have a higher qualification that does not necessarily translate into better education. A better educated man must have better sense of his responsibilities.

Human beings have an innate resistance to obedience. There is a dilution of inner discipline and personal interests overriding organizational interests amongst men. Discipline ensures obedience, instils pride and respect for the authority. It is my belief that our army needs to work harder on cultivating inner discipline. Remove supervision and self-discipline of men declines. Attending a seminar on HR management in the valley, the commander brought out that his survey indicated that forty percent troops were not happy with the quality of food. I stood up to let the men know that while the need for the most hectic day that a soldier may have is about 3000 calories, the army rations provides over 4000 calories per day. That every soldier who returns after availing leave loses weight and all of us eat a more balanced diet in the army than at home. The management of unit cook houses is entirely by them and they have to blame themselves and no one else. There is a tendency to kick the problem upwards at the first instance rather than solving it themselves. As a divisional commander I carried out a survey of expectations of the men. I was surprised how little appreciation the JCOs and men have of how well the army looks after them.

In a soldier's calling, there is a positive correlation between Spartan living and effective performance. Materialism and comforts beyond a point are counterproductive. The Americans and the French were beaten by Vietnamese, who fought with a rifle and a rice bag hung on the back. What they had was the will and belief in their cause. The Russian and the US experience in Afghanistan were no different. Today, there is undue emphasis on welfare. There are far greater expectations from the army than an equal sense of duty and commitment to the organizational cause. It is important that they understand the cost the army bears and be grateful for what it provides. They came here by choice and must deliver in a manner the army demands.

This change means that the respect and aura that came in the past with the rank, does not come gratis now in the same way. The soldier of today, being much more worldly wise because of technology, media and transparency is demanding more. The immense rise in legal cases from the men is an indicator of the changing trend.

Today, due to reasons of changing times and increasing suicides among men, leave has become more of a right than a privilege. Compare with old days when casual leave was never planned, but taken on occurrence of emergency. The cases of suicides, almost always have their origin in domestic issues that the men find unable to cope with. Thus, timely leave when the soldier wants helps him to address his problems without having a reason to blame the organization for his woes. The inability or the lack of concern of the civil administration towards soldiers' problems, arising out of his being away from home most of the time, to which he cannot attend, adds to his mental discomfort. Land issues, harassment of his family by neighbours or family members, etc., are common problems that they have to deal with.

This notwithstanding, there is a need to check the free flowing of welfare. Soldiers must understand that military by its very nature means restrictions in liberties and freedom. These restrictions must be enforced when necessary, lest they become a habit. The army adequately provides for its families to be looked after even in the absence of the man. It is important that the aura and respect for the authority and the restrictive nature of military life are understood.

What does all this mean for leadership at the unit level. It means higher standards of professional competence and personal conduct by officers. It means being more correct in dealing with men when it comes to their dignity and self-respect. I shall dwell more on it later.

In battle, if the troops trust the leader's competence and believe that he would not unnecessarily expose them to danger, share the same risk and deprivation, his authority and decisions will not be questioned.

> *Look upon your soldiers as you do infants, and they willingly go into deep valleys with you; look upon your soldiers as your beloved children and they willingly die with you.*
>
> —Sun Tzu

## Officers and Troops Relationships

*Good officers devote their time and energy for the troops.*

Army is about that all important 'trust' between officers and men. Trust is a function of many factors that we have spoken of before and it was the strength of our army in combat and combat support arms. The Indian army had incidents of collective insubordination in 1984 post 'Operation Blue Star,' There was a religious overtone to those incidents. There was total lack of appreciation of the environment by the officers who failed to feel the pulse of the men undergoing mental turmoil. The situation was exploited by unscrupulous elements resulting in those unsavoury incidents. Unfortunately, the recent past has witnessed a number of incidents of mass insubordination in combat units. One happened in my division and I was involved in the restoration of the situation. In all these incidents the JCOs consistently failed to play their part in preventing the descent to chaos. Knowing the nature of their involvement in unit routine, it is unfathomable that they were not aware of the developing trouble. Yet, only a few of them have been held accountable, a major organizational weakness.

At the unit level, such incidents are a direct fallout of lack of mutual trust between officers and men where men cannot walk up freely to the officers and be heard. Good leadership creates trust raised on the foundation of strong military values and nurtured by healthy regimentation. A decline in morals and ethics leads to neglect of duty to the unit as well as diversion of the commander's energy to non-essentials. Neglect of matters of importance to men, deviations from the basics, violation of individual dignity in the handling of subordinates and misuse of military resources creates an environment of distrust that just needs a trigger to explode.

The units which had incidents of mass indiscipline were characterized by poor officer men relationship and, as a result, the basics of the battalion had taken a hit. The lack of mentoring had deprived them of the experience, knowledge and the art of handling men. There was lack of empathy. The genuine needs of men were neglected and, above all, in daily dealings, the dignity of the soldier was violated. The shortage of officers and peacetime chores reduces the opportunity of officers-men interaction. While this is factually correct, to blame the problems on this factor alone is only half the truth. In the same environment, some units continue to excel, while others continue to blame shortage of officers for their ills. Three officers in the unit are good enough to feel the pulse of the men if the unit *dastoor* (basics of unit functioning) is followed. A chat with the men as often as the situation permits, PT and games parade done the way it should be is good enough to keep contact. The problem is in grooming of the officers to do the right thing. Shortage of officers is a poor excuse for poor officer-men relationship. More than anything else, it is either the lack of concern or simply not knowing what to do, for want of grooming. One can never disregard the fact that no unit is short of JCOs and senior NCOs. There is simply no excuse for lack of interaction with men by these important functionaries who have decades of experience and interact with men on a daily basis.

Today, the commanding officers are very young. They spend half of their regimental service out of the unit, most of it in the crucial second half, the period when one begins to grasp the command functions. Often they land up learning to command on the job in a short two year command tenure. There is no other officer experienced enough to mentor the juniors. At a JCOs mess function or a *bara khana* (community meal) with troops, it is common to see officers chatting in a group of their own rather than interacting with men. Some officers do not seem to be comfortable in the company of men, which is a shame. The JCOs should be filling this void but unfortunately they failed to rise to the occasion in the units which had problems. Most JCOs either remained bystanders or fanned the fire, making the situation worse.

The onus of regimentation lies on the officer cadre. It starts with a selfless commitment of officers to the unit's interest and genuine care of the men. It has to start from the top and the entire responsibility rests with the commanding officer to ensure the environmental factors do not become an excuse.

Notwithstanding the changing times, our men are a fine lot. They respond to an interactive approach with doubled enthusiasm. An interactive approach breaks barriers.

'As a second lieutenant, I was on a long range patrol with my platoon in Sikkim. Lying alongside the men in a three men bivouac on a cold and rainy night, a simple highlander offered me a *bidi* (local cigarette rolled from tobacco leaves). I said, I have never smoked in life. He said, that is okay, but now you are our platoon commander, we will fight and die together. On your order the whole platoon will be prepared to die.

I had my first and last drag from my soldier's *bidi*. He was thrilled and the next day the whole battalion knew. We became *bidi* friends and he remembered it all his service. I could trust that boy with my life.

During a visit to the divisional engineer regiment as a divisional commander, I spoke to a young *jawan* who was recently married. He had not taken his wife out since he came after his marriage. That evening I sent him a vehicle to take his wife for a movie in the army cinema hall. At the end of my command, I got the best compliment from one commanding officer, quote,' Sir, while the officers of the division will surely miss you, the troops will miss you more.' Building good officer men relationship is not rocket science. It is a simple art; if you genuinely love your men, you will know what to do.

Such small gestures give the men something good to talk about and that builds harmony in relations.

On the other hand actions such as violation of dignity of individuals, mass punishment or ridicule of the troops, hurry-up and wait troops and similar drills that waste time, resting before your men, shirking the responsibility of checking your men's state of affairs, blaming higher commanders to cover your follies or lack of moral courage, blaming subordinates for a unit's failure in any activity, favouritism, etc., are recipe for building resentment. Transparency, accessibility and fairness play a big role in maintaining good officer men relationship.

Lastly, genuine care for the men is a mark of truly good officers. It is the single most important factor that builds good officer men relationship. A negative attitude, prejudice, abuse of authority and self-serving actions are traits that spell failure in this regard. This is a critical element of leadership and it cannot be faked. Troops know when their leader is genuinely concerned about their welfare and they respond to such leaders with unswerving loyalty.

> *A soldier must always feel free to bring his problems to his officers and be heard. The day he stops bringing his problems to you, he is convinced either you do not care or has lost confidence in your ability to deliver.*
>
> —General Colin Powell, US Army

Both are a shame on the leadership.

If you take care of your men, they will take care of you and guaranteed there will never be a problem. Problems occur when we fail to do our duty to them or conduct ourselves as we are expected to.

The article below is titled DUTY PERFORMED PROPERLY. This is a true story. It was first published in The Tribune Newspaper on 7 September 21 and later in the Sainik Samachar.

I would like the readers to analyse this article from an officer-men relationship perspective. Here is a soldier with two daughters less than three, prepared to die for his officer. We have had incidents of mass indiscipline by men where officers were seriously wounded including a commanding officer.

- Why do you think Havildar Mahesh was prepared to risk his life for this officer?
- Why did General XXX, after retirement, with his wife take all the trouble and spent a decent sum to attend the wedding of the son of Havildar Mahesh, twenty years after the NCO had left the unit with a pre-mature retirement?

* * *

## DUTY PERFORMED PROPERLY

*Author: Lt Col Ashok Ahlawat*

An elderly couple was travelling from Delhi to Pithoragarh to attend a wedding. The small bus whirled and bumped through the tunnels of dust on broken roads. Yellow dozers and JCBs worked clearing the debris.

The bus screeched to a halt, raising a shower of dust in its wake. They were at the Ghat bridge. The green waters of the Saryu river raced southward singing over rocks. The elderly had been a much-respected General in the Infantry. A tall rugged man with flowing pepper silver hair, he looked every inch a soldier. His long moustaches imparted to him the aspect of an 18th-century warlord. After retirement, he had started writing books and memoirs about the army service. The books brought him acclaim and satisfaction. He was working on his book when this wedding journey had pulled him away from his desk. He alighted from the bus and offered his hand to his wife and helped her get down.

They saw retired Havildar Mahesh emerge from a chai khana where two gaily caparisoned ponies stood ready for the remaining journey. Behind old Mahesh walked his son whose wedding it was. He carried a tray with teacups and pakoras. He was also a soldier in his father's paltan. The two old comrades met and bear-hugged warmly without a hint of the wide chasm between their ranks.

Mahesh's village lay three hill hours away. Mahesh had been the General's batman over three decades ago.

The year was 1993 and the General XXX then was Major XXX. The paltan was at Sopore, famous for its apple orchards, the Wular Lake and its badminton playing terrorists. It was also called the militants' Rajdhani.

Those days, bulletproof jackets were just being introduced and were in short supply. Issued thirty per battalion, barely 3 or 4 came to a company's share. The officers avoided wearing them thinking that the men didn't have them. The men said, if our officers aren't wearing, we shall also do without them. Such was the spirit of the paltan.

One day in September 93, Major XXX was leading a company column through terrorist haunted Sopore town. He was the first man up in the hallowed tradition of the army. The ominous streets were narrow and houses welded together in rows. The militants started raining heavy fire. Bullets clanged and sparked and ricocheted all around. Major XXX pinned in a doorway fired back at the enemy, but he found himself receiving a tremendous amount of fire and it was only a matter of time before a bullet struck him down. He saw the figure of a man come darting through the spray of bullets and jump in front of him. It was his batman, Sepoy Mahesh, thus shielding him bodily from the shower of bullets.

"Mahesh, what gall... Get back. You got two little kids to look after back home. Get aside and stop shielding me," protested the officer. Major XXX also had two sons aged two and three and a half years. Mahesh then had two daughters about the same age and this son whose wedding it was, was born later.

But the adamant soldier didn't budge. He behaved like a deaf man and ignored his officer's entreaty. Other guardsmen were advancing now, retaliating and picking up terrorists firing from upper storey windows. Gradually the terrorist fire diminished and they melted away. The Guards battalion again started probing through Sopore.

After the day's battle, Major XXX called Mahesh and admonished him sternly, "Mahesh why did you take such a grave risk. Why did you become a human shield for me? It's luck that both of us are alive. Why did you do it?"

Mahesh replied, the simple soldier that he was,

"Saab, I am assigned to you. It is my duty to protect you. If a bullet had struck you without first going through me, I would have failed in performing my duty properly."

* * *

## Creating an Enabling Environment

*A Commanding Officer's first objective is to be continually prepared for war and, second, to create an environment in which every man finds personal meaning and fulfilment. Create a climate where everyone is treated with dignity and respect regardless of race, gender, creed or religious belief.*

*It is only the attainment of the second that will ensure the first.*

(Extrapolated from General Edward C Meyer's quote, cited in book Be-Know-Do, by Frances Hesselbein and General Eric K. Shinseki)

A commanding officer must be an optimist. He must always radiate enthusiasm, confidence and positive vibes. Simple gestures like returning every salute with a smile, no matter how his day has been, does wonders. A good command at all levels starts with creating a good working environment. A commanding officer must understand that he cannot be the only happy man in the unit. For him to be happy, his unit has to be happy and contented.

For a start, do not criticize your predecessor; his environment may have been very different from yours. Do not change anything for the first three months unless you have been sent to fix an existing problem; observe, but do not change anything for the sake of changing.

A good environment dispels fear in the command. It allows free expression and interaction. It allows your command to grow, cultivates enthusiasm, encourages exercise of initiative, builds camaraderie, and esprit de corps. Above all, it spreads happiness, creates a sense of belonging and work becomes fun. Net result, it enhances human quotient and everyone enjoys voluntary contribution towards the common goal.

How does one create this conducive environment? A good environment is a direct function of the commanding officer's approach to command. He must create an environment where everyone benefits from upward thrust generated by the group. A commanding officer who puts himself last in priority for welfare sends an immediate message. A commanding officer who is like a Banyan tree, which only spreads itself and allows nothing to grow under it is a certain failure as a leader, no matter his personal growth.

A common shared vision and inclusive style of functioning contributes towards a good environment. During my interaction with the formation commanding officers, it emerged that a vast majority of them followed democratic and participative style of command. In peacetime, that is the preferred style, as it gives everyone a sense of ownership of unit functioning. A transformational leadership approach will contribute towards building a good environment. Transformational approach allows the leader and the led to raise each other to the next level of motivation and therefore greater achievement. This approach enables the leader to act as a role model, wins the command's trust and respect of the followers. Providing inspirational leadership and intellectual simulation to enable growth of subordinates will provide the right environment. A commanding officer must remember, every soldier in his unit is an individual and must find time for each individual. Every soldier, no matter how small in status, must be treated with dignity and respect, and his aspirations honoured. This will help fulfil self actualization needs and self belief of every individual. A unit environment must be such that the men see it as their first home because of the happiness and a sense of security that it brings by being part of it.

In my long military service, I cannot recall one individual who has not responded to encouragement and recognition. A coercive approach has a short shelf life that works only under supervision. I have seen many unwilling workers converted into willing work horses through this approach, sometimes by exaggerated recognition and appreciation. The command must have the confidence that mistakes committed in performance of duties will be accepted.

Creating an enabling environment is not difficult, yet one often finds establishments who could do better on this score. The commanding officer can do so by simply following the dictum 'the commanding officer eats last,' ensuring that the aspirations of his officers and men are met before his own, and willingness to sacrifice his interests for the good of his command. The commanding officer must protect his command from unwarranted interference from outside.

I have alluded to the importance of a cheerful commander. A commander with a smile is never lonely; there will always be officers around him. A poker faced commander will have to find company. A sense of humour encourages the men to open up and their own sense of humour is the ultimate ice breaker.

In a unit *barakhana*, I realized that the men were sitting quietly and no one seems to be sipping his rum. I asked one generally quiet *pahari*, how was his drink doing? He replied, '*Saab, ek peg issue tha, woh toh kab ka khatam ho gaya. Ab toh, PM (Packing material) leke baithe hain.*' (We were issued one peg that disappeared long ago, now we are sitting with empty PM (Packing Material, meaning tumbler). The company had a good laugh. Promptly, I gave the man my drink and had the battalion given another round of drink. The battalion gave him credit for that extra free drink and that individual was a different man thereafter.

PT and games are important tools towards building a great environment. They must be full of fun that leaves men with something to talk and laugh about. The culture of separate officer PT squads must be stamped out. Regimental games are not about high scoring. They are about rubbing shoulders with men. I remember most of our basketball games in the unit had a score line closer to a football game, but the larger purpose was more than achieved.

In the army we never talk of social differentiation, even though we know who comes from which background. A bite from the plate of the socially lowest soldier does wonders to the unit environment. It was my routine ritual whenever I had the opportunity to eat with the troops. Men must be convinced that you treat them as equals for we are all soldiers and all soldiers are equal.

A commanding officer must be predictable and consistent in his behaviour. It will help create stress free environment and trust in his command. I remember a very senior commander who was known for his unpredictable behaviour. He would walk out of the mess on a flimsy issue. He even walked out of the command mess where he was the chief host. While he may have had a reason to be annoyed, this behaviour did him no good and commanded no respect. Unpredictability and surprise must not be used to prove your intellectual superiority over your command. If you have an idea, give your command time to deliberate over it and then debate the issue.

Every man in the unit is an achiever. He only needs the right environment and an opportunity in his field of competence. A commanding officer must ensure that there is no panic or stress in the unit functioning. Giving a task without suitable guidelines and then changing things at the last minute creates avoidable tension and hurts subordinate confidence. Simple habits will go a long way in avoiding undue tension. Give a good thought before giving an important task. Give the subordinate a clear idea of what you want and the resources required for the task. Ask him to come back to you with his plans, provide guidance and leave him alone. Give a timely mid course correction if necessary and subordinates will enjoy doing the job. Do not breathe down their necks.

A commanding officer must ask himself the following questions: Are you empowering your subordinates to meet the demands of the army and the demands of life itself?

Do your soldiers feel comfortable in your presence or do they sulk away? Do they bring their problems to you without hesitation? Is the command chain honoured in your battalion? What will be the impact of your command beyond your tenure? Will your command stand up when you need them and will you stand up for them when they need you?

If the answers to the above questions are positive, you have created a good environment.

In summary, in a good environment every man feels empowered, feels comfortable and safe, is proud of being part of the group and contributes voluntarily.

Commanding officers must find ways to make the unit routine fun. I joined my unit on commission at Siliguri in 1979. We were having a Sunday family lunch in the officers' mess. Pineapples were common and that was the fruit on the menu. As the last one to be served, I got a small piece of pineapple to eat. My commanding officer, Pup Mann asked me how many pineapples I could eat in a sitting? Small piece that I ate felt good, leaving me wanting more. Without much thought, I said eight. Eight pineapples in a sitting! No one believed that I could. As for me, I did not realize what eight pineapples meant. Tuffy Marwah, the spirited second-in-command laid a bet that I could not, others bet that I would. With number of beer bottles at stake, the stage was set.

The next day eight pineapples were lined up outside the second-in-command's office. Officers, JCOs and NCOs formed an impressive spectator's gallery. I wasn't impressed to see that all the eight pineapples on parade, lined neatly in rows of two were rather raw, poorly peeled and possibly the largest available on either side of Brahmaputra. Tuffy Marwah, had been smart. There was no way he was going to lose the bet. Even though I protested, a Second Lieutenant's protest had no future.

I was not giving up either and started eating the pineapples. With great difficulty I managed to finish one. By the time I got there, my mouth and teeth had become lifeless, unable to even bite the slice of the fruit. The citric acid and thorns from the raw and poorly peeled fruits had cut through my tongue and taken a toll. Blood was dripping from my mouth and over my chin. As I continued to battle valiantly, the commanding officer asked me to stop.

He said the experience will make me a wiser man, and it did. Such incidents are wonderful stress busters and make for good environment in the unit.

> *The state of organizational climate is a true index of leader follower relationship; it is a reflection of the leader's personality, character and ability to influence and direct his command. It is also a major contributory factor in determining the response of the followers.*
>
> —Lt Gen KB Kala, Demystifying Leadership

## Crime, Rewards and Punishment

A commanding officer has the obligation to look after the welfare of his command. He also has the responsibility to uphold the discipline and effectiveness of the unit. Towards that end he has to have a fair and firm approach. Men must not be punished for trivial omissions, they must be corrected. But when they do need to be pulled up, the commanding officer must not hesitate and have no remorse in doing so, no matter the consequence of the punishment on the individual or the unit.

In combat arms, officers serve for long in the same unit. They know their men intimately, and sometimes it becomes difficult to take harsh decisions. When necessary they must be taken in the interest of the organization. Avoiding harsh decisions in the name of unit's image is detrimental to the unit's discipline and well-being.

The commanding officer is responsible for the 'stomach' of the battalion. An individual is responsible for his own and his family's stomach and he must live by military regulations for his own sake. Quite often, disciplinary action is diluted or simply avoided because the commanding officer is uncertain of the legal procedures. That should never be allowed to happen. Legal advice is always at hand in the army and just a phone call away. In many cases serious offences are overlooked because of the so called 'Unit *Izzat*' or unit reputation. I have seen cases of cowardice in the face of adversity being overlooked for the same reasons. The commanding officer needs to remember that every unit has its share of non-performers and men who fall short of soldierly conduct in peace and in face of the enemy. The commanding officer should never overlook indiscipline in the belief that it will harm his career. I guarantee the reputation of the unit or the commanding officer will not be tarnished for taking disciplinary action of any kind. On the other hand, failure to do so is only inviting bigger problems.

Rewards and punishments are two very important aspects of any organization. In the army they are even more because either way it has a huge impact on the soldiers. I am tempted to narrate the closing dialogues of the film The Dirty Dozen, where the hero on being pinned a gallantry medal on his chest says, that as long as you keep giving a medal to a soldier, he will keep giving his life. Because it means so much to him, it is of utmost importance that the system of rewards must be fair and impartial. If it is not, it will cause resentment amongst the men and will result in loss of confidence in the commander. At the unit level small recognition in unit *sainik sammelans* mean a great deal to a soldier. I have often heard officers expressing disillusionment with the system of awards in the army.

Every soldier is expected to do his duty for duty's sake. Will the young officers and men continue to put themselves in the line of fire with the same commitment if there were no awards or incentives? When one is asking a man to lay down his life, worthwhile incentives and recognition that safeguard the future of their families are an absolute necessity. The need is to review awards in peacetime. I have often wondered on the logic of awarding *Sena* Medals in the Army Headquarters or to personal staff officers and not for raising a brigade in field. Any worthwhile officer who reaches a one star rank should not need the motivation of a medal to work. If he does, he is there by default. It is important to remember that undeserved awards tarnish the value of that award for even the deserving winners.

The worst that can happen is faking encounters in pursuit of rewards. This is a grave offence. It is not only the highest form of professional dishonesty, it brings disrepute to the officer class and men lose confidence in them. Above all, it lets the army down in the eyes of the countrymen who hold our organization in high esteem and expect us to live by the highest code of conduct.

Similarly, the principles are almost the same when dealing with punishments. A commanding officer should not punish a man without thorough investigation. Mass punishments are outright wrong which cause resentment amongst men. Fear of the system is necessary in the army. The series of incidents of mass insubordination in the recent past indicate loss of fear of the system. In war, in addition to other factors, it is the fear of the system that keeps the men going.

I have known commanding officers who have overlooked grave omissions or commissions in combat for unjustifiable reasons. I also know a commanding officer who court martialled seventeen soldiers in the first year of his command. He went on to become a Brigadier. Just proves a point that you will never be sacked for setting things right.

Avoiding taking actions to be considered a good man or a good leader is bad. On the other hand unjustified firmness is also counterproductive. There would be situations when demonstrating firmness becomes a necessity. During the Second World War, far too many soldiers were being lost to Malaria in Burma, more than in combat. All warnings and measures failed to arrest the malaria losses. The theatre commander, Field Marshal Slim then started sacking the commanding officers who failed to keep malaria in check. Soon the problem was under control.

For the right reasons mobile phones were prohibited in our division deployed in counter insurgency area, except by explicit permission. There were STD booths in every company base for the men to call home. Many soldiers however kept mobiles despite the instructions. One commanding officer proudly told me that he had punished over one hundred men during his command. Surprised, I asked him on what account? He said mostly for keeping mobile phones. I wonder if that was the right way. One exemplary action against a defaulter would send the right message rather than the commanding officer wasting his time in disposing hundreds of cases. Similar problem was faced in my headquarters. The deputy commander, having given adequate opportunity for the men to deposit their mobile phones, smashed the next two mobiles found in front of the whole lot. There were no more violations of orders on the issue.

Our men respond to financial fines better than they do to minor disciplinary actions. Colonel Passion was commanding a battalion which had expensive imported combat vehicles. The tyres of these vehicles were hard to come by. He frequently noticed that they were underinflated and getting damaged. Instructions and extra duties to the defaulters did not improve things. He then imposed a simple hundred rupee fine on every underinflated tyre. There were no more under inflated tyres. The concerned NCOs would check their vehicles four times a day. There are often smarter ways to correct infringements that take place in the units. Similarly, cases of late from leave were effectively dealt with by asking the soldier to encash twice the number of days of absence from next year's leave. That worked wonders.

Sometimes there will be grave incidents and yet a commanding officer will be at a loss to take action. I had one such experience. During the course of field firing, my battalion was up very early preparing for the day's firing. An outstanding NCO was sent to fix the problem in the jammed gun of an armoured vehicle that had occurred the previous evening. He got into the vehicle, elevated the gun and got to work. Unknown to him, as he was trying to fix the fault, another soldier mounted the combat vehicle to clean the barrel for the day's firing. Blind inside the vehicle and in the morning darkness, the NCO did not realize that there was a soldier on top. He fixed the fault and pressed the trigger to check the weapon, a standard drill.

The morning calm was shattered as a shot rang out and the round pierced the chest of the soldier outside, killing him instantly.

The previous evening, as the last crew was firing, a sudden sand storm blew away everything casting a pall of dark cloud, reducing the visibility to zero.

At the end of the day, the ammunition NCO was left with a belt of fifty one rounds of 7.62 mm ammunition. While the whole day he was issuing every firer a belt of fifty rounds, he rightly gave the last crew of the day the remaining fifty one rounds. Some coincidence that as the storm struck, the weapon got jammed after firing fifty rounds, leaving the last round in the chamber.

I called off the firing to manage the storm and everyone got busy restoring order in the sandy madness.

The ammunition NCO had a hard time taking stock of the ammunition and fired cases as they lay strewn all over covered by sand. The last firer deposited his fifty fired cases, forgetting that he was issued fifty one. In that chaotic melee, the ammunition NCO overlooked that he had given this firer fifty one rounds and not fifty as the rest during the day.

Now, who is at fault in this very live incident?

The outstanding NCO, who was detailed to fix the gun was charged with culpable homicide not amounting to murder. He was awarded loss of three years seniority that effectively eliminated all his promotion prospects to JCO rank. A bright career brought to an end, he left prematurely after becoming a *Havaldar*.

I met this NCO and his family in his village a decade after I had relinquished the command of my battalion. We discussed that incident. And since then, I have been troubled by this thought that under the circumstances in which the incident happened, was I right to punish this soldier? What wrong did he do? Or, was I only finding a scapegoat because we had lost a soldier and someone had to be punished, and he was the convenient one.

My conscience now says, I was wrong to punish him. There were series of unusual incidents beyond anyone's control that led to this tragedy, destiny as some would say. Yes, theoretically, the ammunition NCO should have ensured that the last firer returned fifty one fired cases and all his ammunition was properly accounted for at the end of the day. Yes, theoretically, the NCO fixing the fault should have ensured that there is no one in front of the barrel when he pressed the trigger. But no one knew that there is a round in the chamber. On the other hand, a soldier was dead, and can there be no one responsible for the grave loss in peace time?

The more I think of it, the more I am convinced that he was awarded unjust punishment. How much could the circumstances be accepted as a legitimate reason for the lapses by the crew and the ammunition NCO? While lapses did take place, as explained above, under the circumstances who should actually have been held responsible for the death of the soldier?

Men seem to have an increasing tendency to ignore the military code of conduct when not under supervision. While '*Roko aur Toko*' is an effective way to correct infringements, JCOs and NCOs rarely do so, particularly outside their units. Disciplinary actions are always an option, but better solution is to motivate them to believe in their special being as soldiers and how their conduct affects the image of the whole army. He needs to understand that when out of the camp, he is not *Sepoy* Ram Singh, whom no one recognizes on the street. That he is seen by the public as '*Sepoy* Indian Army' and whatever he does, is seen as a reflection of Indian army. A conviction of this kind, I am sure, can be cultivated in all men provided it is done by superiors who preach what they practice. There also is a tendency amongst commanding officers to take a lenient view on reports coming from outside. They do no good to the cause of the army.

> *'When one consistently imposes severe punishment, men become repulsive to his command, while who is always lenient becomes contemptible. But whoever imposes punishment as deserved becomes respectable. Punishment when awarded with due consideration, makes people devoted to righteousness...,while punishment when ill awarded under the influence of greed and anger or owing to ignorance, excites fury amongst even hermits and ascetics, dwelling in forests, not to speak of householders.'*
>
> —Chanakya, quoted in 'Demystifying Leadership', Author Lt Gen KB Kala

During my long service, I have not seen one man who has not positively responded to encouragement. Remember the old adage, 'praise in public and reprimand in private.'

## Emotional Intelligence (EI): A Critical Factor in Command

EI is a very important aspect of life and leadership, often neglected. It is a vast subject on which a lot of literature exists. It is also a subject of doctorate research. Here, my intention is simply to highlight the importance of EI in command. Officers must study this aspect in detail to optimize their personal and leadership potential.

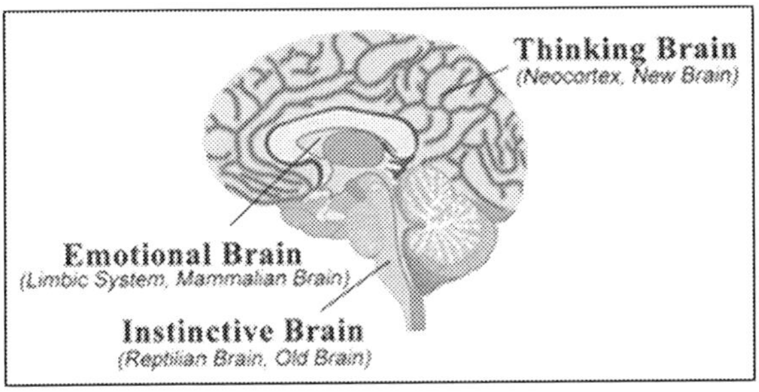


Image Credit: Internet

A basic understanding of the brain mechanics will help to understand the dynamics of EI. As the brain diagram above shows, two relevant parts of the brain concerning EI are the Emotional Brain (Limbic System) and the Thinking Brain (Rational Brain). The latter is located at the front of the brain. Every impulse starts at the base of the spinal cord. It has to first pass through the Limbic System, the place where emotions are generated before it reaches the Rational Brain. So, we have an emotional reaction to events before our rational mind can engage. Pause is a critical element of mind control. An awareness of EI allows that pause that enables effective communication between the rational and emotional centres of the brain, leading to a reasoned response as against an emotional or impulsive response.

When 75 members of the Stanford Business Graduate School were asked to recommend the most important capability for the leaders to develop, their answer was nearly unanimous- Self-awareness. Denial can be the greatest hurdle that leaders face in self-awareness. Egos, insecurities, fears and the inability to see your own reality come in the way. Here is a real example of how most men see things entirely differently from reality. When one professionally very successful man went through a torrid second divorce, he met the counsellor and told him that he thought he had a ' wife selection problem.' The counsellor heard his story and told him, on the contrary, you have a husband behavioural problem. He took his advice and fared well in his third marriage, listening to his wife's well-meaning advice. Most couples have a similar perception of each other's behaviour- I am okay, you are not okay!

The same analogy can be extended to a commander and his command. A majority, under their exalted position, see themselves as the embodiment of all virtues and wisdom. Worse, the commanding officer, fairly young, is the judge, jury and the executioner and his demeanour can deprive him of the advice from his subordinates leading to the reinforcement of the belief 'I am okay, you are not okay.'

Apropos, it is important to dwell on EI as it relates to a commanding officer. Why is EI so important for leaders? EI as a subject of formal study came in pretty late, in the mid-nineties. When EI was first discovered, it provided the missing link in a peculiar finding: People with the highest IQ outperformed those with average IQ only 20 per cent of the time, while people with average IQ outperformed those with high IQ 73 per cent of the time. Research findings concluded that EI was the critical factor for this. While it is believed that IQ remains constant (even though some latest research seems to suggest that it can be improved) throughout life, EI can be improved by awareness and practice.

It is a recognised fact that it is the Emotional Quotient (EQ) and not the IQ that is the true predictor of success in future. As a battalion commander, EI as a factor of success relates to a commanding officer's ability to deal with his and others' emotions in responding rationally to situations. The fact that he deals with over 600 men below and many above him emphasises its importance. This has a direct bearing on his ability to lead effectively.

One time study of EI is not adequate. It needs to be constantly revisited in the mind because the ego can come into play so easily when in a position of authority.

Subconsciously, an average human being in authority detests disagreement by a subordinate and worse, in public. In the Indian culture, seniors expect deference a lot more than any other society. In the military, it can easily become the expectation of unquestioned obedience and compliance and quite often servility.

As a commander, it is easy to disregard the feelings of the subordinates. I have seen Generals do that so often, just because it is one-way traffic and the subordinate does not have an opportunity to respond, except at his own peril. The battalion command is primarily leadership, and, leadership deals with people -human beings who are unique packages of personal challenges and emotions.

I have seen an army commander closely who had no understanding of EI. He would often behave in most erratic ways on minor things. He would walk out of the mess where he was the chief guest or the chief host creating an embarrassing situation for everyone. He appeared to be focused on proving his intellectual superiority by springing surprises. The environment he created was one of anxiety, stress and unpleasantness that prevented the professional growth and contribution of the subordinates. He had no control over his emotions, no awareness or concern for others' emotions and no clue how to deal with them. He is not an exception.

Battalion command is the highest level of direct and independent authority over a body of troops. It is the most critical level of 'contact leadership' where men stare you in the face.

Leadership is not about you; it's about who you deal with and are responsible for. And it is all about you, in the sense, that how you deal with others depends on how you deal with yourself. The emotional state of the leader directly affects the emotional state of his people and his unit/sub-unit. EI is a critical factor in dealing positively with yourself, others and dealing constructively with vicissitudes of command and life itself. It helps a person to make the right choices, right decisions, self-motivate oneself and practice perseverance. It helps a person to be constantly aware of developing emotions and thoughts and how they affect his behaviour and response. So often, we are overtaken by emotions and biases rather than rationale, leading to avoidable conflict or unpleasant situations.

This awareness helps a person to avoid impulsive and emotional responses to an unpleasant stimulus – and that is an important trait in a position of responsibility. How often have we regretted our actions and responses, simply because we reacted on impulse?

Social-awareness, on the other hand, is your ability to accurately pick on the emotions of other people and understand what is really going on with them. Of the hundreds of men under your command, men will be under different degrees of emotional stress due to various factors- domestic or professional. This means perceiving what other people are feeling or thinking (empathy), even if you do not feel the same way. Empathy is important when dealing with men. Every individual is different, they get put off by different things and get motivated by different things. Thus, in an organization where the man is the key element of success, the importance of EI cannot be overemphasized.

My experience narrated below shows that extremely provocative situations can be turned around into a win-win situation with a good application of EI.

I was posted as the Deputy GOC of 56 Infantry Division under raising in a remote location in Northeast India in 2010. Except for the divisional commander everyone dined in the mess.

Lt Col Krishna, Mahar Regiment, a dark skinny decorated officer, who could be blown away by a gust of wind, was an alcoholic and very chirpy after drinks. A good guy, he was a victim of alcohol; one failed marriage and the second in turbulence. He would often say, I am a superseded guy, what can the Army do to me? One day as I walked into the mess for lunch, Krishna with a drink in hand walked up to me, and out of the blue said, "One day I will kick you so hard on your backside, sir, you won't know what has hit you."

A Lt Col telling this to a Brigadier, the Deputy GOC, is very unusual and outright insulting. I was taken aback for sure since there had been no issue with him, though I had been advising him to take control of his drinks. I wondered what led him to behave like this, which for sure was stupid and suicidal.

All officers were stunned and waited for me to explode. I did not. I calmly said, "See me tomorrow in my office at ten," and walked away to have my lunch as if nothing had happened.

The legal officer was asked to produce a written warning and be present. Krishna was marched into my office, almost trembling.

I said, "Look, what alcohol does to you and now you are trembling in my office. Where has yesterday's bravado gone? You often say that you are a superseded guy, what can the Army do to you? My options on your state, that the Army provides can put you on the road. You know what that means with two marriages in trouble. As an alcoholic, you can be out of the Army and struggle for your pension. The same runner and your buddy will refuse to serve you a glass of water if they know that you do not enjoy the establishment support. In this remote place, I will give you no work. You will die of boredom, indignity, and shame.

You are looking to be a time scale Colonel, which is a big jump in pension. All that will disappear, if I choose to get after you. But I do not look at you as a disciplinary case. I look at you as a good man who is losing the battle to his circumstances because of liquor. I look at you as a soldier who has earned a gallantry award, who now needs help and get his life back on track.

I am serving you this written warning, but you can count on me to help you if you come half the way. Now, you have two choices - to continue drinking the way you are and mess up your life and your family's for good or make a decision to get your life back on track. You make the same mistake again; you will see the wrath of this patient man. You make the right choice; I am with you as a friend."

This man became my Man Friday. He would stand six hours in the pouring rain, working. When I was leaving the division, he said with a laugh, "Sir, you had me. No one has got so much work done from me during my whole career. But I loved doing it for you."

Six months after I left, he called me to tell me that he has completely stopped drinking. Sadly, he died in a motor accident later- a teetotaller!

Well, I am not a patient man by DNA. But I have learnt through the application of EI to exercise self-control and manage crises with reasoning and not emotions. This realization helps me feel the turmoil of emotions building inside me and manage those emotions to the overall good of myself and the organization. The bitter truth is that I do not succeed all the time, despite self-awareness. Most men have more good in them than evil. Many become victims of circumstances or poor choices that they make in life. It is easy to condemn them. Getting them back to life is the test of command and that is a function of leadership.

EI helps you to understand yourself and others and get the best out of both.

> *'The most important time to hold your temper is when the other has lost his.'*

## Officers' Mess

Officers' mess is one of the most important institutions in a unit. It is the home of bachelor officers. It is the repository of unit's history and traditions, its achievements and a great deal more. Maintaining a good mess is only partly a function of money. Military decorum, well trained staff, good drills, hygiene and cleanliness and well cooked food need no funds. It is a result of the interest and the pride the unit takes in its officers' mess. Officer messes are falling prey to five star culture which is not desirable. What is desired is military decorum and courtesy. In most armies the privilege of unit messes have long gone. In many, they are outsourced except for the mess sergeant who oversees the mess. Overall, the messes consume a fair quantum of resources and combat manpower one way or the other. The mess is not an eating joint, it is a place that contributes to battle efficiency of the unit, and this it does by grooming of young officers who are the cutting edge of the sword in the battalion.

An officers' mess should be spotlessly clean and hygienic. The trophies, etc. must be properly displayed and well maintained all the time. The mess staff should be carefully selected, properly briefed and well trained in all important aspects like regimental history, mess etiquettes, mess drills, courtesy and hospitality. They should know the history of important trophies and other artefacts in the mess. They should be aware of security aspects and be trained in proper answering of telephone calls.

It was in 1982, as a young captain, that I spent a day in a battalion on the Line of Control in Jammu and Kashmir. The mess was in a makeshift accommodation, what is known as *Basha* in the army. As far as the building is concerned, there was nothing impressive about it. But the drills of the mess were immaculate. The mess staff seemed to be taking pride in leaving a good impression about their unit. I recollect the mess serving me coffee during breakfast in record time after asking me what I wanted. Surely, coffee does not get brewed in a few seconds. The mess staff had taped its drills and speaks volumes of their pride. On the other hand, another unit's officers' mess in a peace station was absolute shambles in upkeep and its drills, notwithstanding the impressive draping of curtains. It was hard to find mess staff, food was poor and the mess staff unconcerned. Sad though, the commanding officer of this unit was nominated for Higher Command course. Not that this is the only criteria, the commanding officer was neglecting what he felt was not giving him personal returns.

What does the officers' mess mean to a young officer? It is here that the esprit de corps and brotherhood is forged and the unit bound into a cohesive fighting unit. It is here that the officers learn military courtesies – the making of a gentleman, conducting with juniors, peers, senior officers and ladies. It is here that they learn about trials, travails and achievements of their units. Portraits of war heroes and history are a constant reminder of the sacrifices of the forefathers that motivate the new generations.

For a young officer, the mess is a minefield of information. He must know all about mess property, in particular, anything that has to do with the battalion history.

I have come across some interesting issues relating to the mess functioning. These have generated some debate in my battalion and are worth narrating here. My battalion was raised in 1960. In its over fifty five years of existence, rum has never been served in the mess. Occasionally, some officers have raised this issue in the mess meetings. The consensus has prevailed that in the officers' mess rum should not be served. Personally, I am a strong supporter of this view. My reasons are; first and foremost, that rum is soldiers' preferred drink. In the unit canteen there is invariably just one or at best two brands that are popular brands. In some units where rum is served in the mess, soldiers are known to harbour a grouse that good rum goes to the officers' mess and they do not get their share of good rum. There will be no grounds for complaint on this score if rum is not served in the mess. Secondly, in my long service, I have rarely seen an alcoholic whisky drinker. They have, barring an odd exception, always been rum drinkers. Of the two, whisky goes better with the decorum of the officers' mess.

I remember an interesting discussion in one mess meeting in our mess. One officer who himself was a whisky drinker raised the issue of serving rum in our mess. He said that some officers were drinking rum in their homes and therefore the unit should consider doing so in the mess. Interestingly, the most vociferous opponent of rum in the unit officers' mess was the officer who drank rum at home. His point of view was simple, what he drank at home was his personal choice. The mess reflects the battalion's ethos and there was no justification to change time tested customs. Later, we put the whole issue at rest once for all, that the status quo will be maintained and this point was never to be entertained in the mess meeting and has not been since.

The next issue is of serving a small or a large drink in the mess. Many battalions, as does mine, follow the practice of serving only a small drink and not to take the next drink till you finished the one in hand. I have religiously followed this habit till date and that has stood me in good stead always. This incident illustrates how.

I was commanding my unit at Bhatinda where power outage is rare. The divisional commander (GOC), a Sikh officer accompanied by his wife visited the unit for the annual inspection. They stayed in our small unit guest room. That evening was the formal Dinner Night. As I entered the mess, my second-in-command gave me the news.

When the GOC and his wife were getting ready for the dinner night, the power went off. The emergency light that was always there could not be found; someone had removed it from the guest room that day itself for some inexplicable reason. The generator would not start as it had not been used for long as the power had not failed in months. When the generator finally started, the electric cables in the guest room caught fire. The guests could not even run for their lives as they were half undressed. In a room full of smoke and burning cables, the high profile couple was in a Catch 22 situation. The lady was half draped in a saree and the General, half way through tying his turban.

The Gurkha buddy, sensing the criticality barged into the room. He grabbed the first thing he could lay his hand on and ran all over the bed to put off the fire as the high profile couple watched with an indescribable expression, glued to the spot. By some Godly intervention the fire died down, of its own accord, and not because of 'beyond the call of duty' charge of my brave Gurkha Guardsman.

When the evening commenced, the ADC told me that the GOC wanted soup served at 8.30 PM, which meant half an hour of drinks.

I walked up to the GOC, 'Sir, I understand that you have all the reasons to be annoyed after all the fiasco, and soup would be served as you desire, but as long as the GOC enjoyed the evening with the excellent jazz and pipe music in attendance, we should continue.'

The GOC replied, 'Not to worry, I am used to such fiascos. We will continue the evening as long as you have a drink for every drink I have.'

The soup was served around three in the morning. By then, between the GOC and me, two bottles of whiskey were consumed. The GOC had twenty six drinks and I had twenty four as per the barman's record. The dinner finished well past four. The case of towering inferno was forgotten and I commanded the battalion ceremonial parade at sharp seven in the morning. And above all, the annual inspection finished after the parade. The GOC said, if the commanding officer can drink the whole night, run BPET in excellent and turn out an outstanding ceremonial parade, the battalion has to be fit for war. I survived the day without a scar just for one simple reason, small drink and one at a time.

I have always been a proponent of 'officer like drinking'; small drink-one at a time and you will always remain in control. Do anything different and you may embarrass yourself and others. More important, an officer should never smell of alcohol on parade, let alone ever appear drunk.

As much as the officers, the mess is also a training ground for the young ladies, as large numbers come from civil background. They need to know the battalion history pretty well and be abreast with battalion customs and traditions. These days there is a tendency to relax on the strict dress code of the mess which should not be done. A strict dress code is part of the officer grooming and inculcates good conduct. Dinner nights and guest nights with ladies go a long way in taping up mess drills and grooming officers and ladies.

The mess customs and traditions must be scrupulously followed. Meaningless traditions should not be continued just for the sake of it. Unit customs in reception of new officers and the newlyweds helps build camaraderie.

**The JCOs mess:** It is also important to remember that the JCOs mess too needs same attention. 'Clean living leads to clean thinking.' JCOs mess could easily deteriorate if the commanding officer or the second-in-command does not keep an eye.

When a sector commander in the valley, I went on a planned visit to the JCOs mess. I noticed a thick a wad of one foot by foot pieces of newspapers. My hunch was bang on; the JCOs were using them as paper napkins. A person's self esteem and confidence is affected by his standard of living. JCOs must pride their self esteem if they want to be taken seriously by the men.

While in command of my division, I was appalled when one brigade commander told me that he was subsidizing JCOs meals from the regimental fund as a welfare measure. When we complain that the JCOs are not pulling their weight, this is absolutely ridiculous. I directed that the practice be discontinued forthwith. The army looks after JCOs and men in a big way and such welfare is most misplaced.

There is one universally neglected issue that impacts the officers' mess, JCOs mess and the troops, and that relates to the standard of chefs in the army. Of them all, the community chefs who cook for the troops are the poorest. We spend lots of efforts on training, but precious little on training of community chefs. Try out senior community chefs and you will find most have progressed little from where they started. Special training to improve his skills must be imparted and better standards demanded. With excellent entitled rations good food for the men is a function of interest that one takes. My division camp had troops from the JAT Regiment. True to their reputation, the cook made fabulous *jalebis*, better than any sweet shop in Meerut. I organized a *jalebi* cadre for the division. The division found that hilarious; a strike corps division conducting a *Jalebi* cadre. Two days cadre later, the division units never bought *Jalebis* from the market. They were healthy, hygienic, cheap and better than any in market. That is what I mean; a little interest can do wonders.

## Secret of Military Happiness

Today's lifestyle is characterized by high tempo with potential stress at every step. It can be caused by smallest of things such as traffic jams to environment in the place of work and home. In recent years, I have witnessed an unhealthy trend. In the old days, officers and men seemed to have a better approach to life. The life style was Spartan, they had much less of material and financial support and their approach to life was very balanced. Importantly, they were not chasing ranks. Today, ambition seemed to have gripped officers no end and failure to get the next rank hits them very hard. The pride of wearing a uniform and the fun of soldiering seems to have been lost. The fault lies at many planes, starting from the individual's attitude to the steep pyramidal structure of the system.

Far too many officers, particularly from the commanding officers to the divisional commanders are chasing two good reports in their short tenures. And that is the bane of the army. I was told that an officer's wife slapped her husband for getting a 'charley' grading on an important career course. One army commander told me how worried he found the young officers doing the young officers course about their grading. And, in my own division, a commanding officer's wife cancelled her birthday celebrations because her husband did not figure in the Higher Command course list declassified that day.

Compare this with olden days when the young officers streaked naked on a bike through the busy streets of Mhow on a bet for a bottle of beer. I have no doubts in my mind which of the two categories will win you the likes of Kargil war.

Posted at the army headquarter, I was asked to conduct a study on the management of non-empanelled officers. I interacted with a large number of them. I was pained to see how severely officers were affected by non-empanelment for the next rank. They saw promotion to higher ranks as the only manifestation of success in life, which affected their families in a big way. That, to my mind, is a recipe for greater sadness in life and does not augur well for the organization. These officers were denying themselves the pleasure that the journey of soldiering provides and the fun of life itself.

As the divisional commander I would talk to my command on the concept of 'Gross Happiness Quotient' (GHQ), on the same lines as Bhutan talks of Gross National Happiness.

Maslow's hierarchy of needs brings out the needs of an individual. That notwithstanding, in the balance sheet of life, everyone has credits and debits. The happiness quotient will be determined by the values one assigns to each major aspect of life. The pie chart of life is made up of numerous aspects. The major aspects are family health and happiness, children's well-being and their career, immediate family issues, financial stability to meet family obligations and the often forgotten aspect of satisfaction from the way one does his job, etc. There is also that important aspect of progress in career by the man. Career progression meets Maslow's hierarchy of needs. It raises the self esteem of the individual and the family. It also brings along some perks and privileges that come with rank. In the army they are visible everywhere, from the shoulders to headquarters with boards stipulating commanding officer's vehicles and staff cars only.

Important as career progression is, non-empanelment is inbuilt in the army hierarchical structure. This being beyond one's control, how much should one allow this to affect one's future.

I too was overlooked in promotion to Brigadier despite an excellent record of service. Looking at my colleagues who had suffered grave tragedies, mine was of no consequence. In six months, three of my officers had lost their young children to accidents. Should I not be grateful to God for all his kindness. When I count my blessings, the list far outweighs non-empanelment. Besides, it is important to ensure that the future is not ruined because of the past, over which I have no control.

One officer asked me, 'What do you plan to do now?'

'I joined the army for the love and passion of uniform. For me passion is not a function of ranks. Besides, the army has not taken away anything it was giving me. The day my passion diminishes one bit, I will quit. Now my aim is to be the best superseded officer the army has ever had," I replied.

The moral of the story is that it is up to the officer to remain in control of his happiness. In the pie chart of life, all factors must be apportioned importance sensibly. Issues that will be a source of lasting happiness are not ranks. Children's future, family health and happiness being the most important. It also comes from loving the work you do and doing it well. No rank is good enough if the former are not in order. Ask anyone who has challenged or unsettled children.

The Geeta concept of life needs to be absorbed; why should King Ashoka or Prince Buddha have renounced their vast empire and life of status and comforts. Purpose should drive life and not ranks. Mahatma Gandhi held no post, yet he was the most revered Indian in the world. In summary, there is life beyond promotion and a lot more to live for, for the happiness lies in this truth.

The journey is always bigger fun than the destination. Unfortunately, fun of the journey of this wonderful profession is being lost in pursuit of higher ranks. The solution lies within the individual, i.e., to love your work, enjoy the journey and keep up the enthusiasm of life for your own good, promotion or no promotion. The respect one commands and self esteem is a function of your contribution to the organization. Respect based on rank alone has a short shelf life.

How does one help officers prepare for this inevitable eventuality? At the unit level, the commanding officer must cultivate the habit of professional study, i.e., reading and writing habits in young officers. By the time an officer completes twelve years of service, the career trajectory is clear. That leaves eight years before he reaches pensionable service in which to prepare for the second career through education and skill development. Distance education and study leave provide the opportunity for self empowerment. Various schemes for making short service commission attractive are being introduced that should enable good career transformation. Realistic assessment of one's promotion prospects and timely preparation will help transition to a second career. Age plays an important role and thus, if an officer has lost promotion opportunities, it is better to move on at the earliest.

Often we let our happiness suffer for trivial things. Being unhappy for own poor showing is understandable. Becoming miserable because someone else is doing well is the most stupid reason to be unhappy. You will be the master of your happiness when you do not place it in others' hands.

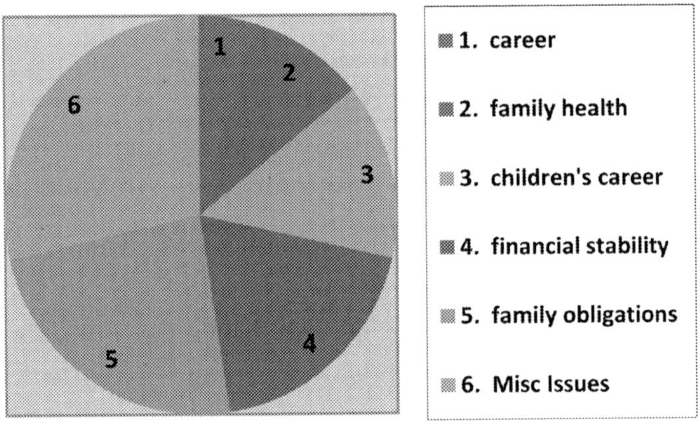


**Happiness Pie Chart**

Happiness depends on the values you assign to each aspect

While happiness is a lot about genes, it is also about your attitude which can be cultivated. Biggest sense of satisfaction and accomplishment comes when a person lives for a purpose beyond one self. The happiest people are those who have dedicated their lives for the well-being of others. Chen Shu Chu, a small time woman vegetable seller in Taiwan, who lives a frugal life in a village, has donated over US$ 330,000, including all the royalty from her book. She says, there is great happiness in helping people in need. And the best sleep that she gets are on the days when she actually donates.

There are only two things that multiply by sharing – knowledge and happiness. Smile is God's special gift to mankind. The world looks better when you smile and it is infectious. An officer is not fully dressed till he wears a smile.

If values are assigned to alphabets from 1 to 22, with A being 1 and Z being 22, there is one word that adds up to perfect 100 and that is ATTITUDE

*Change your ATTITUDE*
*and you change your life...and your family's.*

## The Soldier is at the Centre of Military Command

### *The Battle of Waterloo was Won on the Playing Fields of Eton*

The quote above is ascribed to the Duke of Wellington, commander in chief of the British and allied armies at Waterloo, who was a graduate of Eton College. What he possibly meant was that Britain's military success was based on the value which was taught to the schoolboys in the Public Schools.

Here, I wish to focus on what is generally understood of this quote. The values of character, the ability to deal with success and setbacks with equal grace, team spirit, grit, and many other values that are nurtured on the playfields are most relevant to the military. Officer men relationship, trust and Human Quotient, the most critical military qualities are nurtured when the sweat and blood of leaders and their men mix, on the playgrounds, training areas and the battlefield.

## Command - of Dignity and Shame?

I am aware that there are commanding officers who do not run the Battle Physical Efficiency Test (BPET) with the men, even on the day of the Annual Inspection when the whole unit does it. My take is that the majority of such commanding officers must be physically unfit and do not want to be embarrassed, which itself is a shame.

One officer who had commanded an Infantry battalion told me that this was a culture in some units, as it was in his own. I find it amusing that not participating in a major combat training activity could be a culture. I was shocked to learn that when a commanding officer was asked why he was not running BPET with the battalion on the Annual Inspection Day, his reply was heartbreaking. He said without a hint of remorse or hesitation, "It is below my dignity to run BPET with the men."

Can participating in military activities with the men you command ever be a matter of indignity? The thought itself is sickening and deserves no comment.

To drive home the point that in the military, the men are at the centre of military command, I am sharing a few photos with men as the formation commander.

It is not your brigade commander that you have to impress, it is your men who you must convince that you are worth following:

## ONE AMONGST EQUALS

**The Author as GOC in a Rugby Game with Men**

It is not the Weapons but the Human Spirit that Wins Wars

There is more to Beer than Drinking – Beering our Way to Combat Effectiveness

The Men are Always Fun to be With

**Building the Warriors**

**Happy Families Empower Soldiers-Children Football Championship**

# CHAPTER IV

# UNIT LADIES HAVE A ROLE

## Family Welfare and the Commanding Officer's Wife

*'A lone pillar of strength, fearlessly braving the odds that may last a never ending length.*

*Invisible is her contribution, to the army's noble cause.*

*She will always remain a soldier's strength, that, she always was.'*

—Col Rohan Anand, *Sainik Samachar*, March 2015

An army wife plays an important role. Invariably, she runs the family without or with very little contribution from the husband. The onus of children upbringing in all respects invariably falls on the housewife. If she manages her household affairs well, the soldier can attend to his duties with a free mind. A troublesome home front means a stressful living for the military men. They also provide the support to the unit families who may be living without their men folk.

A commanding officer's wife has an important role to play. Her role lies in two domains, one domestic and the other official, i.e., towards the unit. The commanding officers, however, have to be careful that she does not assume parallel authority and handles the trappings of power with maturity.

The commanding officer is a busy man. Command pressures generated as a result of many environmental factors are a reality. The lady has to be a calming influence on the man. The commanding officer has enough concerns to deal with. The last he needs is a troublesome home front. It is easier for an officer to deal with office stresses, much harder to deal with domestic stresses and it reflects directly in his work. A commanding officer who starts with a disturbed mind from home is certain to be irritable, in bad mood and foul in his conduct and dealings.

The lady needs to be very mature in dealing with domestic issues so that the man is free to deal with his command assignments without other worries. This is equally true for other ladies as well. Let me narrate an incident that best conveys the predicament of a commanding officer troubled by a disturbed domestic front. A very mature officer was commanding a very old proud battalion. The battalion knew that despite the best efforts of the commanding officer to hide his domestic turbulence, all was not well. The battalion was shocked one day morning when they learnt that their commanding officer had shot himself, having been driven to despair by his domestic issues. While this is an extreme case, it highlights the point.

At the end of the day, an officer has to go home. That is where, in the normal course, he spends better part of the day. In the Indian army's context, where a buddy soldier is available at home, precious little remains secret that is not known in the battalion. How can an officer struggling with this kind of domestic atmosphere be expected to do justice to his all important duty as a commanding officer. Who is at fault for the domestic turbulence is of little consequence. In a situation like this, everyone is a loser with disastrous affect on the children. The battalion too suffers in the process in every way. How does one deal with this kind of situation. No easy answers there except that the man has to ensure that his prime responsibility towards his unit is not affected. There are examples where officers have suffered horrible domestic situations but went on to lead a very balanced professional and social life. They are fine examples of personal crisis management. It is a personal matter and each individual will have to find his own ways to deal with it. There are increasing instances of troubled marriages these days, both at the troop's level as well as the officers. A man in uniform finds it even more difficult, for he lives in a closed military society and does not have the benefit of anonymity of a civilian. Further, a professional officer finds little time to contribute to his family. And that makes life difficult for the lady of the house and causes friction. It is important that all officers and men must shoulder their domestic responsibilities, and that will bring domestic peace.

Coming to the first lady's responsibilities in the unit: The lady too has a demanding task at hand. In a peace station, there are demands on a unit on the social front. Lots of them fall upon the first lady to manage and needs support from the unit. Not all ladies in the unit are forthcoming in participation. A few are present without making a contribution. Some are focused on learning the tricks for their time in command and there are a few who whole heartedly put in their best. These days, a large number are working ladies. They are rarely available and that increases the burden on the commanding officers' wives.

One of the important responsibilities of a commanding officer's wife is grooming of newlyweds. In the earlier times, the first lady was mature having been in the army for a decent period of time. These days, they themselves are very young and often with lap babies, with little regimental time to their credit in the unit, and by extension not quite experienced to groom others. I was told by an officer, that in his unit, one of the important parts of grooming a young wife was how to manage herself at home and deal with buddies. I found this interesting that the ladies were advised never to hand over a list of stores or money to the buddy by hand. It should be left on the table for him to pick up. Logic was simple. A lady is not always adequately or formally dressed at home. Sitting lower down and speaking to a standing buddy exposes her to prying eyes, surely best avoided. Similarly, the line which the buddy was not to cross at home was to be made clear, unless called for.

With the changing socioeconomic scene and increasing aspirations, more and more soldiers want to keep their families with them in the unit and provide their children with better educational environment.

The units run what is called a 'Family Welfare Centre', or FWC. Ask any officer and he will be quick to reply that it is a waste of time. That remark is not completely off the mark. Today, soldiers' families are fairly well educated and aware with higher aspirations.

There is a need to review the concept of unit family welfare programs. The commanding officer should be able to stand up and say that this is not what his families want and this is what he would like to do. What then is the need today? Given the higher education of military families and their aspirations, they need opportunity for self empowerment and better education for their children. They need better living conditions than are available today. They need to be able to spend more time with their families. I am of the opinion that if a unit can address these requirements through unit welfare centres, it would have done its job.

Where does the commanding officer's wife figure into all this. The unit welfare programme is a unit project and needs all the support of the unit to succeed. The first lady is the CEO of this project and must ensure its success. The army today has excellent educational facilities both at the school and graduate level. They provide excellent opportunities for career progression of the military children. The unit welfare centre can do a great deal in preparing the men's children to join these institutions and make a career.

The units can contribute by facilitating recruitment in various services through suitable training and preparations. Empowering of families through effective and professionally conducted vocational courses can be very useful.

The commanding officer's wife is an excellent source of feedback on matters relating to the families. Information on domestic violence, maltreatment of families, poor accommodation, lack of amenities, health, etc., can only be obtained by personal visits which are best done by the officers' wives. When the battalion moves out on operations or exercises, the unit ladies have the responsibility to look after the families in the rear. A soldier on the front with the knowledge that his family is well looked after and safe at the rear is in a good frame of mind to perform his duties. Incidents such as the one that resulted in deaths of soldiers' families in J&K in 2002 by terrorists, when the troops were deployed on the border are disastrous for the army.

There is a general belief that a soldier's wife hates a family welfare meet. That is not quite true. There is a natural resentment against anything that is enforced. Since I also believed in that when I took over the battalion, I made the monthly family welfare meet a voluntary affair. After a while we noticed the attendance rising. Surprisingly, ladies with very young babies were also attending voluntarily. When asked why they had come with such small babies, they replied that this is the only opportunity to get out of the house. The battalion tried to practice what I have suggested above with immense success.

Sometimes one hears a remark that the ladies do not come under the army act. Surely they do not. Ladies and officers need to remember that the army families enjoy a colossal amount of benefits and support from the organization, both official and unofficial. It is important that the newlyweds are groomed well into the fabric of the unit and see things positively. Army act or no army act, they have an unquestioned obligation to this organization and the families of their units. A company or a battalion commander is equally responsible for the well-being of troops' families as he is for the men. A military spouse and the officer, as much a team in marital life, must be a team in discharging the military obligations together with a sense of commitment and belongingness. In the present times a large number of officers' wives work, but this is not an excuse not to discharge your obligations to unit families. They need to find time and ways to do so. Amongst other things, the pleasure to see your men and families grow where you have played a part is a matter of immense happiness. It is extreme immaturity not to understand an army wife's responsibility to the unit and its affairs correctly.

Official matters cannot be shared nor should any officer or his performance be discussed at home by the commanding officer. Normally, one can gauge the inter officer relations by observing the behaviour of their wives. Easier said than done, it is in the interest of everyone that the differences between the officers are not passed on to the ladies. The commanding officer should never discuss at home any action, verbal or otherwise that he takes against any officer or men.

The commanding officer's wife can be a very good influence on the young officers and help build a good team by mentoring the ladies and the young officers with maturity. She should see herself not as more equal amongst equals, but as an elder with a mission to build a happy team. A lady should not be too involved with her husband's career. Leave him alone and he will do well by himself.

In an ambush by the terrorists in the Northeast in 2021, the commanding officer of an Assam Rifles battalion was killed. Tragically, his wife and child travelling with him also lost their lives. There have been similar incidents in the past.

Families are an important part of soldiers. Happy and safe families strengthen the soldiers to discharge their duties better. In safe locations, their presence would be empowering, not quite in operational areas. For a commanding officer, the presence of his family in a hostile area can be extremely detrimental to his functioning and a cause of mental stress to both spouses. Operational areas demand a hundred per cent round the clock attention of the commanding officer without distraction or worries.

It is therefore wise to avoid the presence of families, as incidents such as these, have grave consequences and a shot in the arms of the terrorists.

Rommel was an outstanding soldier and spent the better part of the Second World War away from his family in prolonged campaigns. On 6 June 1944, when the Allies made their famous landing at Normandy, which was the beginning of the end of Germany, Rommel was at home in Germany because it was his wife's birthday. This is not to take credit away from that legendary soldier; in such long wars, they deserve breaks and family time too. The fact is he was not there on the most critical day that turned the tide for Germany; for a reason that makes it look worse. When the commander is away from the front for non-operational reasons, the troops naturally tend to slacken down.

The following quote perfectly captures the danger of an over enthusiastic wife in the army, even if in a lighter vein.

"*Behind every successful man stands a woman.*
*The further behind she is, the more successful he is.*"

Today, while women are being inducted into the military at all levels, the army has its own way of conveying serious things humorously. There is an old saying, 'If the army wanted you to have a wife, they would have issued you one.'

# CHAPTER V

# ON MORALS, ETHICS AND MILITARY VALUES

## Morals, Ethics and Military Values

*The men of upright life are obeyed before they speak.*

—Confucius

I was posted in the regimental centre in the mid-nineties. One recruit lost hundred rupees from his locker. He blamed his neighbouring recruit for the theft. The accused recruit repeatedly pleaded that he has not stolen the money. No one heard him. He was punished in front of others.

The next day he was found hanging in the toilet with a suicide note which said: 'I did not steal the money.'

That simple recruit had very high moral standards and the humiliation was too much to bear. That day the Regiment lost a wonderful soldier.

Values are the basic foundation on which our society is built. Values are invisible wealth of the communities and nations that guide them through adversity of life. Where the values decay, the society or the nation will collapse.

*'Moral decay resulted in the dissolution of Roman Empire. The Roman Empire succumbed to barbarian invasions in the large part*

> *due to the gradual* ***loss of civic virtue among its citizens****. They had become weak, outsourcing their duties to defend their Empire to barbarian mercenaries. The character of the soldiers changed from armed men fighting to defend their homes and families to men signing up to fight as mercenaries. Romans, had become effeminate, unwilling to live a tougher, 'manly' military lifestyle.'*
>
> —Edward Gibbon

Civic virtues, morality and ethical conduct seldom come naturally to human beings, for they mean self deprivation, denial and self discipline; an inconvenient proposition. It would thus need constant and relentless reminders and enforcement.

The United Nations and countries all over the world have formulated a code of ethics for the public services based on universal values. In India, there is a Committee for Ethics in both the houses of parliament to monitor and ensure that the parliamentarians live by the ethical code. The ministers take oaths on assuming office, yet they have a reputation of being amongst the most corrupt and unethical. Worse, about 40 per cent of members of parliament have criminal cases against them. In India, Public Services Bill, 2006, attempts to do the same for public services in India. These indicate the fickleness of human character and the need to be constantly reminded of the expected code of conduct.

For the military, there are no institutionalized morals and ethics guidelines in the manner laid down for the civil services through government statutes. Military values and ethics have evolved over the millennia because the extreme calling of the soldiers cannot be sustained without willing adherence to these values. These values are practiced with far greater commitment by the vast majority in the military than any other service or group of people.

Why do we need morals and ethics in the military? The profession of arms makes ultimate demands on the soldiers. War is all about extreme danger where lives of soldiers depend on each other. In such times, unwavering mutual trust is sine qua non for the very survival of the unit and success. Every soldier has to be fully assured that his buddy will stand by him at the cost of his own life. This commitment can only be realized when military values become the glue that binds a group of men into a unit or a sub unit. This must become part of a soldier's DNA from day one in uniform. This extreme calling of soldiering demands uncompromising adherence to military values such as integrity, courage, self sacrifice, loyalty and allegiance, sense of duty, discipline and camaraderie. In peace, these values are essential in upholding the high ethical and moral behaviour, which is the hallmark of this noble profession.

It is that all important intangible, Trust, that differentiates military from the rest of the professions.

Morals and ethics are important for two reasons. Firstly, because it is the building block for good armies. Secondly and, equally important, is the fact that the army is placed on a very high pedestal by the nation. Whether it is rescuing children from bore wells, people perilously stuck in cable cars thousands of feet above the valley floor, riots, devastating floods or earthquakes, they look at their Army as a messiah that can be trusted every single time. It is this trust and faith which is our biggest strength and demands that we live by the highest code of military values, despite the declining values in the civil society. That is why we need a structured moral and ethics code that must be reiterated to all ranks through various forums regularly.

With time there have been drastic changes in the societal environment. A soldier of today is not isolated from the ills of society. Barring a few, the cantonments are intermingling with civilian areas. A large number of men are compelled to live with their families in the civil areas due to paucity of accommodation. The breakdown of joint families has brought added pressures and responsibilities on our men. It has also diluted the values and respect for elders. Materialism has caught up and aspirations have risen in every way. With internet and social media, physical isolation is impossible. In the present day every soldier is confronted by societal paradox. He is expected to live by values which make him a misfit in civil life and do not help him to get by in life. Thus, the modern day soldier is tempted to disregard military values and customs and does not accept the strict codes of conduct so readily.

From day one, an officer and a soldier is expected to live by the high morals and ethics of soldiering and all that goes with this profession. Steadfast adherence to these military values is the recipe for success of military missions. We need moral and ethical insulation of troops. It means creating a 'mental and psychological cantoning' based on the belief in 'military values' and '*nishkam karma*,' through indoctrination and personal examples by superiors. This must become the firewall against the ill influence of society.

While the training establishments play their part, the mentoring of young officers and soldiers must be prime focus of all units. I have always believed that every young officer is a motivated young man, ripe for moulding into a proud ethical soldier. If he begins that way, he will stay that way.

Why are soldiers prepared to die in battle, even though India, unlike other countries, can hardly boast of treating its soldiers and veterans half as well as do most other countries? Political and bureaucratic dispensation towards the military is less than encouraging. How often have the supreme commander or the defence minister reviewed the passing out parades at the military academies? How often has any politician been present at the funeral of a soldier? It took India more than six decades of urging and goading to have a national war memorial. How was the government represented at the funeral of Field Marshal Sam Manekshaw? Sam's lifetime pay as a Field Marshal was handed over to him on his death bed. The British maintain their war cemeteries all over the world from France, Gallipoli, Syria, Egypt, to Kohima and beyond. No wonder, it was the empire on which the sun never set.

A visiting British dignitary invariably lays a wreath at the India Gate, a mark of respect for the Indian soldiers who fought for England over a century ago. They made a memorial for Indian soldiers; Indian government had not till the time of writing this book in 2015.

Why then does the Indian soldier still continue to lay his life, freedom and comfort on the line? The thought of the nation, while always with him, is too distant. That he is patriotic goes without saying. He is brought up that way. To motivate him to risk his all, he needs something nearer with which he can associate himself. To an Indian soldier, his personal honour is of greatest value. Coming from a village, his conduct, good or bad, becomes public knowledge in his village. His regimental pride, the mutual trust and responsibility that he shares towards his fellow soldiers with whom he spends the greater part of his life are the other drivers of why men are prepared to die in battle. To let down your buddy in danger, is to fall from grace in your own esteem. To all this must be added the all important trust in the cause, unit leadership and the belief that the leader will not put him in harm's way without reason and when they do so, he will be prepared to share the same hardships and risks. They shudder at the consequence of failure in battle, the acid test of professionalism of every military unit. They shudder at the failure becoming part of their history, of which they were a part. Therefore, the only thing that matters to a true soldier is victory, no matter the odds. Of all things, not being courageous in battle, irrespective of the dangers, and the loss of honour that it entails is simply too dishonourable for him to bear. These values emanate from the morals, ethics and military values. In the army, these are both moral and functional requirement. These are the sine quo non for military effectiveness.

*'Not for fame or reward, not for place or for rank,*
*Not lured by ambition or goaded by necessity,...*
*But in the simple obedience to duty as they understood it,*
*These men suffered all, sacrificed all, dared all and died.'*

—Inscription at the Arlington National Cemetery

Over-ambition and careerism promotes sycophancy, and interests of men and the unit are sacrificed at the altar of personal ambitions of such officers. Incidents of pursuit of glory through unethical acts such as the infamous 'ketchup colonel' are outright condemnable and do the army incalculable harm, even if they never get exposed. It breaks the officer-men trust. These developments strike at the heart of morals and ethics because it strikes at the very basic military ethos of selfless service. Prolonged employment of the army in counter insurgency brings them in close contact of society. This weakens the aura of the army and exposes them to the ills of society. I remember, one para-military force unit posted in the valley would extract something from passing trucks. A chicken, if the truck was carrying poultry or a case of apple if it was carrying fruits and so on. The public loses respect for the security forces and, not surprisingly, this unit was the chosen target of the militants.

Let us understand some terms relating to morals and ethics.

Values, as the name suggests, is something that is valued by a man. These are the accepted principles or standards of belief that guide the behaviour of an individual or a group. They are like the anchor of a ship that prevents a man of strong values or character from being swayed in crisis, under pressure or under temptation.

In the military, values are standards that can never be compromised. These are integrity, loyalty, camaraderie, truthfulness, self less service, etc. The military values tell the soldier what he ought to be everyday and in every action they take. Army values are the very identity of the army, upon which everything else stands especially in combat.

Moral relates to personal conscience of what is right or wrong and to how individuals should behave, rather than on what the law says. Thus, morality means standards of conduct that are accepted as right or proper.

> *'That which is selfish is immoral and that which is unselfish is moral.'*
>
> —Swami Vivekananda

In the military, moral values cannot be individual standards of conscience, they are universal military moral standards applicable to all, across the ranks.

Ethics is the study of moral standards and how they affect conduct (Encarta). Therefore ethical means conforming to accepted standards consistent with agreed principles of correct moral conduct. Ethics refers to standards of behaviour that tell us how human beings ought to act in any situation in which they find themselves, as friends, parents, citizens, businessmen, public servants and so on.

Military ethics means, code of conduct that dictate military behaviour which is guided by good character, courage, integrity, loyalty, camaraderie and selfless service. Military ethics are also universally applicable across the globe and all armies are expected to follow them. They play a major part in combat.

**Morality and Ethics:** Morality can be an individual set of commitments even when they are rejected by others, whereas ethics relates to a group of people. Morality does not demand acquiescence from others the way ethics does. It is possible to be moral alone. The resignation of Admiral Joshi, the Indian Naval Chief, on a series of naval accidents was a moral step. Another person may not have done so. No political leader except Lal Bahadur Shastri has resigned on moral grounds, because their moral standards are entirely different.

**Character is the essence of a man:** The sum total of a person's virtues or traits forms his character. Character is that quality of head and heart of an individual, through the help of which he masters facts and forces of life in a creative manner and realizes not only self-fulfilment but helps other members of the society. The man of character develops upwards while a man without character slips downwards.

A man of character has morally uplifting values. It means integrity, honour, truthfulness, loyalty, selflessness, impartiality, moral uprightness and dedication. A man of character honours his word. He accepts responsibility and is willing to accept mistakes. A man of character therefore will command respect from all, even his adversaries.

Values get reflected in character. In order to have a society based on ethical and moral values, we need character building at every level in society, particularly in the youths.

Conduct is an outer expression of one's character the way a person behaves, especially when not under observation. Thus, in simple words character is described as 'what a man is in the dark' when not being watched. Character remains the key to the growth of any organization irrespective of the level,

*National Character is the keystone on which rests the fate and future of our public affairs, not this or that 'ism.' Individual honesty must be brought into being before we can hope for improvement of national affairs...Let's gain our character quickly and all will be well -politics, administration and economic conditions.*

—C Rajagopalachari, President of India

**Integrity and Honesty:** Integrity is the utter sincerity, honesty and candour. It is the avoidance of any kind of deceptive, shallow, or expedient behaviour.

It is about doing the right thing, knowing that nobody's going to know whether you did it or not, even at personal cost. People with integrity are those whose words match their deeds and whose behaviour mirrors their values. A man of integrity will have the courage of conviction, be honest, truthful, fair and straightforward, will accept responsibility for his actions. He will be open and transparent in everything he does and not be afraid to open all his functioning to scrutiny. He will be sensitive and not bring discredit to himself or to the organization he belongs. He will practice justice and fair play in all his dealings and acts. This characteristic ranks highest in personal qualities and defines character. It is the inner voice of self control.

Why is it so important in the military than anywhere else is, because it creates mutual trust within one's command. And mutual trust is the foundation of good leadership and brotherhood. Actions of a man of integrity speak loud and instil trust. A man of integrity is predictable and steady in decision and in action.

A man of integrity does the right thing, not because it is convenient or he has no other choice, but because his character allows no less.

**Courage:** Moral courage is the ability of a person to stand by his convictions and for what he thinks is right, irrespective of the consequences and pressures. It means standing by your subordinates when they deserve, despite what it may mean to you. It also means taking a harsh decision when one is warranted. It also means accepting your mistakes and giving credit to others when it is theirs. It also means being a non-conformist when that is in the interest of the organization. Physical courage stands for bravery, valour and intrepidity. A commanding officer has to train himself to look fearless and be fearless, at all times. His body language must exude confidence and optimism at all times. His shoulders can never droop.

> *Values, critical as they are, can only be sustained by institutions. Therefore creation of an Ethics Code is of great importance to promote and sustain values.*

(Compiled from different sources)

While posted at the Indian embassy in Ankara, Turkey, I attended a cultural programme organized by the Japanese embassy. The hall was overflowing and a large number of diplomats and civilians stood watching the show. In that nearly pitch dark auditorium, I also stood watching the show. After a while I saw a person get up in that dark hall and offer his seat to a lady standing near him. I did not recognize that person then. Later as the lights were switched on, it was Colonel Joe Collins, the US Marine Attaché in Ankara. On another occasion I saw him do exactly the same thing and stood for an hour watching the show.

In that multinational gathering where no one knew who was who in that dark hall, he had that character of an officer and a gentleman, who did what was the right thing to do, when not being observed and which would bring him no credit. It brought great credit to US Marine Corps; I saw him do that and many more will read this piece

Compare this with the scene in metro trains in Delhi, young men occupy seats meant for ladies and senior citizens and pretend to be asleep.

**Ideals are like stars:** We never reach them but, like mariners on the sea, we chart our course by them.

Idealism is a difficult path in this non-ideal world. An idealist will find himself a lone ranger digging a lonely furrow, very often at odds with his superiors and the system itself. The Indian Army has been on a high pedestal on morals and ethics. The Indian soldier through his social values and grooming is correct in his behaviour. The modern ills of society are beginning to have an influence on him that must be arrested through grooming, strict discipline and good leadership.

> *'I don't like praising armies. I don't like armies because armies mean wars and I don't like wars. But this (the Indian army) was something... They were great all the way. There was never a black mark...I lived with the officers and I walked, rode with the jawans and they were great. Sure some of them were scared at first; they wouldn't be human if they were not. But I never saw a man flinch because they were scared. There is a tremendous spirit (in the Indian army) and it did one good to experience it...And they were the most perfect gentlemen, I have never seen them do a wrong thing, not even when they saw how bestial the enemy had been."*
>
> —Sydney Schanberg, *New York Times* (quoted by Lt Gen VK Kapoor (Retd) in SP's Land Forces Round up, Jan 2015

Having spoken of morals and military ethics, let us answer some searching questions.

Are we honest in conducting our training exercises or do we resort to unfair practices to show results? Are we honest in appearing in promotion examinations? Are we honest in reporting our achievements or are we fudging figures? Are we honest in inter unit competitions or do we take unfair advantage when the opportunity exists? Are we truthful when things go wrong or do we hide unpleasant facts? How much are you prepared to sacrifice for other officers of your team? Are you a role model for someone in the army? Would your men follow you willingly when life will be in danger? Did you live by the same standards as you expected from your subordinates in probity and use of perks and privileges? Did you command your battalion selflessly and placed the unit's interest before your own?

And finally, the most important one: How would your subordinates respond to you if your command authority was taken away? It is my belief that the response of the subordinates in such a situation would be dictated not by your professional competence, but by the strength or the lack of character.

Unfortunately, ethics is not about what things are but what things ought to be. In the army, the purpose is to minimize the gap between the two to the minimum, ideally to zero.

In the army, occasionally there will be a paradox between the ends and the means. In general, except in war, ends do not always justify the means. Means have to be ethical too.

In command, telling lies to cover up for the battalion is ethically wrong.

# CHAPTER VI

# BATTALION IN COMBAT

The function of a unit in war is to fight and win, The function in peace is to prepare for war. Peace time routine not contributing to success in war is an utter waste.

US experience in Iraq, Afghanistan and Syria yet again proved that, in the ultimate analysis, with all technology and power at our disposal, war is all about leadership and men. Technology can never substitute them. All the wars have also amply proved that there is a direct relationship between Spartan living, frugality and effective soldiering.

**Combat is all about hardships:** And hardship has to be part of training. Is Indian army getting too welfare oriented and soft? I studied in a boarding school (Sainik School, Ghorakhal, Nainital) located well over 6000 feet. It would snow in winters. Morning PT was always conducted in shorts and weather was never an excuse for cancelling PT. These days PT in winters is conducted in many formations in trousers or track suits with balaclava. It is not unusual to cancel PT parade on foggy days. Bad weather is a soldier's ally in battle, get used to it. Our physical standards have sharply fallen.

I remember a staff officer walking up to me with an officer's request for routine leave. When I reminded him that the army commander's visit was round the corner and he was expected to be here, I was told that he had already got his reservation done when he returned from last leave.

Fear of suicides has resulted in ridiculous practices of not issuing ammunition to armed guards. I was amused to learn that in one centre, the commandant had provided Dunlop mattresses for recruits to give duty at night.

As a divisional commander, I asked my Flag Staff House Guard to 'stand to.' They were taken by surprise and had no idea what to do. Clearly, the unit lacked the sense of what they were there for, even though my guards were all tactical and my operational orientation well known to my division. I am sure this is not an exception. Try other places and there will be more surprises. Every guard is there for a purpose. It is there to protect something. There is far more attention to be paid to basics. It must become a habit of every detachment commander to analyze his task, what it involves and rehearse it. There have been numerous incidents where unit's response to terrorist intrusion into unit area has been far from satisfactory. Bull shit and eye wash must be curbed ruthlessly.

> *'War is the realm of uncertainty: three quarters of the factors on which action in war is based are wrapped in fog of greater or lesser uncertainty.'*
>
> —Clausewitz

The present day battlefield transparency, lethality of modern weapon systems and ever increasing elements of warfare will make war fighting a more complex activity. Such an environment will need dynamic junior leadership which is decisive without looking for direction. Thus, the task of a commanding officer is to produce these types of commanders and not followers. A unit which can function well under its seconds-in-command at all levels is bound to prosper in battle. A commanding officer who does not go on leave and thinks that his unit cannot function in his absence is utter failure, for he fails in his duty to train his commanders to function one step higher, a basic need of war. There is no dearth of occasions where the commanding officers and company commanders became casualty early in battle.

The Murphy's law will come into play in battle faster than you think. It has been oft repeated that no plan survives the first contact, therefore leadership that can respond to unforeseen developments needs to be nurtured. Here comes the 'Directive Style of Command'. More on this important aspect later.

Risk taking ability is an important leadership trait. The battle situation will always be marred by uncertainty, chaos and fog of war. This ability helps a leader to be more decisive and exploit the fleeting opportunities. While we expect an officer to be a gentleman in normal course, he must be able to transform into a ruthless 'wily fox' in operations, for all wars are based on deception. This has to be a part of professional training. Ever observed Roger Federer or Sachin Tendulkar; perfect gentlemen on the exterior, ruthless killers on the sports field.

How does a commanding officer ensure that his junior leaders develop in this mould? It starts from the way the commanding officer conducts himself. He must, at all times exhibit the countenance of tiger, a self assured commander, in his thought, body language, conduct and action. A kiss up-kick down commander will never rear tigers. He must avoid micromanagement, accept honest mistakes, punish issues related to integrity and honesty but condone actions that reflect soldierly traits of aggression and offensive spirit. This incident recounted below reflects how you groom tigers and not lambs and lambs won't win you Kargil wars.

Way back 3 GUARDS had an enterprising commanding officer. The youngsters couldn't have asked for more.

One Saturday, the youngsters of the battalion decided to paint the town red. They landed at the club and had a good binge. When they had finished, the bar lay shattered, the crockery was gone and a few pieces of furniture lay in many pieces. The civilian barman survived their wrath with a few broken teeth.

Promptly a report came from the station commander, giving the names of miscreants with a huge property damage bill. He directed that the damage be made up by these officers and disciplinary action be taken against the officers under intimation to the station commander.

The commanding officer called a conference of all officers.

'Welcome to the conference gentlemen,' he said. He read out the report from the station commander. 'This is the first report since we arrived here. These three young men have announced the arrival of the battalion in the station. For the first time since we have come, the town knows that the Guardsmen are here. The total damage is Rs. 3,000/- equivalent of four officers' monthly pay,' he said.

'There are a few things that worry me as your tiger. We have eight subalterns in the unit, and yesterday only three were involved. Gentlemen we have to fight together in war, and unless we fight together in peace, we will not succeed in war. Remember, the Guardsmen live in packs and they must hunt in packs. As for the damage, it will be shared by the bachelors who were absent from the action. Second-in-Command, these three monkeys can proceed on fifteen days leave.'

Justice delivered, no questions asked.

Well, I am not advocating that every commanding officer respond like this. Compare the response of these officers in battle to the one who could not even order the dessert on a normal day. In short, the commanding officers must groom tigers and not pussies, commanders and not followers. Remember, our raison d'etre for existence is success in war.

In operations, supervision and monitoring at appropriate level is very important, simply because the stakes are too high. When things go wrong, someone in the chain has failed to supervise. One has to be careful in the nature of supervision. Too much of it kills initiative and enthusiasm of the subordinates. Supervision as such has another purpose, to send a message that this activity is important to the commander.

I recollect I was part of a brigade exercise, my first in the battalion on commissioning. One of our companies was tasked to lay an ambush on another battalion and fire blank rounds. The company commander asked the Senior JCO to check every soldier's ammunition personally and ensure that they have only blank ammunition. The company commander was given 'all ok.' The company commander decided to check it out for himself. He was shocked to see that one young soldier had a magazine full of twenty live rounds. As has been my experience, a single live bullet often finds a friendly target, and very often it is fatal. What havoc these twenty rounds could have created needs no imagination.

Operations are a test of your peacetime professional integrity. Commanding officers who have been honest to their jobs will create history. For the others, the men will pay the price by losing their lives and the battalion its honour. If the superior commander trusts the ability of the commanding officer, the battalion will get challenging operational assignments, if not, you will get peripheral tasks and that will be an opportunity lost, an opportunity that comes once in a life time.

The military entity that executes the onerous responsibility of defending the integrity of the nation is the battalion. The responsibility to keep the battalion battle worthy is the commanding officer's most sacred duty. To be able to discharge that sacred duty, the commanding officer has to be passionately focused on this single point agenda. He has to be thinking and preparing for war all the time. Other peace time chores that have become part of military life must be managed in that priority.

**Future Operational Contours:** It is often said that most armies prepare to fight the last war. To empower your battalion to fight the next war, it is important to understand the contours of the future battlefield environment. War has always been about uncertainty and chaos and it always will be. Rightly, Patton said, 'No plan survives the first contact.' Murphy's Law will come into play. Whatever that can go wrong, is likely to go wrong. There will be no respite as technology will dictate round the clock engagements. It will be a highly digitized battle where technology will manifest itself at the tactical, operational and strategic levels. The increasing battlefield transparency and lethality will result in intense battle with very high rate of attrition and collateral damage in men and material. There will be new dimensions to the war such as space and cyber in the ever enlarging spectrum of unrestricted warfare. The fifth generation war and the asymmetric warfare are already entrenched in the modern war. In the Indian context, operations in the obstacle ridden terrain with ever proliferating built up areas add yet another dimension. The future war will see new dimensions of human rights issues. The technology will enable the battlefield to be seen in the bedroom without physical presence of the media. The media will play its part, not always in the best interest of the army. Post-war period will witness similar scenarios as those unfolding in the Middle East and Muslim world during the consolidation period – high intensity asymmetric warfare in an extremely hostile environment.

Indian Army's battlefields will remain what they have been. The nature of operations in counter insurgency missions will become more challenging in terms of human rights, use of force and concern for public sentiments with very little margin for error. The army will need to develop more tolerance to public reactions.

The higher level of attrition will demand smarter way of fighting through battle of manoeuvre. Manoeuvre warfare will be the order of the day at all levels in all forms of terrain and warfare. This means fighting small and fighting smart will be the order of the day. Big targets will not survive for too long. Air, space and information power will come to play an ever increasing role in future.

The army could be deployed in a wide spectrum of roles and tasks that range from conventional operations in a nuclear backdrop to low intensity conflict, possibly as part of an international force too. Secondary tasks such as aid to civil authority in restoring law and order and disaster management will remain recurring peace time commitments. The character of future battlefield will continue to change as technology continues to progress. As time passes, technology will drive all elements of war fighting; weapons, surveillance, communication and support systems. The biggest beneficiaries of technology will be the terrorists and their perpetrators making counter terrorist operations more challenging.

The future battlefield will pose different challenges and dictate that things are done differently than we have been doing so far.

In this environment, one change that is often overlooked will be the changed nature of men that we will command. These men, possibly, lack the same degree of mental and physical robustness as the soldiers of the yore. They may be less inclined to blind obedience of orders as the men of previous generations did. The JCOs performance in general has left much to be desired. The confidence in this rank to deliver is less than satisfactory.

The changing nature of the environment notwithstanding, I have no doubts our men will deliver as they have in the past, as long as the leadership is good. I also believe, this generation of men is different from the last in their commitment to military values.

In this kind of complex environment, what are the basic ingredients of success? Simply put, these are, leadership that is in sync with the futuristic environment and the battalion that is trained and equipped to fight the next and not the last war. All elements must comprehend the implications of future battlefield environment.

In this environment the junior leadership will require wider dimensions of initiative and foresight, increased capacity of flexible and autonomous action and decision making ability. This is where better education and not academic qualification comes to play. The present recruitment method will need to change to get better intake.

Junior leaders must be able to comprehend two levels up. Since the future battlefield will put greater stress on the men, there will be a need of higher degree of mutual trust that the officers will need to develop in peace time, based on character, competence and camaraderie. More than ever before, leading from the front will become more important.

The junior leaders cannot suddenly develop initiative at the outbreak of war. This can only be developed by constant nurturing during peace time. Thus, a commanding officer must practice a directive style of command in day to day routine. The junior leaders should be given the task, resources and broad terms of reference and left to themselves. Unless mistakes by subordinates are accepted, they will never grow into independent minded confident leaders. While it is fashionable to talk of directive style, I have rarely seen it practiced. Micro management and unnecessary supervision kills initiative, which, over time becomes a habit.

The complexity of battlefield will provide no scope for micro management. To exploit fleeting opportunities and seize initiative, the junior leadership will have to be innovative, risk taking and empowered to take quick decisions. An armoured column lined up in a drill square fashion to induct over a bridge in present day environment of transparency and lethality has no chance of success.

Needless to mention that there is no scope of learning on the job during the battle. It is during the normal course that the battalion is nurtured in all its manifestations to accomplish the operational task. I shall therefore share some ideas on effective training at battalion level. My general observations on the shortcomings in training in the units are summarized below:

- Neglecting empowerment of JCOs and NCOs to deliver effectively. Kargil war saw disproportionate number of young officers' casualties in comparison to JCOs. When the number of JCOs present in the unit is almost four times the officers, the statistics throw up startling revelations that must be taken note of and addressed. We are proud of our junior officers who faced the brunt of the battle. Without their 'devil may care' attitude it would have taken much longer to win this war and at a much higher cost. But then, there is a serious lesson here, that our young officers possibly did what was the job of JCOs and section commanders and that is not professionalism in the true sense. A battalion is professional when all its elements are capable of performing their mandated tasks and those of one level up, in a fluid situation of uncertainty. It is professional when it can function under all seconds in command. The JCOs must be trained well, given full authority and responsibility and held accountable. It must be understood that the bulk of the functioning of the unit at JCOs' level is repetitive. He has been doing that for decades. Thus, if he has come up the ladder of promotion on merit, there is simply no excuse for not being able to perform the routine tasks satisfactorily. Simply, it is officers' business to make sure that there are no free lunches for anyone.
- Lack of application in making the training operation oriented, interesting and progressive, thus making it a monotonous ritual. NCOs take off levels are much higher and they should be doing far more progressive things.
- Absence of job analysis of a soldier, crew and sub-unit commanders that will identify skills they need to acquire to do

their operational task effectively and serve as a check list.

- Absence of effective operational efficiency audit (op audit) to assess the training standards and institute mid course corrections.
- Poor individual training and inadequate emphasis on night training.
- Inadequate focus on development of leadership at the tactical level.
- Poor technological threshold.

It is evident that weakness in any of these factors is a recipe for failure. Nevertheless, it is the individual training which is the foundation of a well trained unit, most easily quantifiable. These are also the most varied and need most effort on part of the unit. No collective effort will succeed if the individuals forming the team are not skilled in their respective skills. A platoon attack is doomed to failure unless each rifleman, machine gunner, fire support elements, radio operators, fire controllers and section and platoon commanders are skilled in their individual trades. A troop of tanks will get nowhere unless each of the tank drivers, gunners and tank commanders are first accomplished in individual tasks and then work as a team.

The accountability of the JCOs and the NCOs must be demanded in training their sub units. These men who draw a substantial cost to company in cash and kind have to sign for the individual training of men in their squads. Their performance report has to be based on this aspect and unit administration and not on how well he looks after the company commander. The individual job description card that I have talked about later should be his 'ready reckoner' in accomplishing this responsibility.

A recruit is put through nine months of training during which he learns the basics of individual skills that includes drill, physical fitness, weapon handling and firing, field craft and basic tactics. Units do not seem to be entirely satisfied by their standards when they report to the units. Compare that with a terrorist who is put through very elementary training. The field craft of these terrorists is of a very high order and they invariably get the target when they fire. The difference is that the terrorist's life depends on his skills against an enemy far superior in numbers and firepower.

The training therefore has to be realistic, interesting and battle oriented. It is a mistake that we try to make a soldier master of every trade in the training manual. To be realistic, every individual's job description card should have skills in which he must secure A grade, others in which he should secure at least B grade and others in which he could do with a C grade or must know, should know and could know categorization of skills. This will help focus on training in a systematic and prioritized manner.

The last three months of a unit's tenure in a station must be devoted to orienting the unit for the next formation's operational role so that the men are mentally ready for the next assignment and settle down earliest. This is equally important whether you move from Delhi to the Line of Control or vice versa.

Training must never be allowed to become a ritual. Every hour must count, every man must feel a sense of progress every day. The training must be tailored to keep pace with the changing character of warfare-operational role, terrain, technology, enemy modus operandi, trainee level, and threats.

*"He is best who is trained in the severest school."*

—Thucydides, Greek historian.

I was commanding a Rashtriya Rifles sector in a counter insurgency area in Kashmir valley. Initially, I frequently debriefed the parties returning from operations. I realized that the junior leaders, while giving their best did not quite comprehend what to expect when contact was established with terrorists. This resulted in missed opportunities, wasteful effort and sometime own casualties. The JCOs' and NCOs' understanding of the terrorist modus operandi, in general, was poor. The exaggerated fear of the unknown in those dense forests was leading to being unduly over cautious and trigger happy. There was undue emphasis on logistics and many other shortcomings. While no two situations in combat are alike, ten most common combat situations based on the experiences in the valley were identified and possible response actions were formulated. These were then included in the training curriculum of the sector. The training at the unit level was focused on four aspects. One, ensuring that the junior leadership understood the dynamics of the environment and delivered. Two, anticipating possible situations and planning a response in a realistic manner. Three, Field craft as the best aid to survival in that, use of cover and, the last, effective shooting. Use of cover was my personal KRA. Placards reminding the soldier of using cover met his eyes wherever he looked in the company base. A man had to even drink his tea in the operating base behind cover.

Soon, response of the junior leaders showed sharp improvement. While no two situations in combat are alike, preparation in this realistic fashion gave them the confidence and direction to act. Insistence on field craft and use of cover prevented own casualties entirely. The honest truth is that more casualties are caused due to blue on blue, i.e., friendly fire than due to terrorist fire. Not one man suffered a scratch in operations while eliminating a large number of terrorists.

Good field craft protects soldiers from both, the enemy fire and own.

'Think out of the box' was the mantra for the sector. Training pamphlets were put aside and the young officers came out with novel ideas to outwit the terrorists with good results.

Resources in combat are scarce. Of them all, it is the life and energy of the troops that is most precious. All operations are characterized by fatigue, lack of sleep, inadequate food and water. All this saps energy, dulls the brain and slows physical response. Thus 'Do the most with the least' should be the philosophy. The requirement is to make things simple. I notice, today, there is a tendency to train everyone with everything. At the combat soldier level, his mind should not be cluttered with irrelevant technical data which does not concern him. Training a soldier with what is relevant for him will ensure his effectiveness and keep his mind clutter free. Do not make a combat soldier a jack of all trades, better to make him master of his.

> *'Gentleman, we have here a horse. The hay goes in at this end - the mouth. It comes out at that end - the dock. We do not worry about what happens in between.'*
>
> —Major General Scott

This best emphasizes the need for focusing on what is relevant and keeping things simple.

Talk to unit commanders and it is not unusual to hear them say that there is no time to train, as his officers or men are not available for one or the other reasons. I have never been convinced by this argument. A self audit will reveal that a lot can be done in house to overcome most of the constraints.

My question is simple, every man in the unit is availing ninety days leave irrespective of the location and commitment and so are most officers. If they can be spared for this long, there is no reason he cannot be produced for two months of training from the balance nine in the year. The next audit is the feeding strength of the men in the battalion. It is the commanding officers' business to find time and men to train. If his commitments truly make training impossible, then he must walk up to his commander and tell him so.

The commanding officer needs to conduct an honest manpower audit of his unit. He will be surprised by how many men are wasted unnecessarily. The concept of employment of manpower must be task based and not time based. In this, our higher headquarters and senior officers need to do some soul searching.

I was part of the pioneers who raised a new division in an operational area in the north east; not one man was attached in the divisional headquarter. The divisional camp managed the whole show including the Flag Staff house guard. There was much resentment because officers were used to the comfort of excess manpower drawn from the units, who either can't or choose not to represent. In case of war most of these attached men will be returned to units, and in all probability launched in to battle without current training.

In this division, the Deputy General Officer Commanding (GOC) had a staff car and a light vehicle. In that field station he rarely used a vehicle. When he did, it was never more than one vehicle at a time, that too for very brief duration. He called for the staff car driver and asked him what he had done in the last four weeks. He replied, he waits in the division MT park the whole day for orders. That man had simply done nothing but wait the whole month. The Deputy GOC directed that one of the two drivers be dismissed and only one driver will manage both vehicles. When required the second driver will be called for from the unit. This suggestion surprised the staff officers, who gave all kinds of reasons why this should not be done, including the privileges of the Deputy GOC. The direction was implemented without affecting Deputy GOC's functioning or tarnishing his status. This man functioned with just one man, his buddy; no guard and none else. There is huge mismanagement of man power, simply because they are there for free. Any change that reduces the comfort level or the perceived perks is resisted. We need to grow out of comfort and egotist zone and be more honest. Every man in the army has to be multi tasked. Imagine one man dedicated for the photocopier alone where he is doing nothing at all for ninety five percent of the time, or five runners standing outside five adjacent rooms in a headquarter whose farthest ends are less than fifty meters apart. One division commander returned over eighty men attached to the headquarter from units based on the principle of multi tasking and efficient use of manpower. One army commander returned over 30 men from his residential guard; every man had a reserve.

There are three distinct human elements in operational efficiency of the unit. These are officers, junior leaders (JCOs and NCOs) and men. Unlike the US and European armies, Indian soldiers' exposure is lower, so is his ability to function independently. He does his given job well but beyond his domain, looks for directions. Is it a result of how we deal with him in daily routine? Are we curbing his initiative? The age old saying that 'a battalion is as good as its officers are' says it all. The JCOs and NCOs cannot be expected to deliver without good officers, for their standard of competence and leadership will be forged by the standard of officers.

Battalion and company commanders cannot fight a successful battle by a centralized control. There is no scope for a weak link in the chain.

## Operational Oriented Training

The following steps will be useful in organizing effective training in the unit:

- List the operational tasks of the battalion. Carry out task analysis of each task in relation to the terrain. It will break the tasks into specific activities that need to be performed to accomplish each task.
- Based on the above, list out operational Key Result Areas (KRAs) as relevant to the unit.
- From the operational KRAs will flow out the training KRAs. The training KRAs will help identify training that needs to be imparted to each component of the unit. The unit commander must spell out the training objectives for each category of person or appointment holder in the unit. Where feasible, they must be quantified as clearly as possible. It will help evaluate the progress, identify shortcomings and enable mid course corrections.
- Prepare a job description card for each category of soldier as applicable in the given operational environment and terrain.

This must be reduced to SAT (Systems Approach to Training) based syllabus. More like a checklist, it breaks down each task into specific activities that a sub unit needs to perform efficiently to be able to achieve the bigger task. These checklists help in formulating activity based training syllabus.

Training in the units often tends to drift to a routine unless constantly monitored through well defined check points. That should be the prime concern of the commanding officer. A training cell with good junior leaders will be a help. A well conceived and passionately implemented training through CTO (continued training by objectives) for two hours a day is an effective method of training when unit is heavily committed. The commanding officer chooses when and how and all institutions in the unit are closed for this duration. There is no reason why men won't be available. Unfortunately, units are more interested in keeping profit making institutions like the CSD running at the cost of training.

When in command, we were swapping with another unit in a one to one relief. The other commanding officer wanted to leave his soda water factory behind because the unit was earning money from soda water contract in the station. Simply wrong focus for a combat unit, to say the least. Army provides enough funds for the genuine needs of the unit. Unfortunately, these days commanding officers' offices look more like a corporate CEO office and messes and guest rooms like hotels. It appears, senior officers seem to want to leave their legacy more by creating such five star assets with their names on the inauguration boards than in professional fields.

## Centre for Lessons Learnt

Every unit must have a centre for lessons learnt managed by the unit training team. A writing board and a 'lessons learnt' register should be placed at the appropriate place in the unit. Any lessons that need to be shared with others should be entered in the register. The training team should analyze them periodically and co-opt the lessons learnt in the training and record them appropriately for future reference. The commanding officer must create a climate of free exchange of views and accept mistakes. If the environment discourages individuals from discussing their mistakes, the unit loses the benefit of learning from their mistakes, a huge professional loss.

The units must endeavour to learn not only from their mistakes but also from the commission and omissions of other units such as Galwan face-off and the military operations the world over.

At the end of a training cycle, the unit commander should undertake an operational audit at the company level. Aim of the audit is to assess the standards achieved and address the shortcomings. This can be done by a combination of training evaluation, practical tests or through a questionnaire. It is here that the JCOs must be utilized to the full.

In counter insurgency operations, while after action audit must be done after every operation, each sub unit must conduct its operational audit every quarter by taking a few days off from operations. Sit with your men over a cup of tea, discuss important issues, identify shortcomings and address them in the training. One example of an operational audit for MMG and missile detachments is given below. A similar audit questionnaire needs to be evolved for all battle appointments, sub units, crews and individuals for the tasks in the current operational environment.

### Machine Gun Detachments

- Are my gunners competent to engage targets by day and night? Are they proficient in doing so in the laid down timings?
- Do they know the methodology to engage point and area targets?
- Are they efficient in providing fire support to a company in assault?
- Do they understand the need for field craft, camouflage and concealment for safety of the gunners?
- Do they understand the characteristics of beaten zone at different ranges to be able to engage targets effectively?
- Do they understand the affects of terrain on use of their weapon in different operations of war? Is the detachment proficient in maintenance and field repair of the gun?
- Do they understand the ammunition replenishment system in the battalion?

### Missile Detachments

- Do the detachments understand the threat that the unit is likely to face?
- Does the crew understand the way the enemy armour is likely to operate?
- Are they capable of differentiating own armour from the enemy's?
- Is he aware of his own weaknesses and vulnerabilities against enemy armour and ways to counter them?

- Do they appreciate the implications of terrain on missile fire? Is he capable of effectively using the weapon in the given terrain?
- Is he proficient in maintenance and care of the equipment?

The list can be made exhaustive. A similar audit questionnaire can be made out for all categories of soldiers such as rifleman, tank drivers, gunners, sub unit commanders, gun crews and other arms and services as applicable. This will enable junior level commanders to undertake self audit ensuring important aspects are not overlooked. Each unit must evolve an evaluation methodology that practically evaluates the troops' skills in various disciplines.

### *Job Description Card*

Every soul in a unit has well defined duties both during peace and in war. Fog of war is characterized by confusion, chaos, anxiety and uncertainty. In such an environment, what is not practiced in peace will not succeed in war. Murphy's law will come into play when it is least welcome, hence the need for every commander at all levels to know well what his job entails.

It would be a good idea to prepare a job description card for every category of man, crew and commander in a unit. It must lay down all the tasks that an individual will need to perform in battle. For each task, it must spell out skills that need to be learnt by the individual or the crew. It will be useful for the individual soldier, detachment commander and sub unit/unit commanders to evaluate the state of training and identify weaknesses. An example of a job card is given below:

MISSILE DETACHMENT COMMANDER

*Operational Tasks*

- Knowledge of the operational tasks of the unit.
- Knowledge of mob procedures and all connected aspects. List details.
- Integration with the supported formation – liaison, grouping, communication and coordination issues etc.

- Knowledge of the operational area and nuances of terrain that affect his tasks.
- Alternative tasks in other sectors and necessary liaison and coordination and preparation.
- Identification friend and foe.

*Tactical*

- Knowledge of terrain, implications and exploiting terrain to own advantage.
- Coordination with other elements deployed in the area.
- Employment of the weapon in the prevailing terrain.
- Proficiency in field craft, camouflage and concealment.
- Communication with other elements deployed.
- Knowledge of mines and vehicle safe lanes, etc.
- Knowledge of enemy equipment and their tactics.

*Technical*

- Strengths and weaknesses of the equipment affecting their employment in the given terrain and weather.
- Handling, maintenance and field repair of equipment in the given terrain and weather, etc.
- Method of safe storage and transportation of missiles on vehicle and man pack.

*Administrative*

- Documentation of men and material.
- Mobilization procedures (include details).
- Ammunition collection drills, etc.
- Actions in case of casualty of men and equipment.
- Casualty evacuation, combat (medical) survival and ammunition replenishment.

With appropriate details, a job description card will serve as a training checklist to the individual and his commanders. JCOs will find this useful in contributing meaningfully to training of their sub units.

## *Training Junior Leaders*

*"An army of lions led by a deer will never be an army of lions."*

—Napoleon

No unit will succeed in battle by a centralized control. Every soldier is a leader in his own capacity. In his personal life he is the head of the family and takes many important decisions. In the battalion he may be commanding a weapon detachment of three or a section of ten or a platoon. A unit needs a leader at every level.

The task of the commanding officer is to train leaders and not followers; thinking leaders who can analyze situations and take decisions without looking back.

I remember an incident in Kashmir valley that best demonstrates the dangers of not having decision making commanders.

Kashmir valley was on the boil because of some incident. A military vehicle got separated from the convoy. A crowd gathered ominously threatening to burn the vehicle. The company commander on road opening duties saw the developing situation. He contacted his commanding officer for directions, who in turn asked his sector commander for directions. The commander rang up the officiating divisional commander for permission to open fire if necessary. The officiating divisional commander rang up the corps headquarters for permission. By then the vehicle was burnt by the mob and had gone up in smoke.

It is a perfect case of 'CYA' or covering you arse; no one in the chain wanting to take responsibility. The end result the army was made to look stupid. Understandably, the situation was tense but the orders to act in such situations are clear that empower even a NCO to take any appropriate action including use of force to protect life and government property. What can be expected in battle if junior and senior commanders look for directions in such time critical situations. On the ground, the units do face a dilemma. Even though the orders exist, there is immense pressure on units to avoid untoward situations and collateral damage. The troops on ground find themselves in a bind on how to react in difficult situations.

There was an eventful incident in the valley in 2014. Two young boys who violated the barrier in a speeding car, despite being asked to stop, were shot by the check post. The theatre commander was unnecessarily quick to acknowledge the mistake, even before the investigations were completed. This had created a controversy in the army and would certainly create confusion in the minds of officers, wondering what are they expected to do? Though it may not be related, soon thereafter, was an incident of terrorists break-in into a unit resulting in own casualties as well. Never easy for the men on the ground to press the trigger. In fact, mostly units follow the dictum; not to fire till fired at, and that places the troops in great danger. The hierarchy must appreciate the ground difficulties and take that into account. Always a good idea to await the findings of the investigation before jumping to conclusion, when things go wrong. Crisis management remains an important function of all military commanders in counter insurgency areas.

## The Directive Style of Command (DSOC)

All battalion operations, in the ultimate analysis, are actions at sub-unit levels. A company attack quickly becomes several section-based operations. An armoured regiment in manoeuvre is a combination of troop-based operations and so on for all arms and services. The Galwan incident in Eastern Ladakh is a stark reminder of the need to empower the junior leaders to act in the absence of orders. The early death of the commanding officer left the unit to junior leaders to act on their own. Several units in the Indo-Pak Wars of 65 and 71 lost most of their assault company commanders during the attack, hence the need for DSOC.

A centralised functioning in the military is a recipe for failure in operations as it slows down the momentum and curbs initiative. It is critical that decision making is pushed to the lowest appropriate level, closest to the scene of action and implementation. This will help to exploit fleeting opportunities and maintain momentum.

This needs a culture that can be termed the DSOC. The character of warfare is changing rapidly and despite indicators, not enough clarity on what it means at unit and subunit levels. For sure, commanders at all levels will see the enemy earlier, engage him faster, at greater ranges with enhanced lethality. It works both ways. The fast-paced, round the clock operations, will create fleeting opportunities. On the part of junior leaders, this demands adaptability, critical thinking and the freedom of action within the laid down parameters by the higher commander.

This is the essence of DSOC. It is fashionable to talk of DSOC but precious little is done to cultivate or practice it. Many armies implement this concept by different names. The British call it the Directive Control, the US calls it Mission Type of Orders and the Indian Army calls it the Directive Style.

The DSOC is an all-encompassing concept that incorporates facets of leadership, tactics, command and control and senior – subordinate relationship. The approach presupposes intuition, initiative, flexibility, a high degree of commitment, dynamic subordinates and decisive action at all levels.

The tendency of centralization, zero-error syndrome and micro-management work against the practice of this important facet. The successful conduct of this concept at the unit level requires harmony of thought.

Mutual trust in the chain of command from the lowest to the highest forms the basis for the successful execution of DSOC. Mutual trust prevents the need for detailed instructions and enables junior leaders to exercise initiative without fear of criticism or reprimand. As a divisional commander, I remember a young officer telling me how he, as the food member in the mess, did not have the freedom to order dessert on normal days. How does one expect this officer to exercise initiative in battle? His initiative has been effectively killed in the womb. The peacetime routine must encourage officers, JCOs and NCOs to function on their own in their context.

A commanding officer must have no problems accepting mistakes in house. And when the event is being witnessed by a superior commander, a guideline that spells out the commanding officer's mind should be enough. It is disheartening to see numerous rehearsals that are done even for the smallest events that are counterproductive to the DSOC.

In the DSOC the commander gives out his intention and the task. It binds together various tasks and defines the desired end state. He lays down major terms of reference and leaves the execution to his subordinate with maximum freedom of action. In the Arab-Israeli War of 1967, the Israeli armoured regimental commander on the Golan Heights was given this simple order. 'Stop that Syrian Armoured Brigade.' The regimental commander was left to find his way of doing it and he did it, his way, without interference from superior commanders. If we carry out a little analysis of this concept, it brings out the following aspects:

- The subordinates must be fully conversant with the operational environment, understand the mission and their role in the larger scheme.
- The subordinates need to understand their commander's mind and personality so that there is congruity of thought and action. There must be mutual trust and faith in the ability of the subordinates.
- Within the broad parameters, the subordinates are given full latitude to execute the task in a manner they deem appropriate. This will never be entirely the way the commander may have wanted but must be accepted.
- The planning and decision-making process in the normal course, where possible, should be participative. This will ensure that subordinates understand the larger picture and the rationale behind what is being done. This will enable them to act in absence of orders.
- The need for speed in decision making in an environment of uncertainty and fog based on professional judgment and responsibility.

*How does one practice the directive style of command?*

The three basics of successful implementation of DSOC are as follows:

- A high degree of training- both individuals and sub-units.
- A high degree of junior leadership in the unit. Leaders should not only be trained but trained to think critically and arrive at the desired course of action.

- Mutual trust with sub-unit commanders. This can only be developed over time by demonstration of courage and competence to deliver by both.

## The Leadership Environment

The commanding officer must create an enabling environment, where mistakes in the exercise of initiative are seen as learning tools. He must allow junior leaders to fail without becoming failures. Fear of mistakes discourages creativity and exercise of initiative, the basic requirements for successful implementation of DSOC.

The culture of DSOC can only be internalised by nurturing a culture of freedom of action, and exercise of initiative in all aspects of unit functioning in peacetime activities. Units must encourage creative criticism at all levels. Junior leaders must be encouraged to air their views without fear. The practice of detailed instructions, unnecessary supervision and rehearsals for the conduct of events must be done away with. JCOs and NCOs must be allowed to plan and conduct their subunit training and administration. Necessary framework evolved from a combination of Systems Approach to Training, job description cards of every category of soldiers, quantification of training where possible, operational audit of training and operational effectiveness can help JCOs and NCOs do this.

The unit should have a culture of leadership development as an important aspect of DSOC.

The commanding officer himself is the starting point. A cautious, risk-averse commanding officer given to zero-error and centralised functioning will never be able to practice the DSOC. A successful practice of DSOC pre-supposes competent junior leadership. Where that is not the case, as it will happen with some, a mix of DSOC and centralised control or forward command by commanders will be necessary.

Sand model discussions, map board exercises at subunit level and two-sided tactical exercises challenging their intellect and templated thinking will be very useful.

## Disruption Quotient (DQ)

Since combat is all about uncertainty, confusion, complexity, surprises and adversities, it is important to develop the ability to function in this environment which is called the disruption quotient. A plan is the starting point, but once in contact, it will invariably be about adapting and responding to developments, sometimes favourable and sometimes not. A high DQ is critical for success at all levels. Thus, all leaders must be trained to expect the unexpected and respond to the unexpected positively.

### *How does one develop DQ?*

Developing DQ is part of the leadership development process during which subordinate leaders are trained in responding to disruptions by a process called '*positive turbulence.*' Through positive turbulence, you disrupt the planned course of events by creating real-life situations and adversities that force commanders to think critically, adapt, recalibrate their plans and implement them against new frictions and time pressures. A military mind tends to be template oriented and could freeze when confronted with new dynamics unless trained to operate in an environment of disruption at all levels in the unit. They must be encouraged to question the status quo, innovate and think out of the box. They must learn to exploit the theory of indirect approach to find solutions.

At the junior leadership levels in units, exercises such as one suggested below will help to understand the concept of developing DQ.

'The battalion is to occupy defences in mountains. The enemy is likely to advance along Axis A and contact own defences in the next forty-eight hours. I want to inflict maximum attrition and delay him for twenty-four hours before he contacts our defences. I want you to do that on this axis between points C and D. There will be one more platoon deployed for the same task along this axis between points E and F. Work out your plans to cover all aspects and be prepared to discuss after 48 hours.'

The conduct of such exercises must be suitably interjected by real-life surprises and disruptions as are bound to happen. Simple exercises like this with analytical brainstorming will get the junior leaders to apply themselves and train them mentally for disruptions. This concept should be extended to routine peacetime activities.

Standard Operating Procedures (SOP) should only be a guideline, a kind of checklist to ensure that essentials are not missed out. A leeway must be given on the 'HOW' of things to prevent the junior leaders from falling into template thinking and looking over their shoulders.

A dictum that helps the practice of DSOC is 'PLAY TOGETHER - PLAN TOGETHER - KEEP IT SIMPLE'.

### *Young Officers and Soldiers in Combat*

There will often be occasions when young officers and men will be pitch forked straight into combat. In our context, these are more in the form of units in counter insurgency operations, units deployed on the Line of Control with our neighbours and challenging deployments in glaciated terrain. Sometimes it will be in conventional operations such as the Kargil war and other wars India had to fight with our neighbours. I am told a young officer was commissioned into a parachute battalion just before the Indo-Pak 1971 war. The first jump that he ever made without any training was a combat jump straight into battle. All these necessitate a deliberate easing of these young officers and men into combat.

While these youngsters are inexperienced, there strength lies in their enthusiasm, commitment and loyalty. Most young officers acquire fairly good basic level skills and capabilities in the training academies, but the lack of experience can put troops' lives in harm's way in operations.

The young officers must listen and learn. Everyman in the unit has more boot experience and can teach them a thing or two. Young officers will find themselves in command of small sub units in battle immediately. They must ask questions when uncertain. When required to make a decision, young officers must leverage the experience of good JCOs and NCOs and stick to it. Indecision is a fatal flaw in a combat leader and it often causes frustration and needless loss of lives. An officer must display confidence derived from understanding and control of the situation. Overconfidence and arrogance is detrimental and can be fatal.

What a young officer needs to demonstrate is that he is prepared to seek advice and share the same risks and hardships. True respect and confidence is earned through actions and the men will be closely observing him in order to determine his worth as a leader.

The unit leaders must develop virtues of perseverance and tenacity. Unlike a tennis game, in combat you will never know how close to victory you are. Those who have the tenacity and the resolve to persevere will carry the day. I often remember a Tennis match between Roger Federer and Andy Roddick, both top players of the era. Federer was down two sets, and in the third, was trailing 2-6 in the tie breaker. Roddick was a big server and needed to get just one big serve right, but Rogger showed the tenacity and from that brink went on to win the tie breaker and later the match. A fine example of tenacity and self belief.

## Counter Insurgency Operations

Battalion command in counter insurgency operations poses multiple challenges. These cover aspects such as operating among own people where one incident can have a severe fallout. Conflict arising out of constraints and caution imposed by military hierarchy and ground realities. An environment where plethora of agencies are only looking for sensationalizing military errors – the human rights organization who will blame the army without even knowing the facts, the political parties just waiting to pounce on anything that can give them political mileage. Anti national elements who will concoct fictional incidents to tarnish the image of the army. A plethora of media competing for the breaking news and letting their imagination run wild, and above all, pressure to perform in a competitive environment where maintaining an incident free environment may not necessarily mean good performance.

The units are caught in a paradox. A soldier's task in war entails use of maximum force against the enemy. Here he is asked to use minimum force. In war, he is not asked questions if civilians die during the course of battle. Here he may land up in big trouble if that happens, even if unavoidable. In war he can shoot first even without seeing the enemy, here he is only sure of the enemy when he is first shot at. In war he gets rewarded for killing the enemy. Here, he is required to prove that the individual he has killed is a registered terrorist. He knows the conventional war will be short. Here it is a long haul and he will be back here again. In war, the whole nation rallies behind him. Here, part of own countrymen are against him. In war, he does not have to worry about what lies behind. Here, the enemy is all around. In war, there is little chance that he will have to answer in a court of law. Here, he may be defending himself in a court even for false allegations. In war, enemy's culture and beliefs are of little relevance during combat. Here, he is told to be sensitive to local culture and customs all the time, even fight terrorists barefoot. A unit is required to transform from an aggressive fighting military outlook to a people friendly one.

All commanders up the chain are under pressure of some kind. This is reflected as an anecdote that goes around in the valley this way:

*Why are the terrorists hard to find in the month of August?*

Because they know commanding officers' and brigade commanders' annual report is written on 1st September. So they go underground during this period.

A lot has been written on insurgency. My endeavour is to share practical issues that have been helpful in my experience in counter insurgency operations in different capacity.

The lessons from experiences of other countries in Iraq and Afghanistan need to be taken carefully. The major difference in our context is that we are dealing with our own people in our own land. There is no scope for failure, as unlike others, there is no exit clause on the plate. The centre of gravity is the people, thus troop behaviour, application of fire power, collateral damage and human rights etc have serious implications.

I was discussing counter insurgency operations with an American officer when the US had just launched operation Enduring Freedom in Iraq in Mar 2003. Civilian casualties were very high. When I pointed that out to him, his reply was 'shoot first and ask questions later. If someone has to die, it better be the other guy.' America is fighting its wars on foreign soil. For US the worst that will happen is that they can walk out of Afghanistan and leave the country to its fate as they did in Vietnam and Iraq. Compare this with the British, operating in Basra region of Iraq in the same war, they switched from helmets to berets at the first opportunity sending a friendly message.

In this environment a commanding officer has to foremost learn to combat stress and pressures that come to bear on him. These pressures may come in many forms like achieving quantifiable results, collateral damage, untoward incidents such as suicides, etc., and possibly an unreasonably demanding boss. Following guidelines will help in successful command in counter insurgency environment.

- Understand the peculiarities of your environment. On the Line of Control, the key to success are different from a unit operating in hinterland. Environment in hinterland itself differs from sector to sector.
- Focus the training of the battalion in accordance with the peculiarities of your environment. The key to success lies in effective junior leaders, i.e., JCOs and NCOs.
- Effective intelligence is the key to successful operations. Technology economizes troop effort.
- Crisis management is the key function of commanders. Accept the fact that things will go wrong. Do not get pissed off at every incident.
- Do not have to compete with others; focus on your tasks. Develop good trust with your boss based on integrity, truthfulness and sincerity of purpose.
- Create a good positive atmosphere of *Main hoon na*, where your command feels confident, if things go wrong, the commanding officer will handle without a fuss.
- Learn from others' experiences. Use your officers and JCOs as sounding board and be receptive to critique.
- Last but not the least, follow my principles of happy command. This is your last rank; give it your two hundred percent and be scared of no one, not even God.

No commanding officer has been sacked for not killing terrorists. They have been sacked for unethical conduct.

Counter insurgency areas are characterized by a dynamic environment. Understand the dynamics and set the right goals. These areas provide immense opportunity to contribute in different ways and make a visible difference. These relate to upliftment of the people, better schooling for children, welfare projects, perception management, creating goodwill and winning hearts and minds etc that can give the battalion a sense of achievement.

Commanding officer's bring stress and pressures upon themselves by hiding their mistakes. A commanding officer will command without a worry when he keeps his intent right and follows morals and ethics of the army.

Commanding officer's major function is crisis management when things go wrong, which they will. This is only to be expected. Maintaining good relations with local police and village elders come handy in a crisis. During my tenure as the sector commander, one soldier fell into a *nala* and got wet in the freezing winter. He lit up fire with papers lying on the road side. As the luck would have it, those pieces of papers turned out to be Quran pages. A potentially serious crisis was diffused primarily because we had cordial relations with village elders and a junior police official.

When things go wrong, the easiest way out of trouble is to speak the truth and accept the consequences. It will give you a peace of mind.

You will come across different types of commanders. They also have short tenures and are all looking to make a mark in this competitive army. You must handle them smartly and ensure you do not unnecessarily push your men when not warranted.

The battalion must believe and realize the following well known tenets:

- The centre of gravity in counter insurgency operations are the people. The target of the operations should be the cause, ideology and the people's mind. As long as people believe in their cause and voluntarily support terrorists, no military operations will usher a lasting peace.

- These problems have no military solutions. The purpose of the military is to improve security situation allowing reestablishment of civil authority and empower political process. The effectiveness of military must convince the people and the terrorist organizations on the futility of the path of violence to achieve their political ends.
- The centre of gravity being the people, the entire orientation of training and conduct of operations has to be on winning the hearts and minds of the people. This must be repeatedly emphasized.
- Perception Management is an important tool of warfare at all levels. Today, the all pervading social media is a powerful medium for perception management. It provides opportunities and challenges. Used imaginatively, it can be a force multiplier and extremely effective soft kill weapon. In our context, perception management has been by and large left to the army alone. It has to be a national effort.

The populace must see the army as honest, empathetic, impartial, firm yet courteous and for the people force. Good troop behaviour, extending the same courtesies to elders, women and children as we do to our own folks back home is the most cost effective perception management tool.

When you conduct a vehicle check, it is not a bad idea to say, 'Sorry for the inconvenience and offer them a glass of water or toffees to the kids.' You will leave a lasting impression that will more than neutralize the inconvenience. In an Indian family the man is seen almost as a demi-god by his wife and children. Insult him in front of them and the family will never forgive you, and possibly turn into terrorist sympathizers, if it was not one. This is an aspect that needs to be repeatedly reiterated.

Soldiers must understand that terrorists will dry up only if the people stop supporting them. Often, I have heard criticism of locals for not sharing information on terrorists. We need to appreciate the risks the locals bear. Put yourself in their shoes and the picture becomes clear. Your challenge lies in generating intelligence in this environment.

*Insurgents can never defeat a professional army,*
*But the army can easily defeat itself.*

Geneva conventions lay down the code of conduct in war, yet morals and ethics are often sacrificed in war. Indian army derives its values from the rich Indian culture. Human values are universal and apply whether in conventional or internal security scenario. No army should ever forsake morals and ethics in combat. All these leave emotional scars that take generations to heal, as evident in bilateral relations between China and Japan. In the Indian context, the army will always operate amongst its own citizens. Remember, a terrorist's brother is not necessarily a terrorist and very few mothers voluntarily send their children to their death in this fashion.

**Handling of Weapons and Fire Discipline:** A simple skill should need no emphasis. Yet, the need for this simple aspect is best expressed by the saying:

> 'Incoming own fire is more accurate than incoming enemy fire. There is no such thing as friendly fire.'

As a sector of four battalions in the valley, we had eliminated very large number of terrorists without even a scratch to a soldier in operations. But we lost two soldiers in the company bases to a single bullet each due to negligent handling of personal weapons by our own men. In both cases, the victims were wearing bullet proof jackets and helmets, but the bullet found its way to the unprotected small fatal zone of the body. This is the truth of own fire. While no one acknowledges, majority of own casualties in anti terrorist operations are from either own fire or silly mistakes. And, regretfully, the number of men lost due to non-operational reasons is painfully many times higher.

The importance of weapon handling, particularly by other arms and services cannot be overlooked or else we will lose precious soldiers as we did. I sometime wonder why is it so hard for a soldier to learn such a simple thing as the correct and safe way of unloading a rifle. Many soldiers' lives have been lost due to negligent handling of weapons even when not in contact with the enemy. Simple drill of pointing the barrel in a safe direction at all times and making it a habit is all that it needs. There is no such thing as accidental discharge of weapon; it is negligent handling of weapon which is poor training and must be punished.

It is quite surprising how quickly a soldier becomes rustic with his weapons and training. It is important that all fresh arrivals or soldiers re-joining from leave are put through a refresher training before being deployed even on sentry duty. It will save lives.

At the battalion level, there is no strategy. It is all about executing things on the ground, and on the ground only simple things work, things that have been mastered during training.

The aim of training is to reduce the gap between what happens in battle and what we train for in peace time. It has to be well thought out, well planned and realistically executed. In extreme stress situations, the mind gets sidelined and the training takes over. My view is that we need to do a great deal more on this all important aspect.

When in command of a sector in a counter insurgency environment, I had laid out certain KRAs and specific situations that the men should train on to reduce this gap to the minimum. I found that the training of a particular battalion was not up to the mark. I was surprised that the commanding officer had not even read the sector training instructions which I had painstakingly written personally, reducing them to all practical issues. Consequently, his company commanders also had never heard of my KRAs and the ten situations that we had identified to train the teams for. Result: the battalion was jungle bashing without purpose and direction.

Technology is a friend of anyone who chooses to exploit it. Every commander must think of exploiting technology to economize troop effort and enhance their combat effectiveness. I recollect a sector, through simple innovation kept most of its AOR under night surveillance through live streaming of thermal surveillance devices. Successful operations were effectively launched and controlled through use of technology, bringing relief to troops in inclement weather.

Many officers and men have died peeping over the window in operations in built up areas. One sector exploited simple innovations to save lives and operate more effectively. Radio transmitted video from a mini camera mounted on a six feet stick, to a small TV some distance away and periscopes were used effectively for room entry in built up areas without exposing own troops. These are just a few examples how simple innovations can be life saving. Very often, innovations are made for VIP visits and sometimes some of them have good utility value.

There was a unit which fabricated a good infantry foot bridge to cross a canal. It was displayed many times over the years and credit claimed repeatedly. Once, when a corps commander visited this unit, the same bridge was displayed as a new innovation. Having heard the claims of the commanding officer, the General said, 'I know, many commanding officers have used this bridge to Higher Command course. I guess it has served the battalion well, but has lived its shelf life and can take no more passes. I saw this bridge a decade ago when your battalion displayed it first time.'

As I stated earlier, my single point agenda was training. In training, we insisted on field craft and best use of the ground. There was a lot to learn from the terrorists in this aspect. This experience would help to understand what I mean.

One of the Special Forces team under my command had made contact with terrorists. It was a reasonably open terrain on the foothills without the dense foliage that was characteristic of my sector. We took casualties in quick time, two of them fatal. Despite the high standards of training of these Special Forces troops, no terrorist fire was seen and only speculations were made as to their numbers and location. The men were certain that some kind of underground bunker existed with firing slits because of which the terrorists could not be located. Quickly an effective cordon was established with all the sector resources. As we later found, the nearest part of the cordon was less than fifty meters from the spot where the terrorists were eventually killed. The last fire from the terrorists was heard more than thirty six hours ago. All our efforts to draw fire and locate terrorists failed.

The night passed without incident with the cordon failing to detect the terrorists despite dozens of night sights in a limited area. Nevertheless, the second day was utilized in plastering the limited area with fire of heavy weapons, but to no avail. All attempts to draw fire failed, leading us to believe that the terrorists may have escaped. Nothing else having succeeded, we decided to search the area as the only option to confirm whether they were there at all. The search operations started late afternoon on the third day. Lo behold, a typical terrorist AK-47 burst confirmed their presence. Both of them were killed a little later. The point that I wish to bring out here is that there was no underground bunker as the troops in contact thought. The terrorists were stuck up in a limited area without too much cover. They were watched by a cordon of over four hundred men from close range with all kinds of surveillance devices. All efforts failed to detect the terrorists for over two days. The terrorists made excellent use of folds in the ground to avoid detection and survive the heavy onslaught of fire without water or food for over two days and nights. They maintained strict fire control, keeping us guessing whether they were there at all. Quite easily we could have walked away believing they had escaped.

Great lesson in field craft and fire control.

For every piece of equipment in the unit, there is someone accountable. But the commanding officer alone is accountable for the standards of training in his unit.

## Why Some Armies Tick and Some Don't?

Cohesion remains the key to why sub units do well. The Regimental system of our army is our strength till it becomes parochial. The famous battle of Rezangla, where a company of 13 KUMAON, in the finest example of courage and valour, lost 114 out of 124 men defending Chusul, while the rest were wounded but refused to let go. 5 GUARDS, fighting the battle of Thembang against the Chinese without any support, fought till they ran out of last round of ammunition, losing ninety two officers, JCOs and men and over 120 injured. The commanding officer Lieutenant Colonel Jai Singh refused to leave. Finally, when ordered to withdraw, the battalion withdrew in an organized manner in complete control despite the grave trauma. The secret is sub unit cohesion that comes from good leadership by officers, good organizational environment and regimental pride. A sense amongst the men that the officers will stick and fight till the end with them - Trust. Without this critical aspect there is no way units will stick in a manner they did.

Studies on some other armies that engaged in war clearly highlight what succeeds in war and what does not. (Source: excerpts from the book, 'Crisis in Command' by Richard A Gabriel and Paul L Savage.)

The American army in the Vietnam War gave a poor account of itself. The cases of fragging, desertion, suicide, drug pedalling and other unbecoming conduct by soldiers were higher than ever before, while the stress of combat was not higher than World War II or for that matter Korea. The authors in this book on the US Army in Vietnam bring out some interesting deductions. According to them, the US army suffered from lack of cohesion at sub unit level. The reasons for this are many. First, the officers avoided combat service and risks of combat soldier. Since military service was compulsory, those who could do so managed softer options in the comfort of headquarters way behind. To a soldier going through the grind of combat, these headquarters looked islands of comfort and luxury; officers clubs with extravagant life style. Infantry, which did the bulk of combat amounted to only twenty percent of the strength in Vietnam which meant more money was spent on the comforts of the tail than on the cutting edge teeth. The second major point they bring out was the policy of rotation. While the troops served tenure of twelve months, officers were turned over after six months. The careerism came to inflict the officer corps, who used this opportunity to push their careers by what came to be known as 'ticket punching,' i.e., getting all important endorsements on their CV for promotion. The troops were seeing too many officers of poor commitment and competence made responsible for them. The next aspect they point out is the unwillingness of officers to face the same hardships and same risks to life and limb. In essence, they lay the blame of poor performance in Vietnam on the poor quality of officers, obsessed with career obsession and ticket punching, neglecting the basic tenets of soldiering stated earlier.

War College Study on Military Professionalism on Vietnam brought out the following:

> 'Officers of all grades perceive a significant difference between the ideal values and the actual or operative values of the officer Corps. There is also concern that the army is not taking action to ensure that high ideals are practiced as well as preached... that the Army has generated an environment that rewards relatively insignificant, short term indicators of success, and disregards and discourages the growth of long term qualities of moral and ethical strength on which the future of the Army depends. They are frustrated by the seniors who sacrificed integrity on the altar of personal success. The study found distorted and dishonest reporting of statistics and officer efficiency."

All this created resentment amongst the men. In the three year period, Army counted 788 cases of assaults with explosive devices, primarily directed against officers, called 'fragging' in the military parlance.

The US military handed out 522,905 medals in 1970 alone.

Can we spot some similarities in our army? Is the Indian Army also giving too many medals, particularly to officers above brigadier rank for routine accomplishments? What is the perception of the environment? How does one compare an Army Chief's (COAS) commendation card awarded against a citation for Sena Medal (gallantry) with those given to the personal staff of senior officers. There is a general perception that distinguished award is more a function of where you are and not as much as what you do. This must be set right.

Careerism was the problem in Vietnam for the US military. Career obsessed and conformist officers are rarely likely to rock the boat. In the Indian Army too, it is my belief that after the middle rung, careerism takes hold of the majority of the officers at the expense of the organization. From the commanding officer to the divisional commander, getting two outstanding reports in the short tenures becomes the only mission for the vast majority.

US army set its house in order post Vietnam War and performed by and large creditably in all their combat engagements including Iraq and Afghanistan, notwithstanding the strategic outcome.

## Israel

The surveys post 1973 Yom Kippur War showed that the men gave overwhelming approval to their officers, notably the immediate commanders. The responses show that the officer 'knew his job' (82 percent), 'gave clear orders' (100 percent), 'was resourceful' (98 percent), 'often praised his superiors' (11 percent), 'was interested in men's personal problems' (85 percent), 'stuck to the letter of his superior's orders' (43 percent), 'gave impossible orders' (3 percent), 'had initiative' (93 percent).

Lieutenant General Haim Bar-Lev stated after the war. 'Here lies the secret of our Army's success in the six day war...I do not know of any single factor, to which, so much of historic achievement can be attributed, as the human and moral quality of our commanders; of which the readiness to go in the van, their personal valour, their audacity, their readiness to risk their lives are direct products.'

It is these qualities that commands the respect of their men and builds the brotherhood and trust which enables them to click in battle.

## Germany

The German army is another fine example of leadership. In the Second World War, the German Army retained its cohesion despite the collapse of the country. Even till the last few days they fought as organized force till they were overrun. The reason, as these authors point out, was the readiness of the officer corps to lead from the front and bear the risk of death in inordinate proportions than their numbers. The men perceived their superior NCOs and officers as men of honour who cared for their men. The German officers were carefully selected and well educated. In 1944, German officers on the front lines constituted 2.86 percent of the enlisted men, but accounted for 3.5 percent of the casualties. One German soldier in 28 killed was an officer, while there was one officer for 34 men. Of the 675 Generals in the German Army, 223 or 33 percent were killed in action. Even though much is said about the German Nazi ideology and nationalism behind German motivation, the army was not motivated by the big themes but by basic sense of responsibility, performance of duty and willingness to take combat risks demonstrated by their officer corps. In essence, the quality of officer corps. Even though their numbers almost reached half by the end of the war, they never compromised on the quality of the officer corps.

## France

The French Army fought under greater stress than did the US Army. The author concludes that France maintained a much better unit cohesion in Vietnam, despite not enjoying the logistics support that the US Army did.

## Great Britain

Britain was the empire on which the sun never set. For centuries they ruled over half the world that had such a wide variety of subjects from Arabs, Pathans of present day Pakistan/Afghanistan borders, and the diverse people of India. The British army was known for maintaining cohesion under extreme stress. It was again the quality of the British officers and NCOs who always led from the front, often died doing so. No wonder, when a soldier was asked about their officers on the front line not being seen, replied 'They may not be here now, but when it is time to die, they will be here.' You cannot get a better compliment and when the officer corps commands such respect, the unit will maintain cohesion under the worst adversity.

The stark experiences highlight the secret of great armies. Unit cohesion was a direct result of the officer corps' readiness to share the same hardships and risks as their men, something the Americans in Vietnam were mostly not ready to. Officers, who will not allow their command to become a tool of their career progression, are the officers who will nurture great battalions.

It will be worth taking stock of where we stand. The Indian officer corps has given an excellent account of themselves at the junior level. The battle casualty figures follow the same pattern as that of German and the Israeli army; much higher casualty ratio than their strength to the enlisted men. The latest example of the Kargil war, 1999, yet again reiterates the unflinching commitment of the young officer cadre. The problem in the glittering example of the Kargil war is the state of JCOs' casualties which were proportionally too low as compared to the officers' casualties.

Such high officer casualties mean two things; one, the lack of confidence in the JCOs to deliver, or the extreme difficulty of combat situation that convinced these officers that success was not possible without them being right up there in the front. Either way, it points to the JCO as the weak link that must be strengthened. The formation commanders can contribute effectively by focusing on the JCOs during their visits to the units.

## Doctrine of Disobedience

Disobedience is not Always Indiscipline.

> '*There are roads which must not be followed, armies which must not be attacked, towns which must not be besieged, positions which must not be contested and commands of the sovereign which must not be obeyed.*'
>
> —Sun Tzu

The commanding officers must be prepared to represent against illegitimate or illegal orders, and if necessary disobey them. Orders that will bring a bad name to our army and uniform if implemented. Orders that will expose your men to unnecessary risks when not warranted; orders that cannot be implemented in the given timeframe, etc. This is easier said than done, for in our army, there are neither adequate safeguards nor much hope of finding support from one's superiors. The officer in most cases is likely to come out battle (moral courage) scarred at the end of the day.

There are many ifs and buts and hard to draw a line. It all depends upon the conviction of the man to make a decision; and if things go wrong, be prepared to accept the consequences. Let me cite two examples of such a dilemma involving my battalion.

My battalion was deployed on Siachen Glacier in mid-eighties. The Divisional Commander (GOC) flew to the battalion headquarters. He spent the night with our commanding officer, Colonel Umang Seth. He directed the unit to capture an enemy post which was way below our positions. Our posts dominated the entire pass and the enemy locations were much lower. The choice of the objective was clearly unsound. The commanding officer explained that he knew that area well and understood the implications, emphasizing that it would become extremely difficult to hold and sustain the post under the enemy's nose. The GOC tried again, this time cajoling my commanding officer that he wanted to give a birthday present to the army commander and that he will personally lead 5 GUARDS with a band if they did that.

Well, Col Seth told him that the plan was clearly made at headquarters by people who do not know the terrain. He proposed that the GOC visit the place with him, and then if he concluded that it was a viable objective, the battalion will capture it. Needless to say that the GOC never went there and the matter was dropped. Well, dropped only for a while. When my battalion got a new commanding officer on the glacier, the GOC was back again with the same agenda. The new commanding officer, Col Ranjit Singh was well briefed by the outgoing commanding officer. He too was convinced of the futility of the operation and had the courage to stand by his conviction. I am certain their moral courage saved the army many problems.

When I discussed this incident with an army commander years later, he said that the divisional commander may have had a valid justification at his level. To this, my reply was, in that case, he should have ordered the unit to do it, despite the commanding officer's reservations and not be pleading.

Can a birthday present ever be a rationale for the choice or timing of a military operation? It was a case of strong moral conviction by both the commanding officers. There was a grave risk that both of them could have suffered irreparably in their careers. Both were men of strong character and prevented a futile expedition and a military blunder.

Let us examine another incident that my battalion had to endure in a warlike situation. In 1991, my battalion 5 Guards, as part of 192 Infantry Brigade, 8 Infantry Division was deployed in a counter-infiltration role in the Poonch sector, 25 Infantry Division AOR. This meant a second-tier deployment in company groups extended over thirty kilometres in mountainous and high-altitude terrain. The cross-border fire was a daily affair. The Pakistan Army in a surprise move occupied an Indian village Kirni on the Line of Control in the 'Area of Responsibility' (AOR) of 19 PUNJAB, of the holding Infantry Brigade. The villagers fled to the safe hinterland.

All peaceful efforts to restore the situation failed. It was decided to attack and take back the village. 10 MAHAR, also from the 192 Infantry Brigade, in the neighbouring sector, was tasked to capture the village with adequate time to prepare for the attack. Our battalion, deployed in the 19 PUNJAB - AOR, was never informed of the operation or the D Day. Apropos, neither was it given any 'be prepared task', nor was the Commanding Officer asked to attend the orders on the D Day. Having learnt of the attack informally, our Commanding Officer chose to attend the orders of his own accord as an observer, as his two companies were deployed in the area from where the attacking troops would pass and he would be required to assist them in many ways.

On 31 Aug 1991, the D Day, the commander of the holding brigade, 25 Infantry Division, was giving orders to his 'O' group (10 MAHAR) for the attack. A most bizarre thing happened during the orders.

The commander was interrupted by a phone call from his divisional commander, GOC 25 Infantry Division. He returned and announced that the attack would now be launched by 5 GUARDS and not 10 MAHAR.

The Commanding Officer of my unit, sitting there as an observer, was struck by a thunderbolt. The first thought that crossed his mind was, what kind of Generals do we have in our army? When he sought a clarification on the D Day for the attack, he was told the attack would be launched as scheduled, the same day. He did not protest there but spoke to his own commander, Commander 192 Infantry Brigade. He projected his problems and the major equipment deficiencies and sought adequate time for preparation.

The commander said that his requirements will be provided in location and he must launch the attack as directed. He made no efforts at all to find out why the change was being made, nor tried to get the unit bare minimum preparatory time.

It was near mid-day. With the battalion stretched over thirty kilometres in mountain/high altitude terrain, concentrating two companies, organizing them for attack from a counter-infiltration mindset to an assault mindset without prior warning and minimum reconnaissance and preparation was an impossible task. The battalion in effect had less than eight hours to do so till the H Hour. Add to that the fact that the battalion was short of major weapons and communication equipment.

The dynamics of a battalion going into an attack—physical, material and psychological are complex. The machine guns and the radio equipment pooled and provided to the unit were not tested by those who would use them in the attack. Ordering the unit to launch the attack in this fashion was plain lunacy.

Notwithstanding the challenges, the battalion took the task in its stride. But, clearly ill-prepared in every way- no reconnaissance, last-minute coordination, no rehearsals, no time for unit battle procedure and drills, no psychological tuning, the battalion launched the attack. The radio equipment pooled from units failed and the battalion was mostly out of communication in no time.

Cutting the story short, aided by heavy rains, the battalion neutralised the Paki regulars and captured the village. Our first casualties occurred when the patrol base of 19 PUNJAB, which was our Firm Base for the attack, opened heavy fire on my battalion as we approached the Patrol Base. And this was when the guides came from the same Patrol Base.

Dominated from three sides in a re-entrant from less than 100 yards, they cut holes through the roof of dhok huts to place their automatics as it was impossible to step out of the huts. They held on tenuously and with effective artillery support, beat back counter-attacks over the next forty-eight hours shredding the enemy. In less than twenty-four hours, the battalion had travelled a long journey; from a sedate counter-infiltration role to an assault on the enemy regulars, having been launched into the attack most atrociously.

There was nothing that indicated that the attack could not be postponed by another day or, if that was not possible, the battalion that was nominated and had prepared should have launched the attack.

The divisional commander had sprung the most unprofessional surprise on the battalion. He needed to justify his decision and be held accountable. What were his compulsions that suddenly emerged during the orders that he did this? Did he get a sense that the commanding officer of the assaulting battalion appeared shaky to accomplish the mission? Whatever dictated this decision and disregard the genuine request of Commanding Officer of 5 GUARDS for more time, given his difficult circumstances, was never shared or known.

The fact that the battalion succeeded without too many losses is a credit to the resilience of the battalion, but of no relevance here. The question is, should the Commanding Officer of 5 GUARDS have declined to attack the same day and insisted that he gets at least twenty four to forty eight hours for the attack? It is my firm belief that he should have done that, given his circumstances, and when he was not being told why the battalion was being rushed into the attack in that manner. The Commanding Officer deserved to know that so that he could explain that to his men. In this case, when the command chain was unresponsive, the Commanding Officer should have sought permission to speak to the next superior commander. This would be moral courage and not cowardice. There was nothing that indicated that the attack could not be postponed by another day or, if that was not possible, the battalion that had prepared for ten days went into the attack.

I am certain, the Commanding Officer would have been morally right to represent against that order.

What role did the two brigade commanders play in this fiasco? Both were present when all this happened. Mute spectators, none of them legislated the righteous cause for minimum preparatory time for the unit for attack. A case of despicable moral and professional bankruptcy! The brigade commander of 5 GUARDS was morally and professionally bound to ensure that his battalion is not forced into this dangerous situation. I also wonder where the Corps Commander was during this all important operation in the corps zone. While it is right to let the Divisional Commander run the show, he would be knowing which battalion is attacking and the change must be known to him. If I were him, I would have spoken to the assaulting battalion commander to wish him good luck, and check if I could help in some way. If he had done so, he would have known what was happening and intervened appropriately.

Full credit to the Commanding Officer, 5 GUARDS to lead his battalion to a successful attack in most difficult circumstances and later, having the courage to reflect the truth of the unprofessional manner in which the battalion was launched into the attack, despite pressures from higher headquarters. The reason why the battalion did not get the credit it deserved.

Similar situations occurred again during the Kargil war when the battalions were rushed into operations ill prepared in the most difficult environment. Senior military leadership is expected to show more wisdom and moral courage in war and peace.

In war when there are serious issues involved, a commanding officer or a commander must stand up and be counted. There can be no better illustration than the dilemma faced by Brigadier John Dalvi, commander of the Tawang Brigade in Indo-China War of 1962.

As a man fully conversant with ground realities, he fully realized the madness of orders being passed from Delhi regarding a tactically insignificant piece of ground to be occupied on the border. According to his memoirs, *The Himalayan Blunder*, he strongly protested against the directions to occupy an innocuous and indefensible feature with no military significance, dominated by Thag La ridge occupied by the

Chinese in large strength (possibly the trigger for the 1962 war). Given our all round lack of preparedness, this decision ultimately led to national humiliation despite a huge sacrifice by the troops. His superiors lacked the courage to stand up to the diktats of the ill informed decision makers in Delhi. What then were the options open to this commander who was assigned impossible tasks by people located thousands of miles away and who had no clue, about the reality on the ground. His options were: One, to resign in protest; two, to ask to be relieved in view of his convictions; three, to use his judgment and occupy the defences that he could defend. While he contemplated resignation, he chose to continue. He felt that his troops will be thrown to despair, as the clouds of war were gathering fast and the new commander would not have the time to understand the dynamics of the situation. From the book, it is evident that Brigadier Dalvi conveyed his point as strongly as he could. May be resignation or a call to be relieved could have forced a change of decision at Delhi and saved the country the disaster. His concern for his troops got the better of him, and despite odds, he stayed for his men.

Everything looks clear in hindsight. For a commander on the spot it will always be a difficult decision, because such an act can easily be construed and portrayed as disobedience in the face of enemy, cowardice or worse. Brigadier Dalvi made all efforts to redeem the situation, but given the circumstances, he chose to stick on for his men. A good soldierly decision.

Sometimes one finds himself in a tricky situation even in peace stations. In peace, lives will rarely be at stake, it is the commander's reputation that may be. General Passion was commanding a division. One day the corps commander called to tell him that the Army Chief was annoyed that in his division, the commanding officers and brigade commanders were being called to the formation headquarters too often, leaving them no time to command their units. General Passion apprised the corps commander that the Chief's information was factually incorrect. It was necessary that the Chief also knew the truth and questioned his source on the report. With the corps commander's approval General Passion wrote to the Chief clarifying the facts and defended his commanders, who in Delhi had to execute many tasks of national importance which needed close involvement of the commanding officers and the commanders. He also drew the attention of the Chief to the doubtful credibility of the source which, if continued to be blindly trusted, could bring disrepute to the Chief's office in future.

Moral courage is the most essential quality in a commander, and also the rarest, that will sustain the honour and dignity of the armed forces in war and peace.

## Battalion Command in Combat: Demystifying Leading from The Front

Between May 2020 and November 21, the Indian Army lost three commanding officers, killed in action. One in counter-terrorist operations in Kashmir, one in the face-off against the Chinese in Galwan, Eastern Ladakh, a no-conflict scenario and one in an ambush in Manipur with his wife and son and personnel of his escort.

In the high-intensity Kargil War, 1999 which saw over 500 casualties that included over thirty officers, no commanding officer was killed in action. The stark contrast demands a dispassionate review and draw lessons for battalion commanders in combat.

After the death of the CO 21 Rashtriya Rifles in May 2020, a debate raged on social media on the merits of commanding officers leading from the front in a high-risk environment. I had expressed my views on the subject in an article titled '*To Lead or Not to Lead from the Front*' on Mission Victory India, a digital magazine. I would like to share a few more of my thoughts on the subject.

It is important to understand the implications and the application of leading from the front at the level of a commanding officer of a unit. The bottom line is that no directions/restrictions can ever be legislated for commanding officers or commanders in combat at any level, for every situation is different and command is a personality issue. Field Marshal Rommel was famous for appearing on the front lines in the heat of the battle. Many were of the view that the top-ranked commander being so close to the action at one place could result in a lop-sided view of the larger perspective. We are aware that this was not the case and there were other successful Generals like Patton in the same mould in the Second World War. I was fortunate to hear firsthand the story of Lt General Ashok Handoo, the former Army commander, Northern Command. As a brigade commander during the 71 War, he stood erect amid artillery fire, after pulling out his GSO(3) who had crawled under a vehicle. That act dispelled the fear from his officers and men for the rest of the war. If he had been killed during shelling, it would have been criticized as a foolhardy act of bravado.

However, a commanding officer needs to remember the following:

- He is the commanding officer of his unit on whom rests the ultimate responsibility for the mission. He is solely responsible for the orchestration and synergy of all tangibles and intangibles towards mission accomplishment in the most cost-effective manner-lives and blood of his men, resources and time.
- It is **not** his job to lead a company. Getting involved in a firefight by choice or chance will hamper him from doing his actual job and that would be an invitation to disaster for the unit.

Different operational environments would demand different command dynamics. Counter-terrorist operations are entirely different from conventional operations. In these operations, a commanding officer led QRT may find itself drawn in intense, decisive combat actions which in the normal course would have been the purview of subunits led by Junior or Non-Commissioned Officers. Despite all precautions, commanders and commanding officers may find themselves confronted by terrorists in an unknown hideout, snipers, suicide attacks, IEDs and ambushes. Different types of operations in different terrain pose different challenges. The commanding officer's position would be dynamic. Thus, there can be no template for where the commanding officer should be arrayed and command from. It is always the commander's call where he needs to be to make the biggest impact. In deciding his location, he has to consider the following:

- His location should facilitate effective monitoring of the situation and expeditious orchestration of resources accordingly.

- Should preferably be least likely to get involved in a firefight during the initial stages of the planned action.
- Should not get so close to the action that he loses the larger perspective.
- His presence does not interfere with ongoing operations and place an additional burden on the subordinate commanders.
- Every commanding officer must focus on his job which is unique to his position and responsibility.
- It is not a bad idea to be seen where the worst shit is flying, when possible, keeping the above aspects in mind.

Going way back in history, Alexander the Great was successful because he always led from the front and launched himself at the most critical place in battle, however dangerous. His very first battle against the Persians on the Granicus river during 334 BCE, east of Dardanelles in present-day Turkey, nearly proved fatal for the young emperor. As a Persian swung his sword at Alexander's neck, his bodyguard managed to intercept at the last moment chopping off the hand of the attacker, still shearing Alexander's metal helmet. He never changed his approach. The rest is history.

Leadership in battle is personality-driven. The commanding officer's safety, while important, cannot dictate his position. It has to be dictated by the need of the hour and the attendant risk is part of the job. The dynamics of operations being what they are, on a day, one could get away with a dozen 'faux pas.' On another day, one could pay a heavy price for just one.

For a commanding officer, leading by personal example does not mean accompanying the bayonet charge of the leading company. In peace, it means setting the personal example for the standards and values that he expects from his command and placing himself at the bottom of the welfare ladder. In combat, it means, being at the appropriate place from where he can effectively control and respond to battlefield developments and doing what is necessary to give his battalion the best chance to accomplish the mission at the least human and material cost.

It also needs to be reiterated that the commanding officers must avoid the temptation to be at the centre of action in pursuit of a gallantry award or personal glory. Such selfish actions often result in avoidable casualties. If that is the need of the hour for the success of the mission, it is fully justified, however, that risk must be worth the cause. In counter-terrorism operations, a couple of terrorists are not worth a commanding officer getting killed in action; risking his life to save one of his soldier's life is.

There would be times in battle when troops could get immobilized by fear, stiff opposition or heavy casualties. In such scenarios the commanding officer may well have to set the example, assuming the role of the 'pied piper' leading the assault, as Rommel did so often successfully as a Panzer division commander, breaking the impasse into which the leading units had got stuck. Thus, the decision of a rational commanding officer on the ground is the right decision. In hindsight, things always are much clearer.

## Lessons from the Galwan Face-off

The full truth of the Galwan incident will never be known for shortcomings at every level are dusted under the carpet. The sacrifices at the unit level are used to cover the shortcomings of higher leadership. After action reports tend to get modified to coincide with the directions of higher-ups and true lessons are rarely known.

The border incidents are always unpredictable and have the potential of quickly spiralling out of control. However, in such situations, the commanding officers must avoid jumping into the ring on the supposed premise of 'leading from the front.' He must position himself to monitor and respond to the developing situation and contingencies.

In such scenarios, the senior leadership must not breathe down the commanding officers' neck and give him the leeway to accomplish the task. Combat situations tend to evolve at their own pace which cannot be fast-forwarded beyond a point. The terrain can make things worse.

Unwarranted pressures and interference from higher commanders can lead to undesirable developments. Every unit must sharpen their battle drills, train their seconds in commands at all levels and respond at the appropriate level. Yet, the battle situations are dynamic and unpredictable and commanding officers can easily be sucked in as early responders. **It is of utmost importance that the commanding officer's security is ensured at all times by the best men in the unit, professionally trained and equipped.**

The death of a commanding officer's wife and son in an ambush has important lessons. The presence of families in such an environment is detrimental to unit functioning and is best avoided.

A commander's death in battle is not a stigma as long as it is not a result of inaction or unit ineptitude. It is widely considered as a demonstration of good leadership culture. The loss of a commanding officer is a setback of immense proportion, and could adversely affect morale. Militaries are good at absorbing losses and moving on and it mostly spurs the units to greater commitment, for it is a matter of honour to make such a sacrifice count.

No 'one size fits all' directive can be instituted on this score. It will always be situation and personality-driven. Having said all this, when in doubt, **better be well forward than be back.** Nothing like the sight of the commanding officer in your trench when shit is flying. It will lift your men to achieve the impossible.

*Sometimes, a General in a coffin will do more to motivate men than his talks.*

## Beyond the Borders

The test of the battalion begins beyond the forward assembly area. You will reap what you sow in peace time. There is little that can be set right of what has been neglected before. Certain basic guidelines that must be remembered are discussed here.

Everyman must be clear of the task, the hurdles and the contingencies that lie ahead. Every weapon must be checked for serviceability by the man who is going to use it. He must know what is expected of him and his sub unit over the next three days so that he can continue to operate in absence of orders. If possible rehearse in the dark what they are expected to perform in the dark. Maximum troops must see the objective if possible, and if not, the technology virtually enables you to walk through the objective.

The most critical responsibility of the commanding officer beyond this point is decision making.

I have talked of the issue of passing orders earlier in the book. It is here that the consequences of unclear orders will be most devastating. Most orders beyond the borders will be passed orally and there is a general failure to misunderstand oral orders. It must be doubly ensured that orders are clearly passed and understood. It must leave enough time for their dissemination down the chain, understood, clarify if necessary and implement. The orders passed in battle must be followed up in writing to reach the subordinates prior to execution so that it clears any misunderstanding/voids that may have occurred. Equally important, it makes clear that the superior has assumed definite responsibility for the orders passed orally. The commanding officer is unequivocally responsible for everything the battalion does, irrespective of who makes the decision in the unit. Accept the responsibility without demur.

An often neglected part is the fact that all ranks must be rested as much as possible. The most affected category is the battalion appointments, the adjutant, the quartermaster, the intelligence officer and important appointments at the JCOs and senior NCOs levels. I have personally experienced and seen men falling off to sleep at very critical times during exercises and counter insurgency operations out of fatigue. The troops must be fully rested before the operations.

The second important part is good food. The vagaries of battle sap mental and physical energy. It is important that men get good meals as often as situation permits in battle. The officers must eat after the men have been fed. It is a good idea to eat with the men so that they know that you eat no better than what they do. Must remember *shaker paras* are emergency rations; do not expect men to survive on them and keep fighting for long. Rested and well fed troops are mentally alert, last longer and can work harder at high pressure.

Never give a big target. A large number of soldiers in a unit died to one artillery shell during the Kargil War, precisely collecting their lunch from the distribution point. In battle, troops have the tendency to seek psychological safety in numbers, particularly in the dark, which leads to bunching and that is fatal.

Field craft is a life saver. Use cover even when you have your food. Make that a habit and you will have lesser military funerals. Do not forget that now you are more visible and vulnerable by night than you are by day.

Under the stress of combat where life is on the line, instant obedience must not be assumed. Fear and the instinct for self preservation are part of natural human response that must be anticipated. Officers must talk about this to the men that there is no shame in being afraid for a while. Shame is in not overcoming fear. Discipline, self pride, self confidence and good training cultivates courage and helps overcome fear in battle. It is also important that the individual fears the consequences of not rising to the occasion in the face of the enemy.

Never allow your battalion to be launched without minimum inescapable reconnaissance and preparation. If an opportunity exists, be sure to exploit, without waiting for undue preparation but make sure you are ready for the enemy when he comes. Logistics in battle is about anticipation and forward thinking. Better be over supplied than be under or delayed supplied.

Every man in the unit is a potential hero. Even the barber, who may apparently have no trade work in war, will be carrying military stores through the minefield under fire. Your biggest asset in battle will be the para-medic. Make sure every section has at least one skilled battlefield nursing assistant. Ensure your sub units are well equipped for the 'Golden Hour' medical support. More lives will be saved by a competent nursing assistant in battle than a super specialist fifty miles behind. Have time for those who work unseen and unsung.

Men in contact have the tendency to exaggerate reports. Nothing is as good or as bad in battle as reported. Move forward and meet troops as much as possible. You will see the correct picture first hand and your presence up there will make all the difference to the men.

It is said, in war truth is the first casualty. Have the courage to stick to the truth. It will save embarrassment and it will save your men's lives.

## Visualize Your Future Battlefield

The routine commitments of a unit can easily lead a commanding officer to get embroiled in the short term, neglecting the long term. For any organization, the long-term perspective remains the most important and when done continuously, it addresses the short term too. I wish to highlight some aspects and leave it to the commanding officers to think critically on 'hows and whys' of it?

- Why did almost 700 officers and men bypass the command chain and knock the doors of the Supreme Court on the issue of the Armed Forces Special Powers Act in 2018? How culpable were the commanding officers preceding this event in the occurrence of this incident? What role could the commanding officers have played in preventing this shame, whilst ensuring that the concerns of the officers and men were expeditiously addressed?
- What are the lessons for units from the Galwan face-off of June 2020 in which twenty soldiers were killed including the commanding officer?
- Despite great asymmetry in capabilities between the adversaries, the US failed in Vietnam, Iraq and Afghanistan, as did Russia in Afghanistan. In the context of the long ongoing insurgencies in the North East and Kashmir, what lessons are there for units from these operations?
- The 2020 Armenian-Azerbaijan war, the ongoing Yemen Civil war and the Russia-Ukraine war have thrown up game changing facets of warfare and seriously challenged the existing paradigms. They have brought the new weapon into sharp focus – the drone warfare, even though the drones have been around for decades. Drones are the Force – multipliers of tomorrow, difficult to counter, with their exploitation limited only by the imagination. Turkey is one of the leaders in Drone technology and Pakistan is

the blood brother of Turkey. Soon, we will be faced with this threat in all spectrums of warfare from all our adversaries including non-state actors in counter-insurgency. How does it affect units of different arms and services and how are you preparing for it?

- The mobile phone is a weapon of tomorrow. In the digital world, it is a functional necessity. How do you visualize the enemy will exploit it against you and how do you plan to counter it. In the same vein, what does it need to ensure that the social media is not misused by disgruntled men to spread malicious material for perceived injustice or grievances.

## Combat Effectiveness Indicators

- What is not mastered in training will not succeed in war.
- Understanding how the changing character of war will manifest at the battalion level in all spectrums of warfare.
- Junior leadership training - young officers, JCOs and Section commanders in the context of the future war.
- Unit used to functioning on centralised control will fare badly.
- Mistakes are not accepted as tools of growth during peacetime.
- Disruptive Quotient- Ability to deal with the unexpected and work through adversities and disruptions.
- Effectiveness of seconds-in-command at all levels.
- Effectiveness as teams at all levels.

# CHAPTER VII

# BATTALION COMMAND: CRYSTAL GAZING

Much is talked of command challenges these days. While I have covered most of the important aspects earlier in the book, let us see what has and what is likely to change in the future.

We have seen the contours of the future battlefield in Chapter VI.

For the army to respond to the needs of technology driven battlefield, the intake pattern of the men will need to be reviewed. The recruitment methodology must enable better minds with better psychological orientation to be recruited.

At the unit level, training challenges will continue to increase as the future soldier will need to be multitask-enabled. In an era of ever diminishing training areas and shortage of resources, opportunities for on ground collective training at the unit level and above will become increasingly rare, affecting battle preparedness.

I believe we do not make efficient use of manpower in the army. Units must undertake an honest audit of manpower and optimize men through the culture of multi tasking and exploitation of technology. Far too much manpower and resources are unjustifiably committed with senior officers, at the expense of units. In this regard, I saw a good system practiced in Turkey. All service chiefs had their residence within the Presidential Estate. The estate security took care of the chiefs as well, saving precious manpower. Turkish military mostly maintained one or two tri-service messes in big stations with pooled resources. Standing twenty five stories tall and managed efficiently, they met all requirements. Similar concept for our formation commanders and senior officers in a station and messes can optimize manpower and resources, rather than each having his own establishment.

With a plethora of commitments, senior commanders must ruthlessly prune down activities that do not contribute to operational preparedness. It is important that formations plan the yearly schedule with diligence and ensure that it is followed. Rescheduling of events upsets the unit planning with snowballing effect. It is important that new activities are introduced after due deliberations.

As the divisional commander, when I raised the issue of never ending peacetime drudgery of my brigades in the capital that impinged on my operational preparedness, I was told that these brigades were brought to Delhi for this purpose. In other words, I was not to complain of what I felt about what my men should be doing. Sadly, I was told by an army commander that there was no need for my units to do collective training every year, despite being an offensive formation.

We have young commanding officers today taking over command in fifteen to seventeen years of service. So were the commanding officers in seventies and early eighties. In fact, the past wars were fought by battalions led by even younger officers. What has changed is that earlier the presence of senior officers ensured effective grooming of officers in the unit. Today, that is not the case and potential commanding officers spend half of their service outside the unit before taking over command, and most of it in the latter half. That is the period to pick up the ropes of command which they miss out. Hence, lack of experience in important aspects of unit command, particularly in handling delicate man management and crisis situations.

The quantified system with disproportionate weightage to command makes the commanding officers defensive, circumspect, and mutes the roar of the tiger. Careerism and stiff promotion ladder tends to increase the zero error syndrome, where some are prepared to dump and lump everything for two good reports. The short tenure of the commanders results in them running against time and forces them to reset the focus of the unit with every change. (Infantry Journal, 2015).

Notwithstanding the short tenures of higher commanders and their short term goals, a good commanding officer should work on a long term perspective. It is possible to align short term formation objectives with long term unit goals as interim objectives of the unit. If commanding officers in succession work with a long term perspective, no one will need to worry about short tenure problems.

Absence of mentoring and grooming has deprived the young officers of the opportunity to learn the job gradually. They are pitch forked into company level commands without having had the experience or training to discharge that duty efficiently.

Shortage of officers is a well known reality with which the units will have to deal with for the foreseeable future. In the same environment, there are units that excel, taking all that as a challenge, and there are others that keep cribbing. Today, a majority of officers join the army for a job without having the passion for the profession. Motivation level of officers could do better and they should shoulder greater responsibility with pride, notwithstanding supersession. There is no scope for casual approach amongst the officers. While on one hand we have highly devoted officers striving to do well, there is an increasing trend of officers who are happy to coast along with no motivation to do well on courses or pass staff college examination. The pass percentage statistics in promotion examinations is far from encouraging. Is it a function of the steep pyramidal structure that discourages officers? Or, is it the assurance of almost equal or, in some cases, even higher pay and pension than senior officers the cause? If this is true, then introduction of the Non Functional Upgrade (NFU) could further encourage this tendency.

Commanding officers' wives too are very young and have spent little time in the unit and, as a result, the grooming of young ladies has suffered. It is common to see babies born during the command tenure of an officer. How much can be expected from ladies with a 'laptop' baby, who themselves have not gone through the mill. A large number of ladies work these days and that will only increase with time. They may neither have the time nor the inclination towards regimental commitments. When necessary, the commanding officer should seek advice from the formation commanders and responsible senior officers of the battalion.

While there are excellent JCOs in all units, a large number of them need to step up and shoulder additional responsibility. As I have stated before, most of what happens in the unit is repetitive and the JCOs must be able to handle all that. Necessary policy changes to make them accountable by authorizing them to sign various documents and hold charge of important stores will elicit better response. The JCOs respond best when they sign for something which makes them accountable. The only answer to the shortage of officers is for the JCOs to shoulder greater responsibilities. This is all within the purview of the commanding officers – better training of NCOs leading to better JCOs, strict selection of JCOs and greater accountability. The organization can strengthen the commanding officers by stricter ACR criteria for promotion to JCOs, as also for extension of service. From twenty two JCOs in the unit in eighties, the number has gone to over forty five. Any further proliferation of JCOs ranks as part of assured career progression will promote mediocrity and be derogatory to unit functioning.

A commanding officer has to deal with a plethora of entities, both inside and outside the unit. This is nothing new and neither so complex. The shortage and absence of senior officers in the unit places a huge burden on the commanding officer. Thus, command of a battalion seems to be becoming more of a management than a command and leadership experience. Ever increasing demands on the units take their toll. The higher headquarters must employ re-employed officers in all such duties and relieve the units. Rules, where necessary, must be amended to enable them to do so.

**Socioeconomic Changes:** The impact of socioeconomic changes is a reality. I have dealt in some detail about the challenges that our men face because of changing social environment and break up of joint family system. Higher aspirations for themselves and their families is a legitimate fallout of socioeconomic changes. Increased responsibility towards the family and aspirations has resulted in greater requirement of leave, job avoidance and poor response to military duties.

The units will need to factor the changes which cannot be wished away. What this points towards is that units will need to be empathetic to their genuine requirements, aspirations and problems. It will be more important than ever before that following actions are avoided; violation of dignity of soldiers, mass punishment or ridicule of troops, blaming the men for a failed mission, hurting religious sentiments, etc.

In the same breath, there is a need for constant motivation and education of these men towards their service obligations and responsibilities. Simultaneously, units must demand strict adherence to military discipline and values and not be hesitant to bring the defaulters to book. Ignoring indiscipline in the garb of protecting a unit's image will only invite more indiscipline.

With respect to societal changes, I am often reminded of the US and British Armies, whose society is far more conscious of their liberties and rights. Yet, their soldiers demonstrate good appreciation of their duties and responsibilities and deliver through immense operational challenges they have been facing over the decades.

The increasing tendency to take legal recourse by men means that commanding officers will need to be legally correct in dealing with disciplinary cases. In the military business, it is important that the individual fears the system. The units must focus on developing self discipline and that is a function of pride in the profession and belief in military values.

Some commanders tend to hold the commanding officers answerable for all omissions or commission over which they have no control. Lining up the commanding officer and the subedar major in formation commander's office for accidents, has a derogatory affect of over ensuring and hiding untoward incidents. Some formations have gone to ridiculous extent of ordering the JCOs to be co drivers in vehicles; surely he has more important things to do. In this case, the solution lies in aptitude based selection of drivers and better training. To give an example, lack of anticipation on the road remains the biggest weakness of all military drivers including those who have been driving for years. Develop this skill and you will reduce half the accidents.

A commanding officer will have to strike a balance between various aspects welfare vs. task orientation, long term vision vs. short term needs, inward vs. upward focus, informal vs. formal, etc. All this looks more complex than it actually is. Most of them can be managed with little application. A fine balance as per the demands of the occasion and time will meet the need.

**Social Media:** Social media has revolutionized the society. Nothing remains in-house any more. It is not possible to deny this access to them. They will have it through a third person. In future, as social values decline, respect for military values by troops is likely to decline too with dilution of inner discipline. A disturbing trend today is the role officers wives seem to be playing in using the social media to air or spread the actual or perceived grievances of officers. Commanding officers must educate the unit ladies to desist from doing so. If officers have grievances, they must have them addressed through laid down provisions.

Wisdom lies in accepting the change and educating soldiers to use them with responsibility. The army's approach seems to be addressing the symptoms rather than the cause. Curtailing the use of social media or placing restrictions is not the solution. There is a lesson to be learnt from the Indian Air Force. The Air Force does not face the same problems, either on this score or disillusionment, in relation to promotions as the army officers class does. This is so, simply, because their policies and implementation has not given their rank and file a reason to complaint. At all levels, transparency and fairness in functioning removes grounds for most grievances.

While mobiles are a help in many ways to facilitate many routine functions at all levels, it remains a communication tool. It cannot replace military drills such as roll calls, order parades, interviews, etc. Command is all about personal equation born out of personal contact between commanders and troops and cannot be substituted by technology.

Anonymous letters have become a weapon of the disgruntled men. The senior hierarchy must use its discretion in taking cognizance of such letters. Anonymous letters, even when lacking merit, puts the targeted officers on the defensive and harms their image.

Incidentally, a percentage of these letters do carry more than an iota of truth. To some extent they serve a purpose of keeping the unscrupulous and self serving commanding officers in check. An honest upright commanding officer who commands a unit with commitment, transparency, fairness and selflessness is unlikely to invite an anonymous letter. A healthy organizational climate, where men can approach their company commanders and commanding officer with the confidence that they will be heard without prejudice, will prevent anonymous letters.

One commanding officer received an anonymous letter through his divisional commander. The man complained about being asked to buy mufti dress and track suit by the commanding officer. His complaint was whether he should buy these or look after his family. Both things put together were costing no more than six hundred rupees. The battalion had ensured the cheapest price for the best quality.

The commanding officer held a battalion *sainik sammelan* and tore the letter in front of the battalion. He said, 'I command this battalion from my heart and give it 200 percent, and have done that for last twenty years. I am responsible to ensure that the unit excels in all aspects, and good turnout and discipline goes with the motto of the regiment. I run the battalion within the military norms. The divisional commander cannot tell me how to command my battalion. I will command it my way and discharge duties entrusted to me. The man who has written this anonymous letter should have come up and told me his problems and I would have found a way to help him. Now he can write again to the division commander and tell him what I have done to this letter.'

As for the division commander, he thanked him for the letter that apprised him of what bothered his men. That notwithstanding, mufti dress and track suits were legitimate uniforms that the men were required to possess as given in the regimental dress regulations. Good turnout and discipline was enshrined in the motto of his Regiment that they were proud to uphold. As the commanding officer, it was his duty to ensure that the battalion maintained highest standards on all counts. He saw no reason to change the orders that he had passed in the unit. The formation commander appreciated this commanding officer's stand on his orders.

Command is an art, thus battalion cannot be commanded strictly by the rule book. The commanding officers will, therefore, need to be conscious of anonymous letters in future. They must be transparent in all their functioning and, in particular, be correct in dealing with promotions, punishments, financial matters and probity. This notwithstanding, a battalion can never be commanded under the fear of anonymous letters. He must do what needs to be done in the best interest of the unit in keeping with military *dastoor*. If he does the right things, he needs to fear no one.

The post-retirement state of soldiers demands that as an organization we empower them to prepare for the second career. Almost fifty percent of the vacancies meant for the retiring soldiers through the Directorate General of Resettlement (DGR) go unutilized because they lack the requisite qualification and fail to pass the mandatory written tests. Commanding officers can play a major role in this field by ensuring that the men are qualified and adequately prepared to utilize the second career opportunities provided by the army.

The battalion command will always remain the finest hour for a professional soldier, notwithstanding the challenges. The changing environment will demand greater time and energy from the officers. The leadership at the unit level will have to be more participative and responsive to the needs of the men, yet must not accept compromise where compromise is not acceptable. Military culture and values remains the bulwark for effective soldiering and that must be ingrained in all ranks. As long as the unit leadership at the officers and JCOs level follow the basic tenets of military leadership, nothing will ever go wrong. The Commanding officers must remember that if they keep their house in order, all will be well. The major challenges facing the battalions are there to stay for the foreseeable future. Do the best you can in the given circumstances without giving excuses. All battalions face the same constraints.

There is an increasing trend of holding frequent long video conferences by the brigade and divisional commanders. These keep the commanding officers engaged during the most productive part of the day when they should be available to the unit. This is criminal as the bulk of training in the unit is conducted in the forenoon.

In the era of officers shortage and increased unit commitments, this makes their job even more difficult. These must be avoided as far as possible. Commanders should command the brigade and not the battalions. In the same fashion, the commanding officers should avoid waste of man-hours by keeping people waiting for any reason- interviews, conferences etc.

As a commanding officer, you will come across many situations that will have the potential to frustrate you about which you can do little. Therefore, do not get too pissed with things over which you have no control. If you do, you will lose control over things over which you have control. Follow this dictum:

> *'God grant me the serenity to accept the things I cannot change, the courage to change the things I can, and the wisdom to know the difference between the two.'*
>
> —Reinhold Niebuhr

Finally, do not base your command approach on the commander. Base it on character, competence, sincerity of purpose and military values. It is a one size fit all approach that will always stand you in good stead and enable you to be the proverbial Tiger.

# CHAPTER VIII

# BATTALION COMMAND: BE A TIGER

I had conceptualized a set of maxims for myself for battalion command. I followed them to the last word which made my command an exhilarating experience despite challenges that this philosophy threw in my way. These are not theoretical postulates but evolved from over two decades of experience before commanding a battalion. I added a few as I experienced during my command. When I relinquished command, I penned them down for posterity, as required of the outgoing commanding officer. This is the way I commanded my battalion and believe a battalion must be commanded. It is not an easy path to tread. Many may be tempted or coerced in to making compromises for one or the other reason depending on one's personality and value system. If one continues to keep the organization's and troops' interest above one's own, one will never stray from this philosophy. Everyone must follow it as it suits his circumstances and his DNA.

## My Concept of Command

Hello Colonel,

> *Good commanding officers derive inspiration from history but look towards the future.*
> *Battle honours on the wall cannot win the next battle, nor can the Gods.*
> *The battle will have to be won by your men and your officers, led by you, under your watch.*

Heartiest congratulations on assuming the command of your battalion. You have assumed the most honourable and responsible assignment in the army, an honour which only the very fortunate have the fortune to experience. Eight hundred men will look up to you for everything. For them the world ends with you. For them you are the God. You will have to prove to be worthy of their trust. When you do that, your men will follow you to their death. This is my concept of battalion command, for whatever it is worth. Apply it as it fits your scheme of things. I followed it in letter and spirit and derived immense satisfaction and enjoyment during my tenure in command. The unit command indeed was great fun

This will be the best period of your professional life. You have a '**Sultanate**' in which you can realize your dreams as a leader. How selfless you have been in command will be reflected in how long your legacy lasts after you are gone and how much your tenure has contributed to your battalion's professional growth. While in command, be guided by the following principles:

- Formulate an inclusive Vision that should be shared by your command.
- Battalion command is a payback time; an opportunity to give and not to take.
- As a Commanding Officer, I would be scared of nobody not even God.
- I would command my battalion from the head but lead straight from my heart. I will place the interests of my battalion, officers and men above everything else. I, as the Commanding Officer will come last, always and every time.
- My battalion will be the best operationally trained battalion in the formation. Anything that impinges in achieving this will not be accepted. On every count, I must leave the unit better than what I inherited.
- This is my last rank; I aspire no more.

Every commanding officer has quotations that adorn the walls of his office. Generally speaking, they reflect his beliefs and values. I had the following that have remained in the office of Commanding Officer 5 GUARDS ever since and have guided the battalion well.

When an officer entered the Tiger's office, he read this quote:

> 'Hello Colonel, Command is a payback time, an opportunity to give and not to take.'

When the officer faced the commanding officer, he saw this one-

> 'No sacrifice is too big for the honour and glory of the battalion'

And when a person left the office, he was left with this thought on the pelmet of the exit door:

> 'A lot can be achieved if it does not bother you who gets the credit.'

Secrets of a good command are simple:

- Command is all about passion; develop this passion for the battalion in all ranks.
- Be a Tiger. To be a tiger as a commanding officer, you will have to live like a monk; in true Spartan style, living frugally. Detach from all materialistic desires that commanding officers often tend to fall prey to. It is better to be known as the commanding officer of the best unit in the formation, rather than a commanding officer who has the swankiest vehicle in town.
- Command is the authority entrusted in you to discharge your duties. It does not sow the seeds of loyalty and commitment, Leadership does. Lead by personal example; there can be no different standards for the commanding officer in any aspect of unit life.
- Prepare for the next war and not the last one: Your most sacred duty is operational readiness of the *Paltan*. **Do not allow anything to come in its way**. Environmental factors must be overcome; they cannot be an excuse. You must be prepared as if you are going to war next week.
- Think Team, Think We: The battalion is all about team work. Develop a happy cohesive team. Exploit every man's strength; harping on his weakness does not do your cause any good. They are your wards, empower them, only then can they contribute to realization of your vision. **Delete the word 'I' from your vocabulary**, it is all about 'We'.

- Be prepared to accept the sole responsibility for all unit failures; credit for success is of the rank and file.
- Think long term: *Paltan* is an ocean and everything is important. There is no aspect of the unit that can be neglected.
- Your most important asset is the human capital. Invest in officers grooming, they are the future of the battalion. Junior leadership, i.e., JCOs/Havaldars are the key to fighting successful battle in any environment. Their all round empowerment must remain the key focus. Give them responsibility, accountability and respect and they will grow.
- Have a large heart. Your biggest strength is in pardon and not in punishment. Do not get perturbed by small omissions. Allow junior leaders to make mistakes without becoming failures. I have not seen one man who does not respond to a pat on the back.
- Your job is to train leaders and not followers. Battalion needs leaders at all levels to succeed in battle. Battalion should be able to function as effectively with all seconds-in-command in charge. There is nothing that you can achieve alone.
- Follow the Directive Style of Command. Develop decisiveness, fearlessness, mental flexibility and perseverance in all junior leaders.
- When there is a serious issue that affects your battalion, have the moral courage to take it up with your superior.
- Understand the nuances and implications of ACRs for the officers and men. They must not suffer because of your ignorance of the environment.
- The commanding officer's wife and ladies of the unit have an important role to play. She must maintain a happy domestic front, help in building a happy team in the unit and attend to the well being of all families. She must play a positive role in proper grooming of young wives. The first lady must never be allowed to assume a 'larger than life' role in the organization and must never interfere in the professional aspects of unit life. Professionally, she must leave the husband alone; he will do well by himself.

**Focus on the genuine welfare of men:** Help men to work towards securing good future for their children through better education and give them quality time with their families.

**Create an Enabling Working Environment:** Smile is the most effective tool in the commanding officer's arsenal for creating good atmosphere in the unit. Develop one, if you are not blessed with one and use it as often as you can.

Command must be fun, 100 percent work and 100 percent fun should be the mantra. Differentiate between office and off-office time. Be predictable and consistent in your style of command.

By the time you finish your command, you may add a few wrinkles on your face. They should merely indicate where your smiles have been – Have fun and enjoy your command, it will be over before you realize. There will be no better time in your career when you can make a direct impact on so many men.

In mind, body language and action, be a Tiger and leave the pug marks of your character and personality in the sands of your unit history.

*'Oh Lord, why can't you turn the clock back in time.*
*So I can be a Battalion Commander, one more time.'*

***

These quotations have found their way into many other battalions and I am told the commanding officers found them to be effective guidelines. In my battalion, they were inscribed in brass by one of my successors and stayed for almost eight years. Then came a commanding officer who, quite surprisingly, removed the one that reminded him that he was there to give and not to take. Any commanding officer with suspect moral fibre will be uncomfortable seeing this board staring him in the face every day.

The quotes returned on the walls with his departure and have been there since.

Those entrusted with the sacred responsibility to command a battalion, would do well to remember that while the command rests with them considerable power and authority, it entails awesome responsibilities. To sustain these, one needs broad shoulders and a big heart. The path of honesty and integrity will often be a lonely trek. The path of idealism will mostly bring frustration in this opportunistic world. Yet, this is the path of professional soldiers that will ensure that you command respect and trust of your officers and men, even long after your authority is gone. These quotes help you to keep direction, when the satanic temptations might wean you up the wrong path and lose all your moral authority to command.

## Men Have the Right to Demand Competent Leadership

It is an irony that despite the exceptional commitment and sacrifices at unit levels, they often land up as part of the armies who lose the strategic war, because of the failings of the higher military and politico-bureaucratic leadership. The Germans in World War II, India in the Indo-China War 1962 and Sri Lanka 1987, the US in Vietnam, Iraq and Afghanistan, Russia in Afghanistan, Pakistan in all wars, the worst being the Kargil War 1999, China in Vietnam etc. are some of the many examples.

It is the right of soldiers to demand to be led by competent leadership at all levels. My three books deal with military leadership at different levels. While all levels are equally important, the most critical is the senior military leadership, for that sets the standards for the rest.

During the period 2018-2020 and beyond, the senior military leadership was inviting consistent criticism because of the manner in which they were handling important issues. I felt the need to write a book on Generalship, titled '*The BE-DO-KNOW of Generalship*' released in November 2020. It takes decades to develop oneself to be an effective General to deliver at the strategic level in a VUCA environment. It is too late to start learning to be one when one becomes one.

This book on Generalship must be read by aspiring colonels and brigadiers to arm themselves to deal with what their job content will be a decade or more later. The world will be a different place then, and no institution can tell you what it will look like, nor teach you to be an effective General for the future. It is entirely a personal endeavour. *The BE-KNOW-DO of Generalship* is a self-help book to help you to develop into one and leave your legacy.

# EPILOGUE: THE RETREAT

*Command of troops is an art, a free creative activity based on character, ability and power of intellect.*

—Anonymous

Battalion command is all about leadership and leadership is all about inspiration. When I was commanding my battalion, I contemplated changing the 'commanding officer's board to 'Leader' board, for I felt that conveyed better sense of the key function of the commanding officer.

The critical part of leadership lies in lighting and stoking the 'fire in the belly' to persevere even in the face of death. Leadership is a choice to live by high professional and moral standards and the price of leadership is sacrifice of self interest. If a man is prepared to make that choice, he can become a better leader. Thus, while some are born with leadership qualities – leadership can be imbibed through sincere efforts.

The army is all about top down-top first and like a fish it rots from the head. All changes must start from the top. If the changes are forced bottom up, then the top has failed the bottom and such changes will surely be embarrassing. The en-masse recourse through the legal route by officers against promotions is a case in point.

One of the shortcomings in our army is the lack of intellectual challenge and higher education at the higher ranks in the organization. Officers are nominated for the Higher Command course primarily based on their performance as battalion commander. There are many imponderables in how well 'theoretically' an officer does in command. I have known officers, who in my reckoning should have been charge-sheeted for incompetence and operational neglect in command and there were units which had incidents of mass indiscipline soon after the commanding officers' tenure finished, and these officers were nominated for higher command course. The present reporting and evaluation system needs a review to get the right man up.

Even though it is not in context of the book, a few important issues need to be mentioned. In the prevailing system, it is my belief that an average officer can rise to a three star by simply doing the very basics well, without being intellectually suitable for higher command assignments. In the present arrangement, officers can become corps commanders without having been assessed in their ability to operationally handle a brigade or a division on ground, thus, implying not evaluated on how they trained and integrated their commands for operations. Does it mean two-thirds of our corps commanders are being promoted based on power point presentations, communication skills, theoretical discussions and peace time activities?

Senior officers form a miniscule percentage of the officer cadre. Are there enough role models around? Ask a junior officer who he thinks fits as a role model and he starts wondering. Conversely, ask senior officers to name officers who see them as role models? Many will start wondering too.

In the perception of the environment, our senior hierarchy has earned themselves little credit in this regard.

Is the present system of assessing character, integrity and leadership traits of the officers reliable? It is my firm belief that the present reporting system does not honestly reflect on the character qualities of an officer, despite dedicated columns on integrity. If it was so, we would not have so many scams involving senior officers. Morality and integrity, or lack of it, is not a trait that germinates after attaining a senior rank. It is part of an individual's DNA that would surface in the long career and be exposed. It is often ignored by the superior commanders for many unjustified excuses, including personal inadequacies that render him morally incapable or vulnerable in taking action.

As far as the senior leadership is concerned, true reflection on them will only come from 360 degree input; and this concept is not knew. The army has not been able to muster the courage to implement it. The fear that this will spawn populism is not well founded. There are many smart ways of doing things with confidentiality as is being done for selection of defence/military attaches. Why does the organization feel the need to get additional inputs for selection of defence/military attaches who are colonels and brigadiers and not rely only on the confidential reports, as being done for promotion to senior ranks or nomination to Higher Command Course and National Defence College? This is an effective method to overcome the infirmities of the confidential reporting system of today. It also highlights the inadequacies of the confidential reports to give a true reflection on character traits of an officer.

Selection of officers to Major Generals and above is as critical as attaches, if not more. An unsuitable attaché can be and have been recalled overnight; a General officer cannot be undone. There is a definite need for inputs beyond the confidential reports for selection to these important ranks. I strongly believe 360 degrees assessment is the need of the times.

Are we any more professional today than we were in the past? Professionalism in my opinion comprises competence to effectively respond to professional challenges and unexpected developments. It means having the character and integrity to command the confidence and trust of the subordinates. It means providing good leadership, that is, personal example. It means moral courage to stand by what is right irrespective of the consequences. It means selflessness and willingness to subordinate your interests for the country, organization and your men. Where are we on this today?

The country reposes its complete faith in the military. We have to live up to its expectations every single time, in peace and in war. Every man in military uniform is its ambassador in the country. While he wears a name plate, for the countrymen this name is just one, Indian Army. His conduct affects the image of the military. All these men belong to one or the other units which are commanded by battalion commanders. The commanding officer carries that responsibility to groom and motivate every soldier to be a good ambassador in peace and an effective warrior in battle. Every component of the army must ensure that we empower this all important man to live like a Tiger, for only Tigers breed Tigers. Reflecting on my career, as I prepare to hang my boots, I was fortunate to have the finest dream teams in all my command assignments.

My team of officers and men in 5 GUARDS set such high standards that all brigade commanders wanted their battalions to emulate us. During my sector command, the sector believed that with me came good luck, safety and immense success. Actually, it was a result of their renewed commitment, training and efforts. My team of commanders, commanding officers and staff made my divisional command the finest command experience one can aspire to. They were like powerful stallions that had to be reined in rather than goaded. They always did more than I asked for, and voluntarily.

Path of idealism in this non-ideal world is a difficult one. One makes his choices in life; I had made mine to live the righteous way. There was never 'yes' said, when the military wisdom indicated that the answer was 'no.' One leaves a difficult trail with the hope that at least some will try and tread it and that will make some difference. This is also the paradox of the Indian Army. You could easily be a 'moral courage' casualty.

My last command assignment, the 22 Infantry Division in 2013 was the icing on the cake of this wonderful journey of soldiering. At the expense of humility, allow me to share the mutual trust we shared in the division, summarized in the following sentiments:

- There are many Generals who are claiming the tag of 'Soldiers' General'. You are our concept of a 'Soldiers' General'. If we were to choose the commander to go to war under, it will be you.
- When my child is born, I will want the GOC to give him *ghutti* (honey). In our society, it is believed that the infant imbibes the character of the man who feeds him honey first, a young expectant army wife.

As for me, no commander could be blessed with better concentration of units, officers and men in one division as I was. They surpassed my enthusiasm and beat my passion. They raised my stature with their dedication and performance. I had the full confidence in their courage, commitment and the skill to deliver in battle.

Leaving the division was as heart breaking as was leaving my battalion.

No better satisfaction than this to end your career. I never joined the army for becoming a General. I joined it for the love and passion of this uniform, to be a Major Saab. I always passed the promotion boards of my command, but not always of the Army and that is all that matters.

I read in the book *Be-Know-Do,* that if you have done it, you aren't bragging.

This is why I am comfortable writing this book.

*God Bless the Indian Army*

# INDEX

*

# OTHER BOOKS BY THE AUTHOR